SECOND EDITION

BRAIN-BASED
Learning

In a gentle way you can shake the world.

—Gandhi

SECOND EDITION

BRAIN-BASED
Learning

THE NEW PARADIGM OF TEACHING

ERIC
Jensen

CORWIN PRESS
A SAGE Company
Thousand Oaks, CA 91320

For information:

Corwin Press
A SAGE Company
2455 Teller Road
Thousand Oaks, California 91320
www.corwinpress.com

SAGE Ltd.
1 Oliver's Yard
55 City Road
London EC1Y 1SP
United Kingdom

SAGE India Pvt. Ltd.
B 1/I 1 Mohan Cooperative
    Industrial Area
Mathura Road, New Delhi 110 044
India

SAGE Asia-Pacific Pte. Ltd.
33 Pekin Street #02–01
Far East Square
Singapore 048763

Printed in the United States of America.

Library of Congress Cataloging-in-Publication Data

Jensen, Eric.
Brain-based learning: the new paradigm of teaching/Eric Jensen.—2nd ed.
    p. cm.
Previously published under title: Brain-based learning & teaching
Includes bibliographical references and index.
ISBN 978-1-4129-6255-1 (cloth: acid-free paper)
ISBN 978-1-4129-6256-8 (pbk.: acid-free paper)
    1. Learning, Psychology of. 2. Brain. 3. Teaching—Psychological aspects.
I. Jensen, Eric. Brain-based learning & teaching. II. Title.

LB1060.J45 2008
370.15′23   2008003612

This book is printed on acid-free paper.

11   12   10   9   8   7   6   5

Acquisitions Editors:	Allyson P. Sharp, Carol Chambers Collins
Editorial Assistants:	David Andrew Gray, Brett Ory
Production Editor:	Cassandra Margaret Seibel
Copy Editor:	Sarah J. Duffy
Typesetter:	C&M Digitals (P) Ltd.
Proofreader:	Caryne Brown
Indexer:	Jean Casalegno
Cover Designer:	Rose Storey
Graphic Designer:	Monique Hahn

Contents

Preface

One of the most exciting fields in the world is brain research. Keeping pace with the explosion of brain research over the past two decades has proved challenging, but astute educators are applying the findings with growing success. The result is a learning approach that is more aligned with how the brain naturally learns best. This dramatic new paradigm, known as *brain-compatible* or *brain-based* education, has emerged with strong implications for teachers and learners worldwide. Based on research from the disciplines of neuroscience, biology, and psychology, our understanding of the relationship between learning and the brain now encompasses the role of emotions, patterns, meaningfulness, environments, body rhythms, attitudes, stress, trauma, assessment, music, movement, gender, and enrichment. By integrating what we now know about the brain with standard education practices, *Brain-Based Learning* suggests ways that schools can be transformed into complete learning organizations.

As many conventional educational models have been shattered like glass, many are saying, "It's about time." The visionary author-scientist H. G. Wells said, "Civilization is a race between education and catastrophe." Indeed, there is an urgency to our planet that we've never before collectively known. At both the local and global levels, we lack the luxury of being able to weather a continued "Dark Age" in learning. Too much is at risk: We must act on the problems facing us now.

> Present problems cannot be solved with the same level of thinking or with the same tools that created them.

This book calls for the initiation of a fundamental shift in thinking. Shortsighted priorities, outdated teacher-education programs, visionless leaders, "program-of-the-week" mentalities, clumsy systems, budgetary bottlenecks, hierarchical infighting, and professional jealousy all contribute to the problem; and they've got to stop. Furthermore, we need to quit playing the victim and arm ourselves with change strategies that work. We can effect the changes called for if we collectively make it important enough to do so. Each brain-based strategy outlined in this book can be achieved by any one of us at little or no expense.

The first step, however, is to make an important distinction between core problems and symptoms. Whereas solving core problems provides a twenty- to fifty-fold return on our investment of resources, solving mere symptoms creates a net loss. When an organization is antagonistic to the natural and effortless way the brain learns, it faces a mind-boggling array of symptoms that result in ever-greater challenges. This means that for every symptom you "solve," you not only miss the real problem, but you wear down an already overburdened staff and ultimately drain valuable resources. Every new program that has come and gone over the past 30 years was likely to be brain antagonistic. Schools must open their collective doors to the simple and fundamental questions that science is now answering for us: How does the brain learn best? How do we create successful learning organizations with the brain in mind?

Why is now the time for a shift in thinking? The research on what works is both compelling and comprehensive. We are all great natural learners. Failing children and failing schools are indications of a faulty system—not a faulty brain—and our schools have taken enough of a beating! When students are provided with a learning environment that is optimal for learning, graduation rates increase, learning difficulties and discipline problems decrease, a love of learning flourishes, administrators focus on the real issues, and learning organizations thrive. In short, creating an organization around the way the brain naturally learns best may be the simplest and most critical educational reform ever initiated. In fact, of all the reforms, nothing provides a better return on your investment of time, energy, and money than developing a brain-based approach to learning.

Now is the time to expand the research to make it school tested and classroom proven. And that is up to us as educators. It is imperative that we share our knowledge and experiences with others.

Even as you read this, learning organizations across the globe, determined individuals, cooperating teams, and whole communities have successfully implemented brilliant,

> As in most change efforts, the first thing we face from others is indifference followed by ridicule and opposition . . . and then, finally, respect.

innovative, low-cost, brain-based learning solutions. Thus, it's no longer a question of "Can we?" We know we can provide learners with brain-compatible environments and curriculums that support their natural learning abilities. The question now is "Will we?"

> Brain-based learning is a way of thinking about the learning process. It is not a panacea, nor is it the solution to all of our problems. It is not a program, dogma, or recipe for teachers. And it is not a trend or gimmick. It is, however, a set of principles and a base of knowledge and skills upon which we can make better decisions about the learning process.

People who teach and train others make a vital contribution to the preservation of humanity. We must become a world of learners and begin to value learning as much as freedom, liberty, justice, shelter, and good health. We are obliged to take this assignment seriously—our collective future, in fact, depends on it. I invite you to start now. If you can't do it by yourself, ask for support: Start a network. Determined people everywhere have done it. They've simply said, "Let's get all of these people talking to each other and see what comes of it." As they shared what works for them, they realized a success rate that exceeded the norm.

You can make a significant difference. You are a once-in-forever biological event. This planet gets only one opportunity to experience your unique and powerful contributions, so share all that you are capable of at this moment. Can you step up to the challenge and accept your historic role? Go on, join the learning revolution; you've got nothing to lose and everything to gain. Find other like-minded people and organize yourselves for greater impact.

> As Margaret Mead once said, "Never doubt that a small group of concerned citizens can change the world. It is, indeed, the only thing that ever has."

Are you the exception as an educator or now in the mainstream if you are buying into this new approach? How reputable is brain-based education? Harvard University now offers both master's and doctoral degrees in it through the Mind, Brain, and Education (MBE) program. Every year, the program produces about forty graduates with master's degrees and two to four doctors of education who go on to interdisciplinary positions in research and practice. Its mission is to build a movement in which cognitive science and neuroscience are integrated with education so that we train people to make that integration both in research and in practice. The director, Professor Kurt Fischer, helps oversee this new intersection of biology, cognitive science, and pedagogy. Does this sound like a fad to you? It's not.

For many, like Howard Gardner, brain-based education has become a new focus in education. Interest in Harvard's brain-based degree programs is enthusiastic in Canada, Japan, Australia, South Korea, England, South Africa, New Zealand, Argentina, and other countries. There's also a peer-reviewed scientific journal on brain-based education. The journal, which is published quarterly by the reputable Blackwell Publishers and the International Mind, Brain, and Education Society (IMBES), features research reports, conceptual papers, reviews, debates, and dialogue.

This book is written for those who want to know not only what works but why it works and how to incorporate the methods. I have written it in nontechnical terms for new as well as veteran teachers or trainers. When positive habits are formed early, the job of teaching becomes significantly easier. When what we know intuitively works is validated, we are rewarded with great satisfaction. So everyone will benefit no matter what your level of experience. By picking up this book, you've already taken the first step. Turn the page and take the next. If not now, when? If not you, who? Carpe diem.

Acknowledgments

To you who are just getting started, may you enjoy both the journey and the destination.

Many thanks to my wife, Diane, for her priceless support. I would also like to acknowledge Tricia Louvar for her guidance, patience, and insights in guiding this manuscript through the process.

About the Author

Eric Jensen is a former teacher and current member of the Society for Neuroscience and the New York Academy of Sciences. He has taught at all levels, from elementary through university, and is currently completing his PhD in human development. In 1981, he cofounded SuperCamp, the nation's first and largest brain-compatible learning program, now with over 50,000 graduates. He has since written *Teaching With the Brain in Mind, SuperTeaching, Deeper Learning, Arts With the Brain in Mind, Enriching the Brain,* and 21 other books on learning and the brain. A leader in the brain-based movement, he has made more than 45 visits to neuroscience labs and interacts with countless neuroscientists. He founded the Learning Brain EXPO and has trained educators and trainers in this field for 25 years. He is deeply committed to making a positive, significant, lasting difference in the way we learn. Here are some resources you may find helpful:

Staff Development: Currently, Jensen does staff development, conference addresses, and in-depth training worldwide. Contact diane@jlcbrain.com or call (808) 552-0110.

Follow-Up Support and In-Depth Training: Jensen provides in-depth training on the principles in this book. He offers a complementary monthly newsletter with teaching tips, PowerPoint presentations, and more. Go to www.jensenlearning .com for more information.

Part 1

Fundamentals of Brain-Based Learning

1

What Is Brain-Based Learning?

The human brain seems so wondrous, mysterious, and powerful. For centuries scientists have tried to decipher its inner workings. They've mapped the circulation, noted the electrical activity, exposed glucose metabolism, measured and probed its parts, and even traced neuronal growth. Still, the vast complexity of our "thinking organ" has left scholars short of an efficient explanation of how it works. Over the years, however, a few metaphors have emerged to aid the process. The brain has been compared to a hydraulic system, a telephone switchboard, a massive city, and a high-powered computer, with each subsequent analogy reflecting the most current technological innovation of the time. For starters, let's trace the lineage of the field of brain-based education. It may help us gain some perspective on the movement.

> **The essential understanding here is that** the brain continues to be the new frontier. Our old way of schooling is fading fast as our understanding of the brain increases. Everything you do uses your brain, and everything at school involves students' brains. It's the most relevant understanding for educators to have right now.

WHERE DID BRAIN-BASED EDUCATION COME FROM?

During the 1970s a new genre of books emerged. Suddenly the word *brain* was appearing in popular self-help books instead of the word *mind*. Two highly successful books appeared: *Use Both Sides of Your Brain* by Tony Buzan (1974) and *Drawing on the Right Side of the Brain* by Betty Edwards (1979). In the 1980s, brain-based education finally emerged as a whole new field based on what we were learning about the brain and how it might interface with education.

At least part of the driving force behind the related new fields of neurobiology (neurology and biology) and cognitive neuroscience (cognitive science and neuroscience) was technology, drugs, and biomarkers. New technology brought us imaging tools to see inside the brain, such as magnetic resonance imaging (MRI), functional MRI (fMRI), and positron-emission tomography (PET). For the first time in history, we could analyze the brain while its owner was still alive. And the impact of the drug pharmaceutical industry cannot be underestimated; a massive influx of dollars poured into research labs around the world to find the next Coumadin, Zoloft, Celebrex, or Viagra. The stakes are high, and the money funds the work of scientists to better understand how the brain works. Finally, biomarkers allow us to better track any changes, processes, or events that occur. In some cases, researchers inject harmless dyes into the brain, individual neurons, and even genes to create a tracking system for measuring changes. They can follow the flow inside a brain of processes such as disease development, gene expression, or neurogenesis. These new markers, some made from simple jellyfish, have revolutionized neuroscience.

In 1983, a new paradigm established connections between brain function and traditional educational practice. In a groundbreaking book, *Human Brain and Human Learning,* Leslie Hart (1983) argued that cognitive processes were significantly impaired by classroom threat. While not an earthshaking conclusion, the gauntlet was thrown down as if to say, "If we ignore how our students' brains work, we will risk student success." Many have tied brain function to either new models of thinking, as Howard Gardner (1983) did in *Frames of Mind: The Theory of Multiple Intelligences,* or classroom pedagogy, as Caine and Caine (1991) did in *Making Connections: Teaching and the Human Brain.*

By the 1990s, neuroscience had exploded into dozens of mind-boggling subdisciplines. Suddenly, seemingly unrelated disciplines were being mentioned in the same science journals. Readers found immunology, physics, genes, emotions, and pharmacology seamlessly woven into articles on learning and brain theory. The voices that we were hearing were those of biochemists, cognitive scientists, neuroscientists, psychologists, and educational researchers, and they generated brand-new journals. From the field of psychiatry, we now have *Biological Psychiatry*. From sociology, the *Journal of Social Neuroscience*. From the field of nutrition, the *Journal of Nutritional Neuroscience*. There is also a peer-reviewed journal, *Mind, Brain, and Education,* which embraces brain-based education. And Harvard University offers both master's and doctoral programs in brain-based education. Finally, a new field has emerged, and it is starting down the path toward becoming a more established domain with its own values, precepts, and criteria.

Defining Brain-Based Learning

Since all learning is connected to the brain in some way, what is meant by a brain-based approach? Brain-based education is best understood in three words: *engagement, strategies,* and *principles.* Brain-based education is the engagement of strategies based on principles derived from an understanding of the brain. Notice I do not say that it is based on strategies given to us from neuroscientists. That's not appropriate. Nor do I say that it is based on strategies exclusively from neuroscience and no other discipline. The question is, are the approaches and strategies based on solid research from brain-related disciplines, or are they based on myths, a well-meaning mentor teacher, or "junk science"? Brain-based education is learning in accordance with the way the brain is naturally designed to learn. It is a multidisciplinary approach that is built on this fundamental question: What is good for the brain? It crosses and draws from multiple disciplines, such as chemistry, neurology, psychology, sociology, genetics, biology, and computational neurobiology.

BRAIN-BASED TEACHING is . . . E.S.P.
E—the active ENGAGEMENT
S—of purposeful STRATEGIES
P—based on PRINCIPLES derived from neuroscience

It is also a way of thinking about learning. It is a way of thinking about your job. It is not a discipline on its own, nor is it a prescribed format or dogma. In fact, a "formula" for it would be in direct opposition to the principles of brain-based learning. Although a brain-based approach does not provide a recipe for you to follow, it does encourage you to consider the nature of the brain in your decision making. By using what we know about the brain, we can make better decisions and reach more learners, more often, with fewer misses. Quite simply, it is learning with the brain in mind.

Brain-based education considers how the brain learns best. The brain does not learn on demand by a school's rigid, inflexible schedule. It has its own rhythms. If you want to maximize learning, you first need to discover how nature's engine runs. This singular realization alone has fueled a massive and urgent movement worldwide to redesign learning. What we thought was critical in the past may, in fact, not be very important at all. Perhaps our past instructional methods really emerged because they were measurable. Think about this, though—you can have the most efficient net in the world but aren't going to go home with a big catch if you're fishing in the wrong place.

> The brain is poorly designed for formal instruction.
>
> In fact, it is not at all designed for efficiency or order.
>
> Rather, it develops best through selection and survival.

Is Our Old Paradigm Outdated?

The importance of this paradigm to those who teach or train is stunning. It's no less than the rethinking of our old models of instruction, which proposed that the best means for molding individuals was operant conditioning (through rewards and punishment). This was popularized in the 1950s and is still used in some schools today. As an example, some school leaders believe the best way to reduce school violence is to build high fences, install metal detectors, eliminate student-to-student contact, and create stiffer and stiffer rules. A school in Fairfax County, Virginia, has banned all student-to-student contact, including high fives. Heaven forbid a student touch another, a teacher pat a student on the back, or anybody get a hug.

But humans are creative and emotional; some kids will try to beat the system, and others will just plain get resentful or shut off any love of learning. A more brain-based approach would be to increase classroom engagement, greet all students with a smile, increase (not decrease) social connectedness, and boost involvement in school activities like martial arts, theater, music, and ballroom dancing. Adamant "old school" policymakers still insist that achieving the highest possible rank in test scores (instead of producing happy, well-adjusted human beings who can think, care about others, and innovate) should be the top priority in our school systems.

Yet human beings are not rats; to account for our unique condition—which includes our propensity to be creative, depressed, oppositional, and motivated, as well as to make conscious choices—a bit more sophistication is required. Consideration must be given to these factors and the diversity of our experience and backgrounds. How then would you integrate a simple reward/punishment system with such diverse human learners? Shouldn't the student who is living with abuse, rage, brain insults, or distress, for instance, be evaluated on an individual basis? How can educators possibly account for all of these differences? The answer is that we can't—at least, not with a simple model that uses either a carrot or a stick to impose learning. The vast range of learners in today's school environment are subjected typically to one of the following three models.

Survival of the Fittest

"You can lead a horse to water, but you can't make it drink." This old adage reflects the thinking of some educators that their responsibility ends at leading the horse to water. Thus, if children don't learn to read in the standard program provided, they are deficient. The thinking is that if the students can't cut it (or don't want to), that's their problem. This model reduces the teacher's accountability and allows many learners to fall through the cracks.

Determined Behaviorist

"With enough punishment and rewards, you can get any behavior you wish." This model basically views learners as rats to be manipulated by the whims of the establishment. If scores are too low, the thinking is that you bribe students to achieve higher ones. If there's violence, the thinking is to put in more guards and metal detectors. This model manipulates learners and reduces the classroom to a place where students have little voice or choice.

Brain-Based Naturalist

"How can we make the horse thirsty so that it will want to drink from the trough?" This shift in thinking reflects the approach of brain-based educators. A teacher following the brain-based model would think, "How could I discover the learner's natural impediments and built-in motivators so that desired behavior emerges as a natural consequence?"

Giving the Brain an Appropriate Model Environment

Nature's biological imperative is simple: no intelligence or ability will unfold until, or unless, it is given the appropriate model environment. From a biological perspective, it is important to realize that the human brain, like the immune system, is designed solely for survival. Students will do what they need to do to survive in the "schoolyard jungle." The "negative" behaviors they learn—put-downs, deceit, attacking, avoidance, and peer pressure—are to be expected as long as students perceive that their survival is at stake. This precept calls for dramatic changes in the way we organize formal teaching and training. As you continue to read this book, keep in mind this basic brain-based principle: the brain is designed for survival, not typical formal instruction.

Having said that the brain operates naturally on a selection principle, can it still learn through instruction? Of course it can. And it can learn optimally in the most conducive environment. Every day, learners worldwide develop new skills and knowledge based on a brain-compatible model of instruction. Brain-based education is about the professionalism of knowing why one strategy is used over another. The science is based on what we know about how the brain works. It's professional to use research-based practices. Keep in mind that if you don't know why you do what you do, it's less purposeful and less professional. It's probably your collected, refined wisdom. There is nothing inherently wrong with that, but some of the collected, refined wisdom has led to some bad teaching, too. Although I have, for years, advocated brain-based education, I have never promoted it as the exclusive or only discipline for schools to consider. That's narrow-minded. But on the other hand, the brain is involved in everything we do at school, so to ignore it is irresponsible.

It has now been well over 20 years since this "connect the dots" approach called *brain-based education* began. This brazenly optimistic field holds that we use our brains in everything we do, so let's learn more about the brain and apply that knowledge. It is from this perspective that this book begins. The following chapters are devoted to the exploration of discoveries about the brain, applications to the classroom or training environment, and strategies for implementing what we've learned about learning.

2 How Your Student's Brain Learns

This chapter introduces you to a bit of neurobiology. For the most part, the high-level science behind how we learn is not necessary for any educator. But you should know the basics. For example, how do we learn and what can we do to make it happen more often, even on cue? How do emotions and stress affect the learning? These questions become more illuminated when we explore what goes on in our brains.

At times, educators get a bit overwhelmed by all the biology, particularly if they lack a science background. My promise is to keep it brief and keep it relevant. I am reminded of a true story about a physicist, Richard Feynman, who talked about how he gained his science background. He said he would read a text until he got to something he couldn't understand. Then he would take a break, then back up, and read it again. Each time he restarted, he could get a bit further, and eventually he gained more and more background knowledge. Feynman went on to receive the Nobel Prize for Physics in 1965 for his discoveries in quantum physics. In this chapter, if you need to, just take a break from any paragraph. When you come back to it, you'll be ready for more.

> **The essential understanding here is that** the brain can be characterized many ways. But for our purposes, we can say three key things. First, it is highly connected in that events in one part of the brain affect those in other parts of the brain. Second, it is a learning miracle; it's just that much of what it learns may not be what is intended by a teacher. Finally, it is highly adaptable and designed to respond to environmental input.

HOW THE BRAIN LEARNS

Here's an abbreviated tour of the learning process. In this case, we'll assume that the new learning is overt and explicit, or what we call *classroom learning*. This is critical because the brain processes different types of learning through different pathways. For words, text, and pictures, input to the brain arrives from our senses or it may be generated internally.

Routing Information Through the Brain

This input is initially processed first in the thalamus (see Figure 2.1), the "server" or central switching area of the brain. Simultaneously, it is routed to other specific areas for processing because time is of the essence. Your life is happening in real time, and the moment just might be an emergency! Visual information is routed to the occipital lobe, language to the temporal lobe, and so on. The brain quickly forms a raw, rough sensory impression of the incoming data. If there is any threatening or suspicious data, the amygdala (our "uncertainty activator") is activated. It will jump-start the rest of the sympathetic nervous system for a quick response.

Typically, however, the frontal lobe holds much of the new data in short-term memory for 5 to 20 seconds. This new information is filtered, dismissed, and never gets stored. It may be irrelevant, trivial, or not compelling enough. If it is worth a second consideration, new explicit learning is routed to and held in the hippocampus, two crescent-shaped structures in the midbrain area.

Figure 2.1 Medial view of the brain

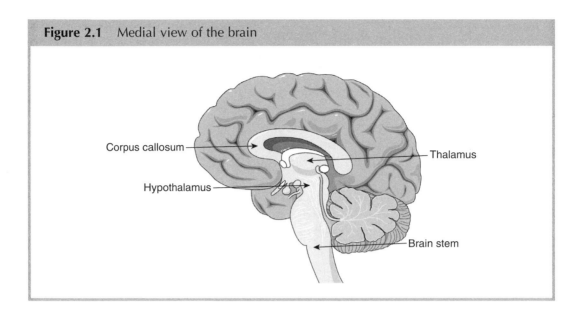

If this new learning is deemed important, it is organized and indexed by the hippocampus and later stored in the cortex. That's the quarter-inch, barklike wrinkle covering the brain. In fact, it is stored in the same lobe that originally processed it—visual information in the occipital lobe, language in the temporal lobe, and so on. The original processing takes place at lightning speeds, but the subsequent stages and storage process can take hours, days, and even weeks. Now, let's dig a bit into the "bit players" in your brain. But first, a reminder: there is no single pathway or process for *all* learning in your brain. Different types of learning (e.g., emotional, the big "aha," spatial, vocabulary, skill learning) each take unique pathways. And although they may share parts of a pathway, we are each unique, and the different input is processed differently. (See Figure 2.2 to review the brain's mapping of content.)

BASIC ANATOMY OF THE BRAIN

The brain is the most complex organ we possess. Cell counts vary widely among humans, but generally speaking, a person's brain contains between 50 billion and 100 billion (100,000,000,000) neurons. For the sake of comparison, consider that a monkey has about 10 percent of that, a mouse has about 5 million brain cells, and a fruit fly has about 100,000. Individual cells don't make us smart; it's the connections that do. When linked together, the number of connections our brain cells can make is estimated to be from 100 trillion to as much as 10 followed by millions of zeroes (more than the estimated number of atoms in the known universe).

Brain size and weight also vary among humans. The average weight is three pounds, and a healthy adult's brain may range from two to four pounds. Albert Einstein, who developed the theory of relativity, had an average-size brain, but the French writer Honoré de Balzac had a brain that was 40 percent larger than

Figure 2.2 How the brain learns new content

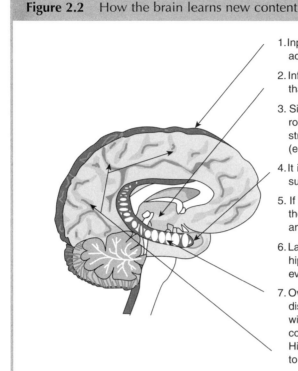

1. Input begins from our senses or is activated by thinking or memory.

2. Information is first routed to the thalamus for initial processing.

3. Simultaneously, the information is routed to the appropriate cortical structures for further processing (e.g., occipital lobe, temporal lobe).

4. It is also immediately routed to subcortical areas (e.g., the amygdala).

5. If it is an emergency stimulus, the amygdala will respond immediately and recruit other brain areas.

6. Later, information is sent to the hippocampus for more subtle evaluation and held over time.

7. Over time, the hippocampus will organize, distribute, and connect the memories with the rest of the appropriate areas of the cortex for long-term storage. High-bias content is more likely to be saved than low-bias information.

average. While the process of learning involves the whole body, the brain acts as a way station for incoming stimuli. All sensory input gets sorted, prioritized, processed, stored, or dumped on a subconscious level as it is processed by the brain. Every second a neuron can register and transmit between 250 and 2,500 impulses. When you multiply this transmission ability by the number of neurons we're estimated to have (approximately 100 billion), you can begin to fathom just how unfathomable human learning potential is.

A normal, living human brain is pink-beige colored and soft enough that it can be cut with a butter knife. Distinguishing the outer surface of the brain, the cerebral cortex (Latin for *bark* or *rind*) appears as folds or wrinkles about the thickness of an orange peel. Rich in brain cells, this tissue covering would be about the size of an unfolded sheet of newspaper if stretched out flat. The cortex's importance is highlighted by the fact that it constitutes about 70 percent of the nervous system: its nerve cells, or neurons, are connected by nearly one million miles of nerve fibers. The human brain has the largest area of uncommitted cortex (no particular required function) of any species on earth, which gives humans extraordinary flexibility and capacity for learning.

Cells of the Central Nervous System

All of us lose some brain cells all the time as a result of apoptosis (cell death). Scientists estimate that this loss of neurons adds up to about 18 million per year between the ages of roughly 20 and 70. For two reasons, however, this is not a problem. First, even if a person were to lose half a million neurons per day, at this rate, it would still take centuries to "lose" his or her mind. And second, in spite of this naturally occurring pruning process, new research (Eriksson et al., 1998) suggests that we can also grow new brain cells, at least in the hippocampus. Brain cells come in many varieties: chemicals, proteins, fats, and connective tissue. The most commonly known cells are neurons and glia.

Glial Cells

At birth, we have as many as one thousand billion glial cells (see Figure 2.3)—that is, one hundred times the number of known stars in the Milky Way. An autopsy of Einstein's brain revealed that, although it was of average size, it had more than the average number of glial cells. The roles assigned to glial cells seem to be multifaceted and likely include the production of myelin for the axons, structural support for the blood-brain barrier, transportation of nutrients, and regulation of the immune system. There are four primary types of glial cells—astrocytes, oligodendrocytes, microglial cells, and Schwann cells—and each plays a significant role in the learning process. These cells are about 10 times more concentrated in our brains than their neuronal counterparts are. In the past, glial cells were thought of simply as support cells, but this is no longer believed to be true. Today, we know that they are equal to neurons in their capacity, function, and importance. Amazingly, neurons grown with glial cells in a lab culture are not just slightly, but a whopping 10 times more active than neurons grown alone (Allen & Barres, 2005).

Figure 2.3 Glial cells

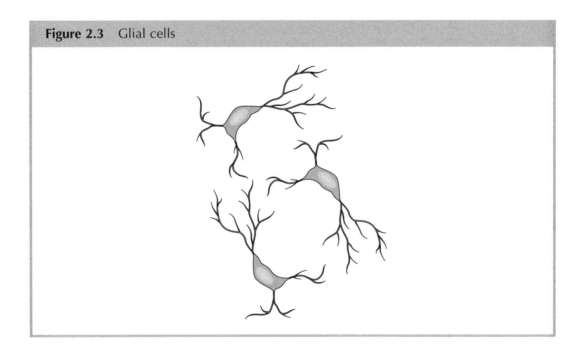

Neurons

A neuron (Greek for *sinew* or *bowstring*) is a basic structural and processing unit of the nervous system. It has three primary functional areas: the cell body (soma), the outbound projection (axon), and the inbound "feeder systems" (dendrites). Its structure and properties allow it to conduct signals by taking advantage of the electrical charge across its cell membrane. Neurons cannot be seen with the naked eye and come in many sizes and structures.

A normally functioning neuron continuously fires, integrates, and generates information across microscopic gaps called *synapses*, thereby linking one cell to another. No neuron is an end point in itself. Rather, each acts as a conduit for information. Always busy, neurons generate a hotbed of activity. In fact, a single neuron may connect with 1,000 to 10,000 other cells. As a rule, the more connections your cells make, the better.

Adults have about half the number of neurons found in the brain of a two-year-old. A single cubic millimeter (1/16,000th of an inch) of brain tissue has over one million neurons, each about 50 microns in diameter. As you can see, learning begins on a cellular level.

Dendrites. Dendrites are branchlike extensions protruding from a cell body. They are the receivers of the input that gets passed along from neurons to cells (see Figure 2.4). The sum of all the synaptic reactions arriving from the dendrites to the cell body at any given moment determines whether that cell will, in fact, fire. In other words, learning involves groups or networks of neurons. There's a threshold to reach, too; the cell needs enough activation to fire, or it will remain dormant and no memory will be activated.

Axons. Although the cell body has the capacity to move, most adult neurons stay put and simply extend their single axon outward. Some axonal migration is genetically programmed, and some is a result of environmental stimulation. Axons normally only talk to dendrites, and dendrites normally only talk to axons. When an axon (which is a thinner, leglike extension) meets up with a dendrite from a neighboring cell, the eureka moment of the learning process occurs.

To connect with thousands of other cells, the axon repeatedly subdivides itself and branches out. Neurons serve to pass along information, which flows in one direction only. The dendrites receive input from other axons and transmit the information to their cell body. Then the information moves out to the axon, which communicates it to another cell through dendritic branches.

An axon has two essential functions: to conduct information in the form of electrical stimulation and to transport chemical substances. Axons vary in size, with the longer specimens stretching to about one meter. The thicker the axon, the faster it conducts electricity (and information). Myelin, a fatty lipid substance that forms around well-used axons, is present around all axons to some degree. Myelination seems to not only speed the electrical transmission (up to twelvefold) but also reduce interference from other nearby reactions. Along with myelination, nodes along the axons can boost electrical impulses to speeds of 120 meters per

Figure 2.4 Axon and dendrite model

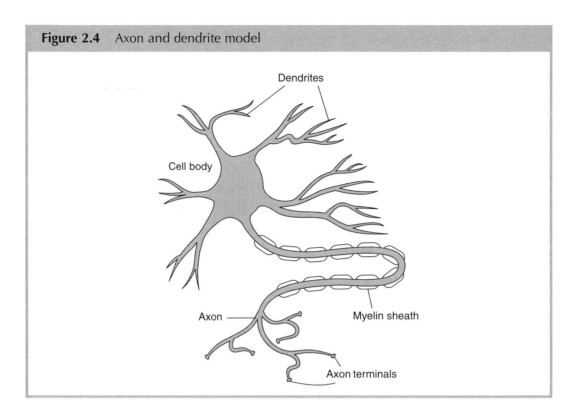

second or 200 miles per hour. The smallest axon probably receives no advantage from myelination.

Figure 2.5 shows the basic physiological process for learning. An electrical impulse travels down the axon, where it triggers the release of neurotransmitters into the synaptic gap. In the span of a microsecond, the chemicals travel across the gap (about 50 microns) and are absorbed into receptor sites on the surface of the receiving dendrite. The neurotransmitters are released, absorbed, and reabsorbed via the thousands of rapid-fire impulses activated every second.

Neurotransmitters influence the synaptic reactions and result in learning impairment, enhancement, or no effect. For example, a low level of the stress hormone cortisol during a learning session has no known effect. Moderate levels, however, enhance synaptic efficiency, and high levels impair learning. On the other hand, the neurotransmitter noradrenaline seems to have the opposite effect. Low levels have no effect, but high levels enhance learning and memory. Progesterone, testosterone, and dozens of other hormones also impact learning. For example, testosterone seems to support spatial learning, but only in moderate levels. A teacher can influence some neurotransmitters (e.g., adrenaline is increased by the type of risk, urgency, and excitement that can happen in a classroom competition), but others are not easily modified (e.g., glutamate seems impervious to our behaviors).

> Get it, get it right, and strengthen it. This is the basic learning process that builds intricate neural networks and makes them uniquely our own.

Figure 2.5   Synapse and neurotransmitters

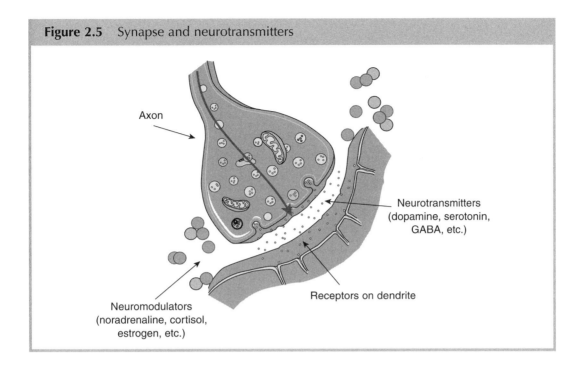

Divisions and Functions of the Brain

The brain comprises four different regions: brainstem, cerebellum, diencephalon, and cerebrum. Together they work as the central command center for the body to move, think, and react.

Brain Stem

The brain stem is the lower part of the brain; it connects the spinal cord to the brain. It houses several loosely defined areas including the pons and the medulla oblongata. This critical area regulates the automatic and nonconscious behaviors essential to life such as breathing and heart rate.

Cerebellum

Our brains need to guide us through life, literally. The area of the brain most associated with balance, posture, and motor control is the cerebellum. It's located in the back of the brain, just under the occipital lobe, and is about the size of a small fist. The cerebellum takes up just one-tenth of the brain by volume, but it contains nearly half of all its neurons (Ivry & Fiez, 2000); the neurons are so compacted that they can form an immense number of connections. This amazing structure may be the most complex part of the brain. In fact, the cerebellum has some 40 million nerve fibers—40 times more than even the highly complex optical tract. Those fibers feed information from the cortex to the cerebellum, and then they feed data back to the cortex. Most of the neural circuits from the cerebellum are "outbound," influencing the rest of the brain (Middleton & Strick, 1994) via a pathway from the cerebellum to the parts of the brain involved in memory, attention, and spatial perception.

Amazingly, this part of the brain, which processes balance, posture, and movement, is the same part that processes much of our learning, too. The reasons for this connection are simple. We learn early on in life to predict (which requires data analysis) each of our movements before we execute them (that's you moving) so that we control them better (Flanagan, Vetter, Johansson, & Wolpert, 2003). This ability suggests that all motor activity is not purely mechanical; it's preceded by quick thought processes that set goals, analyze variables, predict outcomes, and execute movements. Pulling this off requires widespread connections to all sensory areas—a relationship with the cerebellum in such mental processes as predicting, sequencing, ordering, timing, and practicing or rehearsing a task before carrying it out. The cerebellum can make predictive and corrective actions regardless of whether it's dealing with a gross-motor task sequence or a mentally rehearsed task sequence. Recent research suggests a strong relationship between motor and cognitive processes. The cerebellum is the key link between the age-old mind–body link. It's actually the link to how we move and think.

Diencephalon

The diencephalon is the region of the brain that includes the thalamus, hypothalamus, pituitary gland, and other smaller midbrain structures. This region is located at the midline of the brain, above the brain stem. The thalamus serves as the primary incoming relay and sorting station for all sensory information except smell. The hypothalamus performs many vital functions, acting much like a thermostat, sensing environmental input such as temperature, humidity, noise, and stress. At the same time, it signals hunger, thirst, stress, and sex drive. The pituitary gland secretes hormones regulating homeostasis and sexual desires. It is directly next to and functionally connected to the hypothalamus.

Cerebrum

The cerebrum is made up of four primary areas called *lobes*: occipital, frontal, parietal, and temporal (see Figure 2.6). The occipital lobe is located in the middle back of the brain and is primarily responsible for vision. Connect visual areas to language areas, and you can see what you hear and say. That's part of the essence of reading—high visual-auditory connectivity. The frontal lobe is located in the area around your forehead and is involved with purposeful acts like judgment, creativity, problem solving, and planning. The parietal lobe is located at the top back portion of your brain. Its duties include processing higher sensory and language functions. The temporal lobes (left and right) are above and around your ears. They are primarily responsible for hearing, memory, meaning, and language, although there is some overlap in functions between lobes.

Figure 2.6 Lobes of the human brain

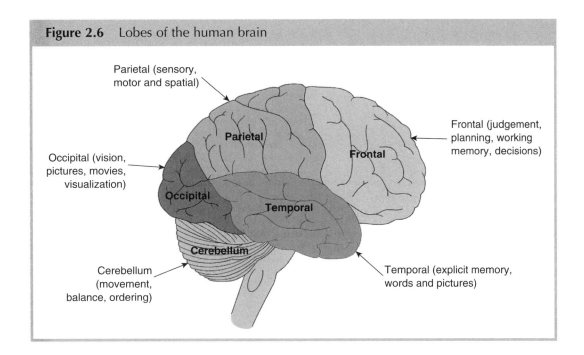

THE MICRO LEVEL OF LEARNING

There's more to learning than synaptic focal points firing away in the brain. Most of the communication in the brain takes place outside the axon-to-synapse-to-dendrite connection. In spite of the time we invest in learning about the physical structure of the brain, it is the processes that are the workhorses of communication. Trillions of bits of information are stored in chained protein molecules called *peptides*, which circulate throughout the brain (and body), transmitting their knowledge to available receptor sites on each and every cell in the body.

The development of neural networks of cells that have fired together often enough to "wire together" are activated by complex interactions between genes and our environment, and are modulated by countless biochemicals. Remember that to truly understand new content, we must move from the micro to the macro and back to the micro world. In this process, information may become oversimplified and out of context, but as elaboration occurs, the pieces of the puzzle reunite to form an accurate picture that results in accurate learning. Now that you are armed with the basics of how the brain learns, let's find out how this knowledge informs the teaching profession.

3 Brain Dominance in Learning

The brain is a self-organized structure that is highly connected. Its communication is both dynamic (through the brain's "subway" system of hormones, peptides, and neurotransmitters that swirl through the blood stream) and static (through the vast and complex networks of nerve fibers called *axons* and *dendrites*). The largest concentrated bundle of these fibers is in the cerebellum, which guides our balance, posture, and movements. The next largest bundle of connective tissue joins the two hemispheres of the brain. The left and right sides of the brain are vastly different in the functions they perform. Yet in a pinch (through injury or removal), one side can compensate fairly well (though not perfectly) for the other side.

The essential understanding here is that the brain works well because it has multiple and dynamic pathways supported by redundant systems. It is adaptive, flexible, and surely *not* fixed from either birth or even our teen or midlife years.

RELATIVE LATERALIZATION

Old myths die hard. Much of the original work of Nobel Laureate Roger Sperry, who discovered the functioning differences between the left and right hemispheres of the brain, remains valid today. But the spin put on his research also remains. Forty years after his discovery, we still hear people talk about "left-brained people" and "right-brained people," which is not just anatomically incorrect (unless one has had a hemispherectomy), but can also be pejorative labeling. We have become used to the associations for each of the hemispheres; some are positive and some are not. To some people, *left-brained* means focused, on task, verbal, analytical, and logical (not true); to others, anal, obsessive, boring, uncreative, and stuck in the mud (not true). To some, *right-brained* means flighty, flippant, random, unreliable, dingy, and new age; to others, creative, fun, expressive, artsy and eccentric. All of these clichés may contain some truth, but as a whole, they are blanket stereotypes that have no place in your vocabulary.

The prevailing research in neuroscience avoids the definitive left-versus-right labels. Scientists now use the term *relative lateralization*: the brain is designed to process spatially from left to right hemisphere, but it processes time (past to future) from back to front. In short, on any given day, you'll use most of your brain, most of time. How you use it, and how much time you spend using any area of the brain, is a whole different discussion. In addition, newer research (e.g., Proverbio, Brignone, Matarazzo, Del Zotto, & Zani, 2006) suggests that gender, occupation, and handedness can also affect lateralization.

The challenge, however, has been in finding and keeping the proper perspective. Some have oversimplified the conclusions or taken them to an extreme, creating a split in thinking that is unwarranted by the literature. Some books have even drawn battle lines between the "old left-brain way" and the "updated right-brain approach." It is an oversimplification to say that an individual is left-brained or right-brained. We are all whole-brained (but see Figure 3.1 for a list of attributes that are characteristic of each hemisphere). Each area of the brain senses what is needed and interacts with other areas in a symbiotic microsecond. What we can safely say about each hemisphere of the brain is this:

> **The Left Side processes** "parts," language, and it does so sequentially.
> **The Right Side processes** "wholes," spatial information, and it does so randomly.

Events occurring in one hemisphere can influence developmental events occurring at the same time in very remote parts of the other hemisphere. For example, in some brains with left-hemisphere damage, language will reposition itself in the right hemisphere. In nontraumatic cases of experience-driven learning (e.g., playing a musical instrument over time) the brain may "remap" itself, using up abnormal areas of neural real estate. It is best to consider brain-side specificity in a more metaphorical sense. To pigeonhole all behaviors in a blueprint of left

Figure 3.1   Left-brain and right-brain dominant learners

Left-brain-dominant learners, more often than not, may
- prefer things in sequence
- learn best from parts to wholes
- prefer a phonetic reading system
- like words, symbols, and letters
- rather read about a subject first
- want to gather related factual information
- prefer detailed orderly instructions
- experience more internal focus
- want structure and predictability

Right-brain-dominant learners, more often than not, may
- be more comfortable with randomness
- learn best from wholes to parts
- prefer a whole-language reading system
- like pictures, graphs, and charts
- rather see or experience a subject first
- want to gather information about relationships among things
- prefer spontaneous, go-with-the-flow, learning environments
- experience more external focus
- want open-ended approaches, novelty, and surprises

versus right may help us understand how we process information, but it leads to faulty interpretation.

Here's an example of how complex brain-side specificity can be. Listening to someone speak may seem like a left-hemisphere activity since the left side processes words, definitions, and language. The left hemisphere has no biological mandate for language, but it does contain soft biases in information processing that are preferential to language skills. However, evidence suggests that the right hemisphere processes the inflection, tonality, tempo, and volume of the communication—elements that are actually more critical to the meaning of a conversation than the words themselves. Further, the female brain processes both language and feelings at the same time far more efficiently than the male brain does. Thus, gender may be a factor as well. While there is some clear-cut specialization, each side often uses the other complement its overall functioning. The corpus callosum (see Figure 3.2), which also includes the anterior commissure, develops at a fairly slow rate and is often not mature until our late teens.

The Paradox of Left-Brain Creativity

The notion that one side of the brain is logical and the other side is creative is outdated. We can become very creative by following and using logical sequences, patterns, and variations. DeBono's (1970) work on lateral thinking reminds us that one can use "left-brain systems" to be creative. For years, he has articulated

Figure 3.2 Corpus callosum

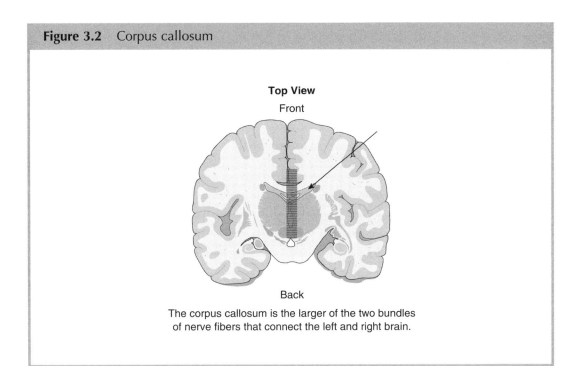

Top View

Front

Back

The corpus callosum is the larger of the two bundles
of nerve fibers that connect the left and right brain.

processes to arrive at creative solutions through sequential methods. Music is a right-brain experience? Think again! Researchers discovered that musicians typically process music to a greater degree in the left hemisphere, while nonmusicians process it more in the right hemisphere. This paradox points to the complexity of our brain functions. In this case, since musicians tend to analyze music more novices do, their left hemispheres are engaged to a greater degree.

Positron emission tomography (PET) and electroencephalography (EEG) scans provide researchers with a look at what specific brain locations are engaged during particular activities, moods, or thinking tasks. For example, these scans show that, as a generalization, the right hemisphere is more activated when the learner is feeling depressed or stressed. While there are some gender- and handedness-related exceptions (Schiffer et al., 2007), when the learner is feeling a healthy optimism about life and the future, the left hemisphere is more engaged.

Detailing the "rules" about how, when, and where emotions are found in the brain has been quite a puzzle for scientists. One idea is that the right hemisphere is dominant in the perception of emotional experiences, but it is the level of activation of the right hemisphere that determines whether the emotional experience is positive or negative. Too much involvement of the right hemisphere can lead to negative emotional experiences, while much less involvement is correlated with positive emotional experiences (Hellige, 1993). This suggests that left-hemisphere activation might merely be an "overflow" of right-hemisphere activation. It is plausible that the left hemisphere functions to regulate the intensity of the emotional reaction, creating an active scan.

What You Can Do

This suggests a two-part approach. You can hold class discussions to help students vent or discuss emotions, engaging the right hemisphere. But more important, when students learn effective ways to process negative moods or events, their learning time is optimized. Teach conflict resolution, social skills, and even learning to say "no." On the other side of the brain, optimism comes from mastering conflict resolution and experiencing a sense of belonging and acceptance. Engage learners in visualization and goal-setting activities, decision-making scenarios, case studies, and exercises that require logical thinking, brainstorming, and mind mapping. Even simple sequential activities such as counting and marching can activate more positive left-hemisphere activity.

The Paradox of Right-Brain Logic

The right side of the brain can intuit many logical things. Drawing, composing, and painting may seem like right-hemisphere activities, yet artists show bilateral activity. In the planning of artwork, they follow their own logic and rules about shapes, colors, and sounds. Artists can express anything they wish on canvas, clay, glass, metal, or paper, but to be acceptable to the masses, they must consider very specific (though unwritten) rules of proportionality, color, balance, and order. The right hemisphere, it seems, prefers its own kind of holistic order.

Current brain research tells us that we generally use both sides of the brain most of the time. Nevertheless, the right-brain emphasis produced the proverbial pendulum swing, which resulted in a hyperawareness of the brain's lateral processing tendencies. To ensure optimal learning, we must facilitate learning activities that include the strengths of both hemispheres. Ideally, our efforts ought to be focused on whole-brain learning.

What This Means to You

Provide learners with global overviews as well as step-by-step instructions. Represent the learning plan depicting the big picture, followed by details representing the subtopics. Alternate between the big picture and the details.

4 Rhythms of the Brain

Have you ever felt so tired in the afternoon that you wanted to take a siesta? This is a common experience; you just hit your low point in energy levels for the day. All of us have different internal rhythms or time structures (chronomes), which we must be cognizant of to perform and learn at peak efficiency.

Your biocycles influence overall physical strength and body temperature, immune system, alertness, and even memory. This chapter reveals those rhythms and what you can do about them. The bottom line is that every brain varies throughout the day, month, and year. Understanding that fluctuations are typical and healthy is important. But even more important, you can use strategies in the classroom to ameliorate any of the temporary adverse effects of these rhythms.

> **The essential understanding here is that** the brain is not designed to work as "on or off." Its intensity and capacity vary throughout the day and night in sheer electrical activity, chemical levels, and the types of jobs different structures can do. This understanding means that it's not very well designed to be focused, locked in, and riveted on class work for six hours a day. You can entice it to do that for a short time, but its natural rhythm is activity and rest (or, if you wish, focus and diffusion).

THE WHEN IS AS IMPORTANT AS THE WHAT AND WHY

The brain cannot function on full throttle all the time, though many people have tried to make it do so. There's always a cost to pay, and the body and brain eventually crash. The quantity and complexity of our ups and downs have been well chronicled. Both males and females have many rhythms:

Ultradian: < 20 hours (90–110 minutes), high to low to high energy

Circadian: 24 ± 4 hours: at night, it's sleep time

Infradian: > 28 hours

Circaseptan: about a week

Circadiseptan: about two weeks

Circatrigintan: about a month, 30 ± 5 days

Circannual: a solar year

The relevance of these rhythms is simple. During the day, there are times in which students are simply not good for class work and times in which they are good for it. Can you influence these rhythms? To a degree, yes. Circadian rhythms are those that occur once a day and relate to the sun; the one that dominates our activities is the sleep/wake cycle that people experience every 24 hours. Ultradian rhythms happen many times per day, every hour or so. Infradian rhythms are monthly cycles, such as menstruation in females; illness and death have been correlated to infradian rhythms, with more deaths occurring in the second half of the menstrual cycle. The circannual rhythm is a yearly occurring one; you may notice that some people get depressed or periodically gain or lose weight at certain times of the year. Each of these rhythms can have an effect in the classroom, too.

Every two hours, hormones released into the bloodstream can dramatically alter our mood and impact learning. Our performance is dramatically affected by our biological rhythms, which are regulated primarily by the hypothalamus, the suprachiasmatic nucleus, and the pineal gland, which are in turn influenced by our genes, sunlight exposure, and other environmental factors.

Based on measurements of psychomotor tasks, intellectual tasks, affective state tasks, and physiological function tasks during various times of the day, research reveals that overall intellectual performance (thinking, problem solving, debating) peaks in the late afternoon. Although comprehension increases as the day progresses, reading speed decreases.

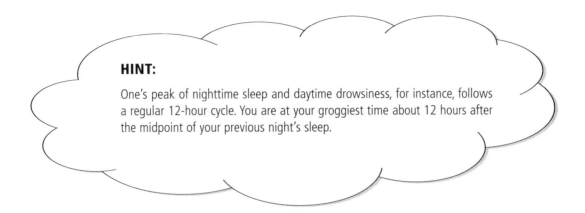

HINT:

One's peak of nighttime sleep and daytime drowsiness, for instance, follows a regular 12-hour cycle. You are at your groggiest time about 12 hours after the midpoint of your previous night's sleep.

Researchers have also discovered that mineral, vitamin, glucose, and hormone levels can vary as much as 500 percent in a given day. This fluctuation can profoundly affect the brain's efficiency and learning effectiveness. In general, our short-term memory is best in the morning and least effective in the afternoon, as opposed to our long-term memory, which is generally best in the afternoon. This personal knowledge can influence not only what you do but when you do it as well. For example, the potency of medications one takes varies depending on the time of day. For maximum effect, a person should plan to take them two hours before his or her daily blood-pressure rhythm peaks. When medication is maintained on this schedule, lower doses can achieve the same effect as higher doses taken during a low point or drop in blood pressure.

Even our breathing happens in predictable cycles throughout the day and night. On average, we breathe through one nostril for about three hours until the tissue becomes slightly engorged; then we switch to the other side. The nostril we breathe through affects which brain hemisphere we use. When our breathing is left-side dominant, our learning will be right-brain dominant, and vice versa.

> We may be underestimating the ability of students if we test them at the "wrong" times of the day.

Attentional Cycle

You may have noticed that you have natural attentional highs and lows throughout the day. One of the brain's key cycles is about 90 minutes. This means we have about 16 cycle revolutions every 24-hour period. The odd thing is that while we are used to "light and deep" sleep rhythms, we rarely connect this with the typical high and low arousal-rest cycles we experience during the day. Some students who are consistently drowsy in class may be at the bottom of their attentional cycle. Movements such as stretching or marching can help refocus their attention. Students should be encouraged to stand and stretch (without attracting undue attention) if they feel drowsy.

As this 90-minute high/low biocognitive cycle alters blood flow and breathing, the brain alternates between more efficient verbal and spatial processing abilities (Khalsa, Ziegler, & Kennedy, 1986). The differences are significant. One study exhibited a verbal-task score increase on average from 165 to 215 correct answers, and a simultaneous downswing of 125 to 108 correct answers on spatial tasks (Klein & Armitage, 1979). This oscillation suggests that we will get lower scores if we test students at the wrong time; giving learners choice in the assessment process may reduce this inherent discrepancy.

The nature of our biocognitive cycles and how they impact learning and assessment makes a good case for alternative assessment measurements, such as portfolios. Portfolios, which reflect learning over a span of time, may provide a more accurate analysis of learning. Not only do they provide a more inclusive means for assessing performance and improvement, but they also better accommodate the highs and lows of biocognitive rhythms.

The message our brains receive at each low end of a cycle is "Take it easy." In fact, some research suggests that in congruence with our biocognitive cycles, productivity increases when learners are given mental breaks several times a day. This recommendation aligns itself well with the bottom of a 90-minute cycle. Students need brain breaks, too. And running from one classroom to another between periods does not necessarily constitute downtime. What we know about biocognitive cycles supports the argument for block scheduling at the secondary level. If classes lasted longer, the teacher would be able to provide students with time to stretch or relax quietly for 10 minutes during each 90-minute period.

The brain's right and left hemispheres alternate cycles of efficiency—from high spatial/low verbal to high verbal/low spatial—every 90 to 100 minutes. In other words, learners switch from right-brain to left-brain dominance 16 times throughout the day. Naturally, teachers will get more cooperation and understanding when they work with students at the peak of their cycles. The students' natural "low" period often coincides with the teacher's low time, which can be good or bad depending on whether the teacher is aware of the situation.

Ultradian Rhythm

Another of our biocognitive cycles, the ultradian rhythm, or the B-R-A-C (basic rest-activity) cycle, corresponds to our rapid-eye-movement (REM) state of sleep. REM, which makes up most of our time spent dreaming, alternates with non-REM rest periods throughout the night. This cycle continues through the daytime as well.

Carol Orlock, author of *Know Your Body Clock* (1998), suggests that our ultradian rhythms coincide with the periodic release of hormones into the bloodstream and regulate our hunger and attention span. Sensitivity to pain, appetite, and learning varies with the cycle. Orlock cites experiments in which subjects consistently headed for the refrigerator or the coffee pot about every 90 minutes. She also notes that hemispheric-dominance oscillations, which also occur every 90 minutes, seem to impact thinking, reasoning, and spatial skills test results.

Some assert that this 90-minute cycle may provide the perfect opportunity for suggestions and affirmation. Why? The changeover may be a time when the body is switching gears and entering a neutral time that is highly receptive to change and healing.

What This Means to You

In some cases, problems in learning might be a result of the learning taking place at the wrong time of day. Learners who are at the peak of their right- or left-hemisphere dominance may need cross-lateral activation to "unstick" them. Proponents of cross-lateral physical activity suggest that exercises that encourage limb movement across the body's lateral center can stimulate both sides of the brain and energize thinking. You can do this with your students: have them reach over with the right arm to touch the left shoulder or elbow and then do the same thing with the other arm. Also, providing options for assessment at varied times of the day is important for accuracy in measuring learner performance. And it is important to vary your presentation/lecture times and other scheduled activities. Provide learners with choice and a diverse menu of activities to suit their biocognitive cycles and learning styles.

DUAL CYCLES RUN THE LEARNING BRAIN

Our brains consistently run on two learning cycles: a low-to-high-energy cycle and a relaxation-to-tension cycle. Learners often focus better in the late morning and early evening, and are more pessimistic in the middle to late afternoon. Our thinking can get unrealistically negative at certain low times, yet swing to the positive side during high cycles. These patterns, or rhythms of learning, coincide with the ultradian cycles described by many researchers.

Can these patterns be modified? Are they consistent? The answer to both questions is yes. Learners can be taught to modify the rhythms by varying their sleep, exercise, diet, and exposure to sunlight. Personality differences also influence pattern variations. For example, introverts report higher tension during the first two-thirds of the day, while extroverts report greater tension during the last two-thirds.

What This Means to You

Help learners become aware of their own best times for learning. Emphasize the importance of repetition and investing effort at various times of the day. Discuss how nutrition, rest, and activity impact learning as well.

The "Pulse" Style of Learning Is Best for the Brain

Allan Hobson of Harvard University discovered that the ability to maintain learning attentiveness is affected by normal fluctuations in brain chemistry. As discussed earlier, these fluctuations occur in cycles of approximately 90 minutes throughout the day and night. At night, we all experience periods of deep sleep, REM sleep, and light sleep. During the day, these cycles continue, but at a level of greater awareness. Even animals exhibit this cycle of basic rest and activity—a natural learning pulse.

> Learning is best when focused, diffused, and then focused again. Constant focused learning is increasingly inefficient.

Requiring learners to be attentive for a long period of time is counterproductive because much of what we learn cannot be processed consciously; it just happens too fast. Internal time is needed to process information and create meaning, as meaningfulness is a process generated within each individual. This settling time after each new learning experience will also reinforce the imprint on one's memory.

Breaks can be structured; they don't have to simply be free time. They can consist of a diffusion activity, a content break, or an alternate form of learning, such as a peer teaching session, a mind-mapping session, or project work. Deep breathing and physical relaxation are useful strategies for sustaining energy. Figures 4.1 and 4.2 represent the variables related to optimal content/rest cycle periods.

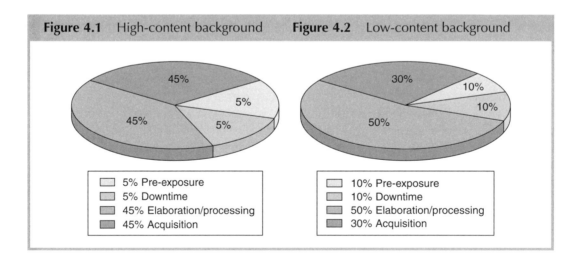

Figure 4.1 High-content background

5% Pre-exposure
5% Downtime
45% Elaboration/processing
45% Acquisition

Figure 4.2 Low-content background

10% Pre-exposure
10% Downtime
50% Elaboration/processing
30% Acquisition

In scheduling time for content acquisition and processing, how do you know what will be optimal for most learners? Two critical variables need to be taken into account. First, consider the novelty and complexity of the material. High complexity and novelty mean more processing time is needed. Second, learner background is critical. Low background on the content being learned means more time is needed, and of course, high background means less time is needed.

What This Means to You

In working with young learners, limit content, lectures, and cognitive activities to periods of 5 to 10 minutes each. In working with adolescents, limit content sessions to 10 to 15 minutes each. And with adults, no more than 25 minutes is recommended for content sessions. After each focused learning period, conduct an elaboration activity, such as mind mapping, pair shares, or model building. Provide downtime with activities such as walking, stretching, deep breathing, cleanup, or recess.

Part 2

Physiological Effects on Learning

5 Biological Differences in Learning

Two generations ago, it was very politically incorrect to talk about how male and female brains were different. Today, it's old hat, and after years of research, dozens of eminent scientists have noted physical differences between the male and female brains. These structural differences may account for behavioral, developmental, and cognitive-processing differences between males and females. And while many differences are reliable, keep in mind two things. First, all differences are on an overlapping bell-shaped curve with both genders. This means that while some brains are more "extreme" male or female, there is an overlapping area where some males have more "female" brains and some females have more "male" brains. Second, many of the differences that have been discovered are anatomical, structural, or chemical. But these differences suggest links only to behavioral differences. We are not yet at the point where we can definitively say a bigger corpus callosum in females means more intuitive behaviors. This chapter fleshes out some of the differences.

> **The essential understanding here is that** our brains are unique, and, while some may still consider it politically incorrect and others may stick to their old understandings, the neuroscientists who study gender differences agree with the model of differences. What is in dispute is how different the male and female brains actually are and what that implies for educational policymaking. For some, it's easy; simply have same-sex schools. For others, it raises questions about who should teach, class size, and instructional strategies.

IT'S NOT THE BRAIN SIZE THAT COUNTS . . .

For starters, in general, males have 10 to 15 percent larger brains than females. When a control for body size is established, studies still indicate that male brains are, on average, 100 grams heavier (Ankey, 1992). In addition, men have about four billion more cortical neurons than women do (Pakenberg & Gundersen, 1997).

The corpus callosum was originally thought to be much thicker in females than in males; however, recent research has debunked the earlier studies (Driesen & Raz, 1995). Another, lesser known bundle of interhemispheric fibers, the anterior commissure (see Figure 5.1), however, is clearly larger in female brains (Allen & Gorski, 1991). This advantage may allow females to tie together verbal and non-verbal information more efficiently. Variances within the same gender group do exist, but certainly not to the same extent as those found between the sexes.

Developmental neuroanatomists have found that, in the early years, brain growth rates vary from a few months to five years both within and across gender groups. Some believe that this may be the reason boys generally outperform girls on spatial task measures and girls outperform boys in verbal and reading skills early in life. Other functional differences show up as well (see Figure 5.2).

Functional Differences

Although we can acknowledge the physiological differences between the genders and note performance variances overall, additional research is necessary before we can draw more definitive conclusions. Additional functional differences that impact learners of both sexes are outlined in the next couple of pages. Be aware, however, that these are general differences and not absolutes.

Figure 5.1 Interhemispheric connections

In females, the anterior commissure is generally larger and carries more inter-hemispheric neural traffic

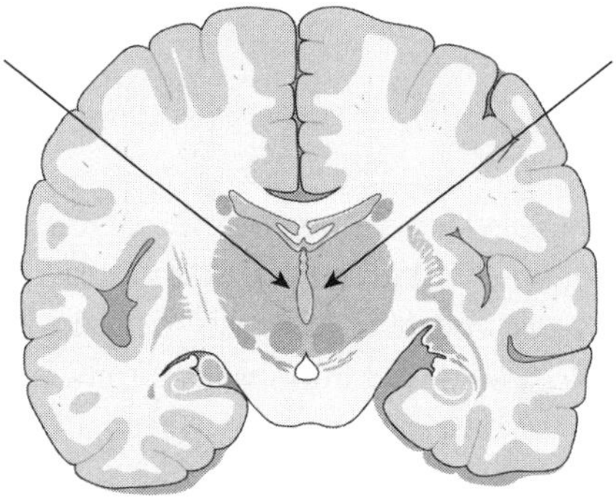

Figure 5.2 Gender differences in performing skills and tasks

Females generally outperform males in the following skills/tasks:
- fine motor skills—ability to move fingers rapidly in unison
- computation tests
- multitasking
- recalling the position of objects in an array
- spelling
- fluency of word generation
- tasks that require being sensitive to external stimuli (except visual stimuli)
- remembering landmarks along a route
- use of verbal memory
- appreciation of depth and perceptual speed
- reading body language/facial expressions

Males generally outperform females in the following skills/tasks:
- targeting skills
- working vocabulary
- extended focus and concentration
- mathematical reasoning and problem-solving aptitude
- navigation with geometric properties of space
- verbal intelligence
- habit formation and maintenance
- most spatial tasks

We should not confuse equality of opportunity with equality of outcome. Often the most objective criteria for a standardized test (e.g., SAT, LSAT) may result in higher scores for males or females due to general differences. Some advocate altering aptitude tests so that scores don't waver widely across genders, calling that the true "unbiased" measure. The PSAT, for instance, adopted a policy that, instead of weighting the math and verbal scores evenly, used an index called *two times the verbal score plus the math* to try to raise girls' scores. Adding a writing skills subtest to the PSAT has also been tried. These alterations, however, have still not offset boys' generally higher scores in math (Arenson, 1998).

Hearing

The female ear is better able to pick up nuances of voice, music, and other sounds. In addition, females retain better hearing longer in life. At 85 decibels, females perceive the volume twice as loud as males do. Females have greater vocal clarity and are one-sixth as likely as males to be monotone. They learn to speak earlier and learn languages more quickly. Three-quarters of university students majoring in foreign languages are female. Women excel at verbal memory and process language faster and more accurately. Infant girls are comforted by singing and speech to a greater degree than males are. In contrast to this summary of research, however, Klutky (1990) says that females have shown no significant auditory advantage in his studies.

Vision

Males have better distance vision and depth perception, while females excel at peripheral vision. Men see better in brighter light, while women's eyesight is superior at night.

Females are more sensitive to the red end of the spectrum; they excel at visual memory, are superior at interpreting facial clues and context, and exhibit greater ability to recognize faces and remember names. In repeated studies, women were able to store more random and irrelevant visual information than men were (Velle, 1992; Williams & Anderson, 1997).

Touch

Females have a more diffused and sensitive sense of touch. They react faster and more acutely to pain, yet can withstand pain over a longer duration than males can. Males react more to extremes of temperature. Females have greater sensitivity in their fingers and hands. They are superior in performing new motor combinations and in fine motor dexterity.

Activity

Male infants play more with objects, and more often, than females do. Females are more responsive to playmates. The directional choice, called *circling behavior*, is opposite for men and women. In other words, when right-handed males walk over to a table to pick up an object, they are more likely to return by turning to their right; right-handed females are more likely to return by circling around to their left.

Smell and Taste

Women have a stronger sense of smell and are much more responsive to aromas, odors, and subtle changes in smell. They are more sensitive to bitter flavors and prefer sweet flavors. A significant advantage in olfactory memory was found by Klutky (1990). Differences in the brain also relate to the effects of contaminants from beauty products. And by using neuroradiological imaging to assess brain shrinkage, Harper and Kril (1990) found that women are more susceptible to the damaging effects of alcohol than males are.

Problem Solving

Kimura and Hampson (1993) say that males and females have very different ways of approaching and solving problems. For decades, Kimura has been a pioneer in studying the anatomical and functional differences between the sexes. But what does this tell us about learning? Although there are some documented functional differences between the genders, there are also cultural and social biases that begin impacting us at birth. While some parents and administrators have opted for same-sex schools to better meet their students' needs, the effectiveness of such an intervention on cognition and social skills is unknown. There are some things, however, that educators can do in coeducational school settings to support gender differences in the learning environment.

Gender Tips for Teachers

- Be aware of how gender differences may impact learners.
- Be patient with learners who may not show the same brain development that others do (especially with boys who usually learn language skills one to two years later than girls do, or girls who are not as skilled in the spatial or physical tasks as early as boys are).
- Respect differences and appreciate each learner's uniqueness. Use differences as opportunities to teach about respecting our own and others' developmental time lines. Refrain from labeling students "slow learners" or "hyperactive."

What This Means to You

Becoming familiar with gender differences and their potential impact on learners is a good way to move toward meeting the gender-specific needs of all learners. Equal education does not mean that everything should be done the same; it means providing equal opportunity. There are real, physical differences between the sexes. Many male/female behaviors make much more sense when considered in the context of brain development. Eliminate groupings by age or grade. They tend to cause feelings of inadequacy because learners are being measured against those with developmental advantages instead of by effort. Change expectations. Keep students in age clusters, such as ages 2–4, 5–7, 8–10, 11–13, and 14–17. Become informed. Learn the differences between culturally reinforced stereotypes and real physical differences. Keep expectations high, and avoid stereotyping. Many problems may not be problems at all; they may simply be an expression of the natural time line along which one's developmental process unfolds.

6 The Impact of Physical Movement on the Brain

Amazingly, many educators are reducing physical activity time at schools because of time constraints and pressures related to the federal No Child Left Behind Act. Yet a large group of studies has linked physical activity with cognition, and they all have solid conclusions about how physical experience affects the brain. A brain-based perspective strengthens the case for maintaining (or even enhancing) physical activities in school. Was all of the research from the realm of neuroscience? No, it was from a wide range of disciplines. But every source still comes back to the brain—is it enhanced or impaired by the proposed strategy (physical activity)? The answer is clear: the brain is involved in everything we do at school; thus it benefits from physical activity in many ways.

PHYSICAL EDUCATION AND LEARNING

The evidence is in that physical activity is good for kids. There are clear, peer-reviewed studies from cognitive scientists (Hillman et al., 2006), exercise physiologists (Kramer, Erickson, & Colcombe, 2006), educational psychologists (Pellegrini & Bohn, 2005), neurobiologists (Vaynman & Gomez-Pinilla, 2006), and physical educators (Rhodes, 2006). These studies are supported by applied research that compares academic achievement in schools where kids do and do not have physical activity (Brener, Billy, & Grady, 2003). The President's Council on Fitness and Sports states that all K–12 students need at least 30 minutes a day of physical movement to stimulate the brain, and the research supports this claim. In fact, according to Larry Abraham, of the Department of Kinesiology at the University of Texas at Austin, it is just as important for students to move around in content classes as it is for them to count in physical education classes. Physical education, movement, drama, and the arts all add to, rather than detract from, the core curriculum.

Benefits of Exercise on the Brain

Exercise does several things for the brain. First, it enhances circulation so that individual neurons can get more oxygen and nutrients. This means a great deal when you're teaching content and you need the brain to be at its best. Second, it may spur the production of nerve growth factor, a hormone that enhances brain function. Third, gross motor repetitive movements can stimulate the production of dopamine, a mood-enhancing neurotransmitter. Finally, when done in sufficient amounts, we know that exercise enhances the production of new cells in the brain.

Aerobic exercise improves thinking and learning because of its ability to trigger a fast adrenaline-noradrenaline response, which is critical to facing and coping with challenges. Even a brisk 20-minute walk can be enough to serve both the body and the mind. Getting out and moving around is the key.

 **What This Means to You**

- Use more slow stretching and breathing exercises to increase circulation and oxygen flow to the brain.
- Incorporate energizers every 20 minutes or so.
- Make sure that some of your planned activities have a built-in component of physical movement (e.g., going outside to do a project, working on jigsaw puzzles).
- Provide manipulatives; have students hold, mold, and manipulate clay or other objects.

- Give learners permission to get up without permission to move around, stretch, or change postures so that they can monitor and manage their own energy levels.
- Facilitate hand movements each day with clapping games, dancing, puzzles, and manipulatives. Invent new ways to shake hands or greet each other. Engage learners in cooperative activities and group work.
- Provide activities that offer varying levels of physical and mental challenge with plenty of feedback mechanisms for support.
- Offer novel activities, learning locations, and choices that require moving.
- Encourage student-generated learning goals, ideas, and experiences.

In spite of the data on exercise, an astonishingly low 36 percent of K–12 students in the United States participate in a daily physical education program. We know exercise fuels the brain with oxygen, but it also triggers the release of neurotrophins, which enhance growth, impact mood, cement memory, and enhance connections between neurons. In fact, it is one of the best things you can do for your brain.

Given all the activations happening at once, physical performance probably uses 100 percent of the brain. There is no known cognitive activity that can claim this. Van Pragg, Christie, Sejnowski, and Gage (1999) say that regular exercise may stimulate the growth of new brain cells and prolong the survival of existing cells. In describing the results of studies in this area, they call the differences between the exercisers and nonexercisers striking. More important, the production of new brain cells (neurogenesis) is correlated with improved mood, memory, and learning. While earlier research was done with rats, more recent work by Pereira et al. (2007) was conducted with humans and verifies the earlier data. It turns out that physical education at school is a great idea for many reasons, just one of which is that it builds new brain cells. There are no data that say that about any other class at school!

Growing Up Active

We know that neurogenesis is correlated with improved learning (Shors et al., 2001) and memory (Kitabatake, Sailor, Ming, & Song, 2007), and appears to be inversely correlated with depression (Nandam, Jhaveri, & Bartlett, 2007).

Neuroscientists at the University of California, Irvine discovered that exercise triggers the release of brain-derived neurotrophic factor (BDNF), a natural substance that enhances cognition by boosting the ability of neurons to communicate with each other (Griesbach, Hovda, Molteni, Wu, & Gomez-Pinilla, 2004). When the Irvine researchers examined aging rats that had exercised daily on a running wheel, they found elevated BDNF levels in various areas of the brain, including the hippocampus, which is critical for memory processing. BDNF has been shown to accelerate the development of long-term potentiation (LTP), or memory formation, in young rats. When researchers at the National Institute of Child Health and Human Development bred mice that lacked the BDNF gene, they found that the animals had markedly reduced LTP in the hippocampus. The researchers were then able to correct the defect by reintroducing the BDNF gene into hippocampal neurons in these mice. Other researchers have discovered the potential effects of BDNF on LTP, and they believe that the findings offer new possibilities for studying and treating memory deficits in disorders such as Alzheimer's disease. In short, exercise truly affects the mind, mood, and memory as well as overall health (Dishman et al., 2006).

Beyond the effects found in the research, an ultimate fringe benefit exists as well: exercise can reduce stress. Thus, physical exercise is still one of the best ways to stimulate the brain and boost learning.

What This Means to You

Be purposeful about integrating movement activities into everyday learning. Provide much more than mere hands-on activities. Facilitate daily stretching exercises, walk-and-talks, dancing, role-playing, seat changing, quick energizers, and movement games. The notion of using only logical thinking in a mathematics class flies in the face of current brain research. Brain-compatible learning means weaving math, movement, geography, social skills, role-playing, science, and physical education together.

Sensorimotor Integration in Kids

Many researchers believe that sensorimotor integration is fundamental to school readiness. In one study in Seattle, Washington, third-grade students studied language arts concepts through dance activities that included regular spinning, crawling, rolling, rocking, tumbling, pointing, and matching. Although the districtwide reading scores showed an annual average decrease of 2 percent, the students involved in the dance activities exhibited an increase of 13 percent in six months.

Some believe that sensory stimulation is so important that, deprived of it, infants may not develop the movement–pleasure link in the brain. Although the research makes fewer connections between the cerebellum and the brain's pleasure centers, there is a growing concern that some infants deprived of touch, movement, and/or interaction may grow up to have a violent disposition. Unable to experience pleasure through usual channels of pleasurable activity, their need for intense states, one of which is violence, may propel them toward antisocial responses. With sufficient supply of the needed "drug" (movement), children are fine; deprive them of it, however, and problems arise.

What This Means to You

When students' energy lags, have them stand up while you continue to talk for a few minutes. Then facilitate a diffusion activity or energizer, or ask them to start a relevant discussion with a partner. Once their attentional systems have been reactivated, allow them the choice of sitting or standing.

The Chemistry of Physical Activity

Most of us would say we feel better when we are healthy, exercise a bit, or work out. A brain that is fully engaged is far more efficient and effective. To be at its best, the brain needs the right balance of chemicals. First, a little surge of dopamine is good not only for our mood, but also for our working memory (Knecht et al., 2004). There is evidence that exercise regulates norepinephrine and heart rate, which is significant in terms of increasing blood flow to the brain. Also, norepinephrine is a memory fixative that aids in the ability to remember content (Gillberg, Anderzen, Akerstedt, & Sigurdson, 1986). The harder researchers look, the more evidence we find that exercise stimulates the good chemicals, the ones that enhance mood, learning, and memory.

For students who are "stuck" or at a standstill, engaging in many activities is a smart thing to do. This means standing up for recess, having physical education classes, and engaging in energizers in the classroom. Cross-lateral movements can be the perfect, simple antidotes for engaging both sides of the brain to full advantage, and they are particularly effective for students who are sleepy, overwhelmed, frustrated, or experiencing a learning block.

 **What This Means to You**

When you go for a brisk walk or work out before starting your day, you feel better. This is no coincidence. An active body enhances an active mind. Learners who are active tend to be more alert. Building physical activities into your daily schedule models good learning practice. Take two minutes when you start your class to activate your learners. A short stretching session, a brisk walk, or some cross-lateral movements will all go a long way in activating learning. Also, provide brain breaks throughout the day. They don't have to be long, just well timed. When attention spans start to fade, you know it's time.

7 Stress and Threat

Stress is your bodily reaction to a perception, not reality. It occurs when you experience an adverse situation or person in such a way that you perceive you're out of control, or losing control, and your goals are compromised. If your goal is to get home safely and on time to make a dinner appointment, stress occurs in your body when there's a traffic accident up ahead and your goal of getting home on time is threatened. There is no stress in a school, a building, or a job. It's not "out there." There are exceptions, of course; you may be exposed to toxic levels of chemicals or a "sick building" and that may stress out your body by compromising your immune system. But typically, stress is what occurs in your body as a result of your perceptions. Change your perceptions, and you change your stress levels.

TYPES OF STRESS

All of us have experienced *good* stress and *bad* stress. Good stress (*eustress*), occurs in short bursts; it is simply stress that is not chronic or acute. It occurs when we feel moderately challenged and believe we can rise to the occasion. Under these circumstances, the body releases chemicals like cortisol, adrenaline, and norepinephrine, which heighten our perceptions, increase our motivation, and strengthen our bodies—all conditions that enhance learning. Eustress occurs when we have the following:

- actively want to solve a particular problem
- have the ability to resolve the problem
- perceive some sense of control over circumstances
- get sufficient rest between challenges
- can think of a potential solution to the problem

The negative form of stress (*distress*) occurs when we feel threatened by some physical or emotional danger, intimidation, embarrassment, loss of prestige, fear of rejection or failure, unrealistic time constraints, or a perceived lack of choice. Distress occurs when we

- are confronted with a problem we don't want to solve
- don't perceive a solution to the problem
- lack the resources to solve the problem
- feel the risk levels involved are unacceptable
- have little or no control over circumstances
- experience repeated situations of intense prolonged stress

The Brain in Distress

Threats are defined as any stimulus that causes the brain to trigger a sense of fear, mistrust, anxiety, or general helplessness. This state can be a result of physical harm or perceived danger (usually from teachers, parents, or peers), intellectual harm (unrealistic performance expectations or time constraints; lack of resources, support, or positive role models), or emotional harm (embarrassment, humiliation, or isolation). Under any type of perceived threat, the brain does the following:

- loses its ability to correctly interpret subtle clues from the environment
- reverts to familiar, tried-and-true behaviors

- loses some of its ability to index, store, and access information
- becomes more automatic and limited in its responses
- loses some of its ability to perceive relationships and patterns
- is less able to use higher-order thinking skills
- loses some long-term memory capacity
- tends to overreact to stimuli in a phobic-like way

In the brain, a change in conditions (e.g., from comfort to fears, threats, or danger) focuses selective attention and instigates a subsequent reaction. This initial recognition of uncertainty causes the amygdala to send a message to the hypothalamus, which begins the chemical cascade to the adrenals, and soon the glucocorticoids (e.g., cortisol) and amines (e.g., noradrenaline) prepare you for the event. The frontal lobes also monitor the event. Cortisol is a hormone that is a temporary source of energy, and for half an hour or even a few hours, it can be helpful. But over the course of days, weeks, or months, chronically high levels of cortisol wreak havoc on the brain.

The difference between positive or moderate stress and distress or threat is distinct. Positive or moderate stress is good for learning; distress and threat are not. Chronic stress makes students more susceptible to illness. In one study (Johnston-Brooks, Lewis, Evans, & Whalen, 1998), learners examined just prior to test time revealed depressed immune systems and lower levels of an important antibody for fighting infection. Such findings may help explain the vicious academic performance cycle with which most of us have become all too familiar: more test stress means more illness and missed classes, which eventually means lower test scores, and the cycle of failure repeats. In addition to increased cortisol levels, recent studies (e.g., Casolini et al., 1993) link chronic stress to low serotonin levels, which are suspected risk factors for violent and aggressive behavior patterns.

The amygdala is at the center of all our fear and threat responses. It focuses our attention and receives immediate direct inputs from the thalamus, the sensory cortex, the hippocampus, and the frontal lobes. Neural projections (bundles of fibers) from the amygdala then activate the entire sympathetic system. Under duress, the sympathetic system triggers the release of adrenaline, vasopressin, and cortisol—chemicals that immediately change the way we think, feel, and act.

The area of the brain most affected by high stress or threat is the hippocampus, which is very sensitive to cortisol. Over time, cortisol may weaken the brain's local memory and indexing systems and may narrow perceptual mapping. The hippocampus is also the center of the body's immune system, so the chronic release of cortisol weakens the body's ability to fight disease, too.

> Learners in a state of fear or threat experience not only reduced cognitive abilities but also weakened immune systems.

A chronically high cortisol level leads to significant physical changes in the brain. Stanford scientist Robert Sapolsky (1992, 1994, 1996, 1999) found atrophy levels of 8 to 24 percent in the hippocampus of Vietnam War veterans with posttraumatic stress disorder: "We have known for many years that stress can interfere with neuron production in the fetal brain and that it can damage and even kill pre-existing neurons. Now we have evidence, as well, that when there is neuron production in the adult brain, stress can also disrupt it" (2004, p. 137). High levels of distress can cause the death of brain cells in the hippocampus—an area critical to explicit memory formation. And chronic stress impairs students' ability to sort out what's important and what's not.

For the most part, the brain responds to threat exposure in predictable ways. The moment a threat is detected, the brain jumps into high gear, and new research reveals that threatening environments can trigger chemical imbalances. Especially worrisome is the reduced level of serotonin, which is a strong modulator of emotions and subsequent behaviors; when serotonin levels fall, violence often rises. Threats also elevate levels of vasopressin, which has been linked to aggression. These imbalances can trigger impulsive and aggressive behavior that some researchers believe can lead to a lifetime of violence.

The Distressed Learner

The list of potential threats to learners is endless, and threats can be found anywhere, from one's own home to a neighbor's home, from the hallway outside your classroom to the gang that rules the neighborhood. It could be an over-stressed parent; a boyfriend; a rude classmate; an unknowing teacher who threatens a student with humiliation, detention, or embarrassment; or a combination of these stressors. When the brain is put on alert, defense mechanisms and behaviors are activated, which is great for survival but not for learning.

Many learners who are underperforming may be simply overstressed. At the elementary level, students may not even be cognizant of the problem. To some learners, achieving at a higher level may simply feel like an impossibility. If all you've ever known is poverty, for example, it's difficult to realize an alternative—a necessary step in the resolution process. Identifying the core stress, then creating an awareness of alternatives, and ultimately working toward a desirable change are the cornerstones of empowerment. And it is this foundation that is critical to optimal learning. Remember, if the brain is in survival mode, it won't effectively process and recall even simple semantic facts like a basic math calculation. You can bet, however, that it will remember information such as "Today is Daddy's payday, which means he'll come home drunk. I better stay away from him tonight." Children who happen to be in such a state likely won't complete their homework because their emotions (and therefore attention) are drawn to more immediate matters.

Distressed children typically experience constricted breathing, which can alter how they focus and blink. Distress can impact learners in other ways, too. Figure 7.1 shows how various levels of distress, including a traumatic event, can impact memory. A stressful physical environment adds to the problem. Crowded conditions, fear of violence or peer retaliation, and even fluorescent lighting can impact learner stress. All of these stress factors contribute to the low achievement/low self-esteem cycle of failure that can occur in spite of a child's high IQ or natural intelligence.

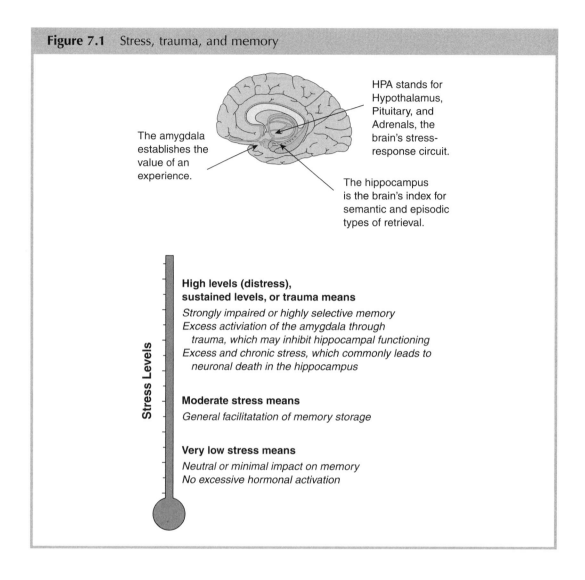

Figure 7.1 Stress, trauma, and memory

HPA stands for Hypothalamus, Pituitary, and Adrenals, the brain's stress-response circuit.

The amygdala establishes the value of an experience.

The hippocampus is the brain's index for semantic and episodic types of retrieval.

Stress Levels

High levels (distress), sustained levels, or trauma means
Strongly impaired or highly selective memory
Excess activiation of the amygdala through trauma, which may inhibit hippocampal functioning
Excess and chronic stress, which commonly leads to neuronal death in the hippocampus

Moderate stress means
General facilitatation of memory storage

Very low stress means
Neutral or minimal impact on memory
No excessive hormonal activation

 **What This Means to You**

Ensure that learners have the necessary resources and support to complete the assignments you give them and, ultimately, to resolve high-stress issues that may be harming them outside of class. Keep in mind that learners will experience undue stress if they do not (1) perceive that a solution is possible, (2) have the necessary resources to solve a problem, (3) have a sense of control over a bad situation, (4) have sufficient time to learn, or (5) have the ability or awareness to manage their stress. Seek help if you suspect that a learner is facing threat and high stress outside the classroom. Routinely incorporate brief stretching, breathing exercises, and purposeful play in the classroom. Introduce activities and games that add an element of moderate challenge, fun, and stress-free learning to your classroom environment.

Quite a few stressors, many of which cannot be avoided, influence our emotional environment. For an adult, it's the noise, erratic drivers, mean-spirited customers, hardheaded colleagues, selfish bosses, broken-down copy machines, insensitive family members, financial worries, and screaming children that provide the emotional stress. For youth, it's fundamentally no different. A typical school day is full of broken promises, hurt feelings, and fear of the unknown. The project that flopped, the low math score, the bully's mean remarks, the insensitive teacher, the pressure to conform, the pressure to perform, the popularity contest, decisions about values and choices, and concerns about money—all of these can be sources of stress that the brain responds to as threats. Accepting our different roles in various social situations can be difficult for adults, let alone youngsters just beginning to grapple with self-identity issues. But if we have a lot of support, we can manage the stress more effectively. Support can come from many places and does not necessarily have to originate at home to positively influence learners.

According to a study by Reis and Diaz (1999), despite lack of parental involvement in the academic pursuits of nine ethnically diverse and economically disadvantaged high school females, the students continued to perform well on achievement tests and in other academic endeavors. The students attributed their success to interaction with other high-achieving students, teachers, and mentors—all of whom helped deepen a strong belief in self. Thus, student achievement may be less related to the parental support factor than to the enrichment factor of the educational setting.

 **What This Means to You**

Social status or popularity, especially among teens, represents a key source of stress for students. For example, a student who may be the top dog at home, but is just one of many in a classroom of 30, may feel stressed out at school. However, such a student may shine if given a leadership role. Since the brain's chemistry can actually change in response to one's perception of social status, it makes good sense to shift leadership roles often to ensure that all students have a chance to lead as well as to follow. Providing an enriched learning environment at school can contribute a great deal to a student's support system. The less support a child receives at home, the more he or she needs to be enriched and supported at school. A simple step you can take to offset the many stressors learners face is to provide more predictability in the form of school and classroom rituals. Predictable events, like a graded paper returned when promised or a peer cheer for completing a project on time, helps put the unsettled brain at ease.

The good news is that moderate levels of stress seem to facilitate storage and retrieval of memories. Moderate stress, such as that caused by an approaching deadline, may also provide the impetus or motivation necessary to accomplish a challenging task. If learners feel capable of overcoming the challenge before them and have the support to persevere through difficult times, the stress state can help establish an optimal learning environment. On the other hand, some studies suggest that low-stress environments increase student receptivity to complex and novel learning.

What This Means to You

Incorporate stretching and breathing sessions, quiet walks, support groups, music, and art therapy in your own life. Give your students and yourself downtime or reflection time to get in touch with your stress levels. Reducing sugar and caffeine intake can help moderate the effects of stress. Only when you are effectively managing your own stress levels can you be at your best for others.

Reactions to Threats

Students often swing or swat at each other to establish rank and control. Such territorialism can be heard in comments such as, "Don't look at me that way!" For the sake of survival, the brain's receptor sites have adapted to the dangers in the normal environment. But misreading danger cues is common for learners who are stressed out. What may be perceived as a friendly gesture by someone who is emotionally well adjusted may be experienced as a threat by one who has lived with chronic threat. While this behavior frustrates teachers, it makes perfect sense to the student whose life seems to depend on it.

There are other costs to threats as well, such as induced or learned helplessness. Because survival always overrides pattern detection and complex problem solving, stressed students are less able to understand subtle connections, patterns, and implications. Under threat, the brain uses less of the reflective higher-order thinking skills of the frontal lobes and resorts to using more of the reflexive nature of the amygdala. In addition, only immediate consequences are likely to be considered in the decision-making process. These results have tremendous implications for learning. Nonstressed learners will exhibit better thinking, understanding, attention, concentration, and recall. Consider, for example, that when you are taking a test (and feeling stressed because of it), an answer can be on the tip of your tongue but not quite accessible. But the moment you turn in the test, the answer pops into your head.

The residue of threat lingers in the body for up to 48 hours. The student who was abused at home on Saturday night is bringing his or her body's stress imprint to school on Monday morning.

Changes in blood flow to the brain also negatively impact the threatened learner. According to Drevets and Raichle (1998), of the University of Pittsburgh, when faced with threat, we experience an increased blood flow to the lower (ventral) area frontal lobes and a decreased flow to the upper (dorsal) area of the frontal lobes. This means that the area of the brain that processes emotions is getting the lion's share of the blood, creating the feeling of being overwhelmed, while the area used for critical thinking, judgment, and creativity doesn't receive enough.

What This Means to You

Avoid calling on learners unless they volunteer. Eliminate discipline policies that are based on fear or threats. Avoid scorekeeping, overt comparisons, or situations that cause embarrassment to students. Never threaten students by saying you'll send them to a higher authority, kick them out, or call their parents. Provide an enriched environment with many opportunities for interactions with caring adults and other learners. Reduce testing and grade stress by providing more frequent reviews, feedback, and remedial support. Make assessments more genuine and meaningful by recognizing the personal challenges of individual students and acknowledging even slight progress.

Putting an End to Threats

High stress or threats have no place in schools. This is a given. The military, which purposely creates a stressful environment for accelerated learning, is a well-known departure from the rule. The very essence of boot camp is to create a stressful environment that resembles a war environment. Thus, threats and punishment are commonplace. However, even the military's teaching approach changes when a soldier is being trained for a technical job or a leadership position that requires critical recall and strategic thinking rather than pure obedience. Teaching soldiers to obey commands at all costs is, in fact, a very different learning task from teaching them to show good judgment and be critical thinkers.

Students who have experienced early chronic exposure to threats and high stress, particularly those who come from violent backgrounds, usually have attention difficulties. Survival behaviors, such as consistent and constant shifting of eyes, voice, and attention, are the norm as these students unconsciously scan the room for potential predators or prey.

What This Means to You

Here are four ways you can reduce the impact of threat on your learners:

1. Increase their sense of safety at school. Encourage discussions about their fears, worries, and causes of stress. Sometimes just the opportunity to talk about these issues helps reduce the burden. Incorporate small-group activities, and model effective communication and problem solving. Increase use of teams and other strategies for developing group identity and support. When necessary, seek outside help and support.

2. Encourage positive relationships among learners. Give them time to relate to each other in ways that go beyond the superficial. Allow for personal choice in the process of creating teams. Once teams are formed, allow learners to remain with the group long enough to develop strong interpersonal relations. Help learners resolve conflicts by being available to offer support, but not enforcing your influence too strongly. Help them with their decision-making and problem-solving

(Continued)

(Continued)

skills, but don't solve problems or make decisions for them. Initiate team cheers, applause, and other affirming rituals that make students feel good.

3. Provide numerous opportunities for learners to express themselves. This can be initiated through the use of art, dance, poetry, singing, sharing, journal reflection, sports, debate, and small-group activities. Give students the opportunity to set their own ground rules and classroom standards. What they help create, they will buy into and adhere to with less resistance.

4. Activate prior learning by reviewing the previous lesson(s). Offer generous feedback, and establish mechanisms for self-evaluation and peer review. If nothing else, this simple strategy will reduce learner stress and increase confidence immensely.

When you create a safe and relaxed learning environment with an absence of threats and high stress, many learners will surprise you. They'll very quickly exhibit improved thinking and problem-solving skills and fewer disruptions and behavioral problems. Although no one can be expected to provide the perfect environment (there is no such thing), providing an emotionally and physically safe environment with plenty of opportunity for enrichment will go a long way toward offsetting life's little (and sometimes big) imperfections.

HOW RELAXATION AFFECTS LEARNING

In a study of 39 older adults conducted at Stanford University's School of Medicine, researchers determined that a memory training course was more effective when students were relaxed. The study compared two groups. The first was taught to relax every muscle in their body, from head to toe, prior to the memory training. The other group was simply given a lecture on positive attitudes. Both groups then attended a three-hour memory training course and were ultimately tested on what they learned. The overall score of the group that received the relaxation instruction was 25 percent higher than that of the control group.

 **What This Means to You**

Physical relaxation may be more important to learning than previously realized. Teach your students about the benefits of relaxation. Better yet, make it part of the daily routine.

The Importance of Rest

The brain may become more easily fatigued when conditions for learning are less than optimal. To get the brain's best performance, deep physiological rest is necessary.

How much sleep is enough? This varies from individual to individual; however, we do know that it is the REM period (the dream state) of sleep that is most crucial. While some adults require eight to ten hours of sleep per night, others seem to function perfectly well on four to six hours. Learners who are short on sleep may perform well on short quizzes requiring rote memorization but not as well on extended performance testing that requires stamina, creativity, and higher-level problem solving.

> Learners who live under stress, anxiety, or constant threats of some kind don't receive the all-important brain rest needed for optimal functioning. Without it, learning and thinking are impaired.

Energizer Ideas

- Use the body to measure things around the room and report the results: "This cabinet is 99 knuckles long."
- Play a Simon Says game with content built into the game: "Simon says point to the South" or "Simon says point to five different sources of information in this room." Ensure that's it's a win-win activity with no risk and no embarrassment.
- Do a giant class mind map, or break into teams and do group mind maps.
- Have students move around the room, for example, for a scavenger hunt: "Get up and touch seven objects around the room that represent the visible spectrum or colors of the rainbow."
- Relate locations to new learning: "Move to the side of the room where you first learned about the food chain related to our pet snake."
- Conduct thinking games and values exercises that require learners to move: "Move to the left side of the room if you feel more like an ant or to the right side of the room if you feel more like an elephant."
- Even simple games we learned as children are great. Have learners jump rope and sing rhymes that reflect new learning.
- Spell difficult words to the tune of "B-I-N-G-O" while clapping out each letter until the whole word has been spelled.
- Wake up the class with a silly stint of Hokey-Pokey, Ring Around the Rosie, or London Bridge. Even adults can benefit from these childhood favorites.
- Conduct a ball-toss game, incorporating content from prior learning. This is great for reviews, vocabulary reinforcement, storytelling, or self-disclosure.
- Have students rewrite lyrics to familiar songs, substituting new words.
- Play verbal Tug of War, in which dyads choose a topic from a list and each must devise an argument. After the verbal competition, the whole class engages in a traditional game of Tug of War with dyad partners on opposite sides.
- Use cross-laterals, such as arm and leg crossovers. Cross-lateral movements activate both brain hemispheres for greater integration of learning. "Pat your head and rub your belly" or "Touch your left shoulder with your right hand" are examples of cross-laterals. Others include marching in place

while patting opposite knees, touching opposite eyes, knees, elbows, heels, and so on.

- Facilitate stretching and breathing exercises. Rotate leaders.
- Provide frequent breaks for water or walking around, or provide this option to learners anytime they need it.
- Ask students to plan and lead a class session, or break into teams and have each present an activity to the rest of the class.

Part 3

Sensory Contributions to Learning

8 The Role of Sight in Learning

All of us in education know that the facilitator–learner relationship is of critical importance to the training and learning environment. Unless this relationship is characterized by trust, safety, and mutual respect, the learning process will be stilted. Walk into any classroom or training facility, and you can very quickly sense the impact of the emotional, intellectual, and social climate. Yet there's much more to the puzzle of learning. How important is the effect of physical environments on our students? You may be surprised!

In San Diego, California, at the recent national convention for the 18,000 members of the American Institute of Architects, the keynote speaker was not an architect; he was Fred Gage, an internationally known award-winning neuroscientist from the Salk Institute. He provoked the audience by suggesting that our environments

have a powerful effect on our brains. He asked the audience to investigate the extent to which architects take this into consideration when they design buildings. Out of this intellectual groundbreaking, a new academy, the Academy of Neuroscience for Architecture, was launched. Times have truly changed.

> **The essential understanding here is that** we have a whole new discipline, one that shapes our brains. Our buildings influence not just how we feel but the physical structure of the brain. This chapter begins to break down how the senses influence people and what that means for educators.

SIGHT'S IMPACT ON THE LEARNING PROCESS

How does your brain know what specifically to pay attention to in the moment? Our eyes are capable of registering 36,000 visual messages per hour. Between 80 and 90 percent of all information that is absorbed by our brains is visual. In fact, the retina accounts for 40 percent of all nerve fibers connected to the brain. That enormous capacity is why it is important to be aware of the environmental factors that influence how we see and process information.

Information flows both ways, back and forth, from our eyes to the thalamus to the visual cortex and back again. This feedback is the mechanism that shapes our attention so that we can focus on one particular thing, like a teacher or a book. Amazingly, our "attention headquarters" gets feedback from the cortex at nearly six times the amount that originated from the retina. Somehow, the brain corrects incoming images to help you stay attentive, but once it reaches its immediate capacity, it demands the filtering-out of incoming stimuli. In other words, the brain has an intrinsic mechanism for shutting down input when it needs to.

The essential elements enabling our eyes to compose meaning from our visual field are contrast, tilt, curvature, line ends, color, and size. These elements, perceived even before learners consciously understand what they've seen, can inform teaching practice and provide a framework for attracting learner attention. While optimal learning involves far more than getting and keeping students' attention, the principles of piquing the brain's interest are useful.

> Attract the brain with movement, contrast, and color changes. Our visual system is designed to pay close attention to those elements because they each have the potential to signal danger.

Color in the Environment

In television commercials, one of the big trends in getting our attention is retro; advertisers use black-and-white ads. Does this get our attention? Yes, but momentarily. The brain is wired to pay attention to novelty, movement, intensity, contrast, and saturation. Black-and-white ads can work, but color is a truly powerful medium, and one that is generally underestimated. A recent study (Vuontela, Rämä, Raninen, Aronen, & Carlson, 1999) measured the relative value of verbal cues versus color cues in learning and memory. In testing memory for verbs and memory for colors, learners better recalled color. And when objects were tested against color, once again, color memory was stronger. Even an intention to remember did not affect the outcome of the experiment.

How a color affects you depends on your personality and state of mind at the moment. If you are highly anxious and stressed, for example, red can trigger more aggressiveness. But if you are relaxed, the same color can trigger engagement and positive emotions.

Our color preferences may say a great deal about us, and they may be innate. For example, you might walk into a room and immediately feel uncomfortable, while another room makes you feel happy and inspired and another makes you feel drained and depressed. It is very possible that the prevailing colors of the rooms are impacting your mood more than you realize. Even in everyday language, it is obvious how strongly color influences us. We often identify people by the color of their skin or the color of their clothing. In general, we remember colors first and content second.

 **What This Means to You**

Use color handouts, and vary color widely on your PowerPoint presentations instead of having the same constant blue background. Consciously choose the colors you use in the classroom; hang colorful posters; and encourage the use of bold color in mind maps, painting, projects, and posters, and softer colors for background.

Concrete Vivid Images

What is the best way to convey information? Is it through discussion, reading material, or computers? No, say Fiske and Taylor (1984). Concrete vivid images are most influential. Neuroscientists theorize that this is because (1) the brain has an attentional bias for high contrast and novelty; (2) 90 percent of the brain's sensory input is from visual sources; and (3) the brain has an immediate and primitive response to symbols, icons, and other simple images.

The brain is wired to identify objects more quickly when they differ from a group of similar objects. These differences are analyzed in parallel by the brain so that while the learner may be observing location, the brain may also be processing property differences, such as color, form, and weight. This evolutionary tendency of the brain provides us with an edge that has ensured our survival. Thus, in the learning environment, working models, project-based assignments, a variety of information media (e.g., computers, videos, books, cameras, writing equipment), and an array of art supplies make for productive learning and a happy brain. We remember best the concrete visuals that we can touch and manipulate.

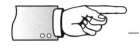

What This Means to You

Visuals are an important key to remembering content. Make lectures or presentations more compelling to the brain by using objects, photographs, graphics, charts, graphs, slides, video segments, bulletin board displays, and color. For maximum impact, change media frequently—from inspiring videos and vivid posters to mind maps, drawings, and symbols. Challenge students to generate evocative images, either through visualization or in the form of artwork, posters, or murals.

The Impact of Peripherals

The brain absorbs information from surrounding peripherals on both conscious and unconscious levels. Many people commonly use peripherals (or items of visual interest in the environment), but they may support learning even more than we realize. Since the brain prioritizes stimuli like colors, decorative elements, sounds, and smells, the importance of these elements should be considered in the planning of optimal learning environments. Peripherals in the form of positive affirmations, learner-generated work, and images depicting change, growth, and beauty can be powerful vehicles of expression. With direct instruction only (lecture), audience recall drops quickly, but with the addition of peripherals, effortless, subject-specific, longer-lasting recall is generated.

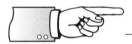

What This Means to You

Assess what factors may be currently influencing your learning space. Consider influences like posters on the wall, room color, concrete visuals, and bulletin board items. A passive approach to surroundings can actually detract from the learning. Make an effort to enhance your visual environment. Add interesting collections, photos, objects, and bulletin boards.

Light in the Environment

Lighting strongly influences vision, which strongly influences learning. Thus, anything we can do to make our eyes more comfortable in the classroom contributes to optimal learning. Although we are rarely consciously aware of it, fluorescent lights have a flickering quality and a barely audible hum, which can have a very powerful impact on our central nervous system. Apparently the brain reacts to this visual-auditory stimulus by raising cortisol levels (an indication of stress) and causing the eyes to blink excessively.

In a study of 160,000 school-age children, Harmon (1951) found that lighting was a major contributor to student health and learning. By the time the children in his study were in sixth grade, more than 50 percent had developed deficiencies related to classroom lighting. Subsequent changes to lighting in the learning environment reversed the results. Six months later, the same children experienced a 65 percent reduction in visual problems, a 55 percent reduction in fatigue, a 43 percent reduction in infections, and a 25 percent reduction in posture problems. In addition, they exhibited an increase in academic achievement.

A more recent study conducted by the Heschong Mahone Consulting Group (2007) focused on 21,000 students from three districts in three states. After reviewing school facilities, architectural plans, aerial photographs, and maintenance plans, each classroom was assigned a code indicating the amount of sunlight it received during particular times of the day and year. Controlling for variables, the study found that students with the most sunlight in their classrooms progressed 20 percent faster on math tests and 26 percent faster on reading tests compared to students with the least lighting. These gains are astonishing considering how hard school districts work to raise reading and math scores. Most districts would be overwhelmed with a 5 percent gain in test scores; a 20 percent gain is unheard of. But that's the disparity between classrooms with the lowest and brightest light.

In the follow-up study, the Heschong Mahone Group (2007) found how sources of glare can negatively impact learning. Classrooms that face the morning sun (east) and have no blinds or tinted windows will underperform compared to classrooms facing north. In subjects with more visual dependency, such as math, students did better when whiteboards were used (versus overhead projectors) since the lighting was better. Schools would do well to heed lighting and student performance research in an environmental context when designing buildings.

> The positive impact of a quality learning environment with strong natural lighting is both dramatic and lasting.

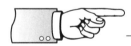

What This Means to You

Soft, natural lighting is best for learning. Provide a variety of lighting types in your room, and give learners a choice in determining where they sit.

Seasons Can Impact Learning

Can sunlight affect learning? Definitely, says Orlock (1993). The length and brightness of daylight affects the body's melatonin and hormone levels and influences the release of neurotransmitters. A portion of the hypothalamus (located in the diencephalon region) gets direct information from the eyes and sets the body's time clock. This affects concentration, energy, and moods. And anything that affects our mental state, in turn, impacts our learning.

A specific condition known as Seasonal Affective Disorder (SAD) was recorded in 1987 by the American Psychiatric Association. This officially recognized biomedical problem, which seems to affect women more than men, is caused by a lack of exposure to sunlight during the winter months. It results in depression and, therefore, negatively impacts learning. Residents who live closer to the equator face less than a 2 percent chance of being affected by SAD, but those farthest from the equator face up to a 25 percent chance. The best time for learning is when the hours of the day are longest—from June to August in the Northern Hemisphere and December to February in the Southern Hemisphere (Liberman, 1991). However, these are the times when most schools break for the summer vacation and the holidays.

A small amount of artificial light or sunlight therapy can alleviate the symptoms of SAD if the dosage of light is strong enough, says Liberman (1991). Phototherapy treatment sessions can last from 30 minutes to 4 hours a day. The good news is that 85 percent of SAD sufferers who participate in light therapy are relieved of the symptoms of anxiety and depression.

 **What This Means to You**

We may be able to improve learning simply by improving the lighting during the darker winter months. Explore your options for improving the lighting in your environment during periods of low sunlight. Ask other teachers if they have witnessed symptoms of SAD among their students. And seek the help of your medical provider if you think you may be suffering from the condition yourself.

9

The Role of Touch in Learning

While many types of obstacles are known to impair learning, heat stress is one of the most preventable. Choice may be the most important variable when it comes to classroom temperature. There is a wide variety of perceptions as to what constitutes a warm or cool room, say Dunn and Dunn (1992). Preference differences exist among individuals in and across the same age groups, and they can change from day to day depending on mood, weather, and numerous other factors. However, 70 degrees (give or take a few degrees) is a good baseline for optimal temperature in the learning environment.

Ornstein (1991) speculates that the evolutionary benefit of humans standing upright and walking is related to the brain's temperature needs. The farther our heads are from the ground (where the temperature is higher), the less likely we are to get overheated. According to Ornstein, "a rise of only 1 or 2°C in brain temperature above normal is enough to disturb brain functions" (p. 58). In fact, as brain size has increased over the past two million years, one of the most important adaptations has been the cooling mechanisms. Our very survival is vested in maintaining normal brain temperature.

What This Means to You

Comfort is important in the process of optimal learning. It is better to be too cool than too warm, but it is best to be neither of these. Provide learners with choice, and be responsive to their temperature needs.

SCHOOL ENVIRONMENTS AND COGNITION

Research suggests that well-planned learning environments stimulate learning and reduce discipline problems. When orchestrated with other sound teaching strategies, brain-friendly learning environments strengthen neural connections and aid long-term memory, planning, and motivation.

Ayers (1999) examined the relationship between high school facilities and student achievement. The researchers used the Design Appraisal Scale for High Schools (DASH-I) to measure the different design variables and determine a total quality score for each school in the study. Based on the results of the analyses, school-design variables explained approximately 6 percent of the variance in English and social studies performance, 3 percent in science performance, and 2 percent in both mathematics and writing performance.

Learning Hurt by Bad Environments

As you might expect, shattered windows, broken-down restrooms, leaky roofs, insufficient lighting, and overcrowding have a significant negative impact on cognition. Such conditions are frequently found in many schools in the United States, and, unfortunately, far too many children, especially those in poor urban areas, are schooled in dilapidated, crowded facilities. According to several comprehensive research studies, including Earthman's (2002) influential paper, school facilities play a significant role in student outcomes.

Findings suggest that quality facilities coupled with strong academic programs are conditions that are essential to student learning. "Educators are under enormous pressure to be frugal in their spending, but short-term cost-cutting when they could be designing the environment to improve learning and amortize the costs over the life of the building," says Scott Milder (personal communication, May 8, 2005) with Dallas, Texas–based SHW Group Architects, a firm specializing in sustainable and brain-friendly learning environments. When schools make positive environmental changes, the return lasts for the life of the school.

Brain-Friendly Environmental Changes

Acoustics. When you build a sound system into the school from the start, it is much less costly. There are no walls to tear down, and any wiring can be hidden. In addition, the rooms can have better-angled walls and smarter use of carpeting to reduce sound reverberation. Each of these is more than just functional; kids learn more successfully, and teachers are happier.

Better Lighting. New vertical solar monitors can harness the natural light and provide 100 percent of daily classroom light. The sunlight is drawn into the light monitor and bounced off a series of baffles to provide soft, evenly distributed daylight throughout the facility.

Temperature/Humidity/Ventilation. Teachers need classroom control to maintain the appropriate comfort levels. Heating and cooling mechanisms should be independent for each classroom, simple to operate, quiet, and controllable separately by each teacher in each classroom.

Optimal View. With over 50 measured variables in school environments, from pets to moldy air to carpeting, you would think that having a view would rate low. But it doesn't. Students do better when they have a calming, distant view of vegetation, as opposed to a close-up view of people walking by (Heschong Mahone Group, 2007).

Staff Areas. Staff members need comfortable spaces where they can get away from the hustle and bustle to think, relax, plan, and reflect. To keep teachers from going crazy, smart schools provide at least three places where teachers can get support: (1) a quiet reflective spot for power naps; (2) a learning center, library, or staff media center; and (3) a destressing area with a treadmill and a floor mat for stretching.

10 The Role of Taste in Learning

How much does what we eat (or don't eat) affect our brains and thinking? Plenty, say researchers. Vitamins and other nutrients are essential to brain development, neural maintenance, and brain metabolism. Glucose, a blood sugar, is the sole source of fuel for our brain cells, yet many learners skip breakfast—our first opportunity to refuel after overnight glucose depletion. And in spite of the fact that alertness, memory, visuospatial ability, attention, and planning/organizational skills are directly impacted by critical vitamins (e.g., A, C, E, most of the Bs, folic acid, lecithin, magnesium, sodium, potassium, zinc, iron, boron, selenium), many learners are deficient in these nutrients (LaRue, Koehler, Wayne, & Chiulli, 1997; Ramakrishna, 1999).

NUTRITION AND LEARNING

Your brain uses tyrosine to make the neurotransmitters dopamine and norepinephrine. These two electrically charged chemical messengers are critical to alertness, quick thinking, and fast reactions, and they help you perform calculations, maintain attention span, and increase conscious awareness. Tyrosine is found in protein-rich foods, such as milk products, meats, fish, eggs, and tofu.

> It's time to take learner nutrition more seriously. An important step is to enhance school lunch menus and provide healthful vending-machine snacks.

Unfortunately, many low-income learners typically have carbohydrates for breakfast (e.g., toast, breads, cereals), which may not provide the boost to thinking that a breakfast of, for example, eggs, bacon, and cottage cheese would.

The Importance of Vitamins

Research supports the importance of taking a daily vitamin supplement in addition to eating your spinach, oranges, bran cereal, seafood, chicken, and vitamin-packed foods. Benton and Roberts (1988) measured visual acuity, reaction time, and intelligence among a group of 90 12- and 13-year-olds, some of whom were given a multivitamin supplement and some of whom were given a placebo. The experiment group showed a significant increase in all scores over the control group.

Vitamin deficiencies as an obstacle to learning remain a serious concern to educators. Even minor vitamin deficiencies can impact learning performance. A study by Sampson, Dixit, Meyers, and Houser (1995) examined the breakfast-eating habits of 1,151 low-income second- and fifth-graders in schools without federally funded breakfast programs. The researchers found that on any given day, 12 to 26 percent of the students attended school without having eaten anything. At least 36 percent of the students were obese, and a significantly greater portion of the students consumed less than 50 percent of the required daily allowance of vitamins A, E, B_6, and folate. And 25 percent of the students were found deficient in vitamin C, calcium, and iron.

LaRue and colleagues (1997) concluded that vitamin supplements can yield cognitive benefits even if the person is already eating smart. Their study followed 137 elderly, healthy participants for six years and found that the vast majority of them improved their performance on memory, visuospacial, and abstraction tests (initially given six years earlier) after taking supplements of vitamins C, E, A, B_6, B_{12}, and folic acid while routinely eating well-balanced meals.

Riggs (1997) conducted a study on the cognitive effects of B_{12}, B_6, and folic acid, and she found that participants with the highest levels of these vitamins in their blood performed significantly better on a battery of memory and spatial copying tests than those with lower blood levels of these vitamins. Vitamin B_{12} is found abundantly in shellfish; B_6 is found in chicken, fish, and whole-wheat products; and folic acid (or folate) is contained in fortified cereals and leafy green vegetables.

 **What This Means to You**

You or your learners may be underperforming due to dietary deficiencies. To boost your alertness and mental performance, include a vitamin supplement in your diet. The best foods for protein are eggs, fish, turkey, tofu, pork, chicken, and yogurt. Eat just three to four ounces, since eating more than this does not further increase alertness. Keep saturated fats low and iron levels normal. Eat a "nibbling" diet of many meals a day, if possible. Too much time between eating can cause loss of concentration and decreased alertness. Allow for appropriate foods in the classroom. Make sure to give learners several opportunities to eat nutritious snacks throughout the day, and talk to them about the positive role that nutrition can play in performance, thinking, and testing. Many important nutrients are often not found in a typical learner's diet.

Nutrition Tips for Teachers

- Vitamin and mineral deficiencies result from either insufficient food intake or inadequate nutrient absorption by the body. Either can cause fatigue, loss of appetite, poor concentration, failing memory, hostility, depression, and insomnia. If you suspect a problem among your learners, seek advice from the health/medical consultant at your school. Vitamin and mineral deficiency can be determined by a simple blood test.
- If your school is located in a predominantly poor area, there is an increased chance that many students are not eating properly. Initiate steps to begin a federally funded breakfast and lunch program at your school if one is not already in place.
- Monitor the menu of your existing cafeteria lunch program, and make suggestions for additional vitamin-nutritious meals.
- Instruct your students on the relationship between a nutritious diet and cognition and well-being.
- Megadoses of vitamins have no benefits and can be toxic. Stay within the required or suggested dosage.
- Vitamin supplements are best absorbed when taken with food. However, caffeinated beverages, alcohol, nicotine, and aspirin and other medications obstruct absorption. (Note: Since high levels of caffeine are known to block vitamin absorption, school district contracts that promote the increased presence of beverage vending machines on campus may be adversely affecting student nutrition and learning.)

Dehydration Hurts Learning

Good nutrition promotes healthy functioning of neurons—the essential building blocks of mental performance. The brain's most critical need is for oxygen and glucose, and the only way to provide this fuel is to consume foods rich in the necessary nutrients. Its second most important need is water—pure water—every day for optimal learning. The brain is composed of 80 percent water and is highly sensitive to variances in pH levels. The transmission of neurons is dependent on the polarity of each cell, which is influenced by calcium, potassium, and water. Typically, thirsty learners drink coffee, tea, or soft drinks, but these drinks are diuretics, and the body processes them as foods rather than water. The sugars bind to the water, and the beneficial effect of the liquid is therefore lost.

As with all animals, we have a "consumatory" prowling behavior that emerges when water is absent or restricted. This behavior increases our stress hormones (cortisol) and our responses to novelty (overreactions). But within five minutes of consuming water, there is a marked drop in stress hormones, and our behaviors become more predictable.

 **What This Means to You**

Students who are bored, listless, drowsy, and lacking concentration may, in fact, be dehydrated. Talk to your students about the consequences of dehydration and the value of water. Remind them to drink water on their breaks and at recess. Allow them to bring water bottles into the classroom. If you teach sessions that last more than 45 minutes, it is especially important to see that students have access to water.

Beyond oxygen and water, Wurtman (1986) says that amino acids set the stage for learning—either positively or negatively. These ingredients in protein are critical to the brain. Tyrosine and tryptophan are two examples: the first enhances thinking; the latter has a calming effect.

Hydration's Importance to the Mind

How important is hydration to physical health and cognition? Water is an essential nutrient required for life. It is the most abundant compound in the human body and makes up between 45 and 75 percent of our body weight. Of all the organs in the body, the brain has the largest amount of water. (Muscles have the next largest proportion of water.) Additionally, the body's regulation of thirst and fluid intake is closely integrated with the brain (McKinley & Johnson, 2004). Yet putting a bottle of water on every kid's desk will not produce high test scores.

Here is the straight story about water. The brain is about 70 percent water, and it is sensitive to bodily fluid levels. When the levels drop, the hypothalamus is activated, and it sends a message to correct the situation. A prompted survival response may impair learning. The blood is also highly sensitive to pH variances.

Too much acid or alkaline is bad. Neuronal transmission is highly sensitive to cell polarity, which is influenced by water. Fruit juice, soft drinks, coffee, and tea are all diuretics—they provide less neutral pH water to the system because, as mentioned earlier, the sugars and other components bind to the water, and it is treated as food by the brain. You get a portion of the water value, but no one seems to know what percentage. So it is best to make sure to consume some pure water.

When the first stage of dehydration occurs, we are not aware of it. Typically we have an adrenal response that's reoriented to consumatory behavior, which means a restless, active state of scattered attention. For some teachers this creates a discipline problem. Students will then have a hyperresponse to novelty and other stressors. During the second stage of dehydration, we become aware of it, but we are often too slowed down to take action. We get lethargic and slow-minded.

When exposed to novelty, the stress response is lower if water has been consumed. Drinking water reduces the body's physiological response to adverse situations. However, the single most important determinant to reducing this stress response is control. Being able to get water is almost as important as drinking it. Adults should drink about 4–6 glasses a day (32–48 ounces) under nonathletic or non-heat-stress conditions. Students should have easy, free access to pure, clean water, but studies suggest that to optimize peak mental performance, they should drink only if they're thirsty.

Participants in McKinley and Johnson's (2004) study were asked to take a thirst inventory. They then performed a rapid visual information-processing (RVIP) task that consisted of pressing the spacebar on a computer keyboard as quickly as possible when they detected an unbroken sequence of three odd or three even digits. The participants later performed the same task two more times at 25- and 50-minute intervals after consuming either a small (120 ml [standard wine glass]) or moderate (330 ml [standard soft drink can]) amount of chilled tap water. (A control group consumed nothing.) The researchers allowed five minutes for water consumption. (Yes, toilet breaks were permitted between tasks!)

The effect of water on the RVIP task was very different between participants who had rated their thirst as "high" and those who rated it as "low." When initial thirst was high, the more water ingested, the higher the performance. When initial thirst was low, the more water ingested, the poorer the performance. This reminds us not to go overboard with pushing water on students every 10 minutes. Drink those eight glasses of water a day only during times when you're really thirsty—or try to stretch out water consumption more evenly throughout the day. A drink of water can improve or impair mental performance depending on small differences in thirst.

About Hydration

Strenuous exercise of up to 60 minutes can result in dehydration, which causes temporary deficits in memory, information processing, and other cognitive performance among adults (Tomporowski, 2003). Scientists also know that physical and cognitive performance is impaired when you experience only 1 or 2 percent dehydration (Kleiner, 1999), directly impacting selective focusing, rapid information processing, executive and high-level decision making, and breathing. Several other factors can also contribute to the likelihood of chronic, mild dehydration: dissatisfaction with the taste of water, a poor thirst mechanism, and environmental conditions (Kleiner, 1999).

To be well hydrated, every day the average sedentary adult man must consume at least 2,900 ml (12 cups, or about 3 quarts) of fluid and the average sedentary adult woman at least 2,200 ml (9 cups, or about 2 quarts) of fluid, in the form of beverages, soups, and food (Kleiner, 1999). Just less than half of the necessary water the body needs comes from solid foods (approximately 1,000 ml [4c] of water) and metabolic processes (about 250 ml [1c] from water oxidation). Mara Vitolins, assistant professor of public health sciences at Wake Forest University Baptist Medical Center, points out that increasing your intake of plain water also helps with weight loss (cited in Conn, 2003). Many sports drinks and soft drinks are heavily sugared; replacing one can of soda with one glass of water can cut as many as 200 calories from your diet. Also, people sometimes have trouble distinguishing between mild hunger and mild thirst. Vitolins recommends that before grabbing a snack, drink a glass of water first. As a result, the sensation of hunger often goes away (Conn, 2003).

What's more, water helps facilitate virtually all biochemical reactions occurring in the body. These include forming the structures of macromolecules (e.g., proteins, glycogen); serving as the solvent for minerals, vitamins, amino acids, glucose, and other nutrients; aiding in the digestion of nutrients and the safe elimination of body waste and toxins; and serving as the body's thermoregulator.

There is no scientific basis for saying that we must all drink at least eight glasses of water a day. Valtin (2002) searched extensively through medical and scientific databases and found no evidence to suggest that the general population is chronically underhydrated. Nor did he find evidence that the diuretic effects of caffeinated beverages like soft drinks, coffee, and tea undermine the body's hydration levels. In fact, overhydration has its own set of potential hazards, including water toxicity and increasing your exposure to pollutants. However, being a student places much higher performance demands on the brain. We know that in conditions of extreme heat or cold or strenuous exercise, more water is required to maintain good health. The same can be said for strenuous learning or studying. That means keep the water available and drink often.

Action Steps

- Drink plenty of fluids, especially during aerobic workouts or on hot days. Fruits and vegetables are also excellent sources of water. People who are not habitual caffeine drinkers should counter the diuretic effects of caffeine with two cups of water for each cup of coffee they consume.
- Be aware of the signs of moderate to severe dehydration: headache, fatigue, vision problems, cold hands and feet, flushed skin, heat intolerance, lightheadedness, muscle cramps, sunken eyes, and dark urine with a strong odor. In addition to physical exertion, severe vomiting and diarrhea can lead to dehydration.

- Should dehydration occur, get to the hospital immediately. Intravenous fluids will often reverse the condition and can save the lives of infants and young children.
- Consider adding water bottles to your list of required training supplies. Trainees who keep water with them will be less likely to miss part of your program by stepping out for a drink. Realize, however, that an increased water intake may require more frequent bathroom breaks!

The Final Word

There are two additional issues to consider. First, children from lower-income families cannot afford a constant supply of bottled water from home. It's expensive and often no better than tap water. Second, plastic water bottles are a terrible storage device because the plastic is made from polychlorinated biphenyl, which is a known health hazard. In fact, many studies point to it as a source for lowering cognition, not raising it. Of the 111 studies on plastic bottles, all that were industry funded showed no ill effects of biphenyl. Yet over 90 percent of all independent studies showed toxic risk levels from biphenyls. Any positive effect from hydrating might be lost by the negative effects of the poisons in the container. Which leads us back to . . . the need for many convenient drinking fountains!

 **What This Means to You**

Ensure that learners have access to water during class. Allow them to bring water bottles into the learning area or to be excused momentarily without embarrassment or hassle. Explain to your students the value of water versus other beverages, such as soda, juice, and coffee. Remind them to rehydrate often. Also discuss the relationship between good nutrition and good brain power. Encourage learners to eat "close to the earth"—fresh fruits and vegetables—and to eat regular frequent meals that include good protein and fiber.

11

The Roles of Smell and Acoustics in Learning

While most of the attention in environments is rightfully given to the big three (sound, light, and temperature), there's more that influences the brain. Just as quickly as with light, sound, or temperature, when we walk into a room, we experience an aroma or know if there is music playing. Both of these may, in fact, be just novel enough to distract us from any glaring deficiencies in other environmental areas. Our sense of smell is so primordial and essential to us. Although ours is nowhere near as keen as it is in many animals, it's usually good enough to alert us to big changes such as smoke, a floral aroma, or food. Add to that the pleasant or irritating sound from selected music, and you've got an immediate reaction in your students. And you can be sure of one thing: it won't be a neutral reaction. Let's jump in and learn what we can do to make it a good reaction.

CREATE AN OPTIMAL ENVIRONMENT FOR LEARNING

Have you ever taken a class or workshop in a stark classroom, conference room, or hotel meeting room? They often feel so sterile and unresponsive. It's possible for some music, aromas, or even plants to shake you out of your doldrums. Scientists at the National Aeronautics and Space Administration (NASA) have discovered that the use of plants creates a better learning and thinking environment for astronauts (Wolverton, 1997). Could this research also apply to other indoor learning environments? Wolverton, who headed up NASA's Environmental Research Laboratory in the 1980s, says that certain plants have improved life for the astronauts (and, he adds, his personal life at home) by removing pollutants from the air, increasing the negative ionization in the atmosphere, and charging the indoor air with oxygen. In fact, he also points out that Federal Clean Air Council studies found that plants raised indoor oxygen levels and increased productivity by 10 percent. A single plant may impact 100 square feet of space. According to Wolverton, the best plants for optimal cleansing the air and enhancing the oxygen in indoor learning environments are areca palms, lady palms, bamboo palms, rubber plants, gerbera daisies, yellow chrysanthemums, ficus benjamina, philodendrons, dracena deremensis, and peace lilies.

Plants not only make the air cleaner and richer, they also enhance the aesthetic environment. Most of us use only 10 to 25 percent of our lung capacity with each breath we take. This is bad because stale air starves the brain. For optimal learning, provide your learners with fresh, uncontaminated, highly oxygenated air so that what air they do breathe in is good air. The ideal humidity level is between 55 and 65 percent. Encourage your students to breathe deeply, and don't forget to do so yourself, especially when you're feeling stressed or pressured.

 **What This Means to You**

We often don't realize the impact of the air we breathe, and the pollutants around us go unnoticed. But these factors are important in creating an optimal brain-friendly environment for learners. Include four to eight plants in your classroom if it's of typical size (approximately 900 square feet), and more if it's larger.

Aromas May Boost Attention and Learning

Aromas are especially important because they take one of the most direct pathways to the brain (Dhong, Chung, & Doty, 1999). Pauli, Bourne, Diekmann, and Birbaumer (1999) reported that undergraduate psychology students experienced significant cognitive enhancement in word-association and word-naming tests after being exposed to a background odor of vanilla. Similar results were noted by Schnaubelt (1999), who studied the effect of lavender scents in learning environments. And in a 40-minute test of vigilance (similar to that needed for air traffic controllers and long-distance drivers), production workers who received 30-second bursts of peppermint or lily of the valley every 5 minutes showed a 15 to 20 percent improvement in performance (Dember & Parasuraman, 1993).

A direct link between the olfactory glands and the nervous system sets up a vital connection that can aid learning. Smells in our environment can influence our mood, anxiety, fear, hunger, depression, and learning. Olfactory dysfunction is among the first signs of Alzheimer's disease and is often observed in other brain-related disorders such as schizophrenia (Moberg et al., 1999; Vance, 1999). Research examining the effects of smell on cognition is ongoing, but preliminary evidence points to a positive connection. According to Sullivan and colleagues (1998), patients with brain injuries performed equal to that of healthy participants in the control group in a vigilance test after receiving periodic whiffs of peppermint.

The olfactory regions are also rich receptors for endorphins, which generate feelings of pleasure and well-being. People can distinguish odors with tiny variations in the chemical structures of the odor molecule. Try experimenting with various aromas in your classroom or training environment. Ask learners what they think. Do they feel energized and more alert after a whiff of peppermint? How do they feel when surrounded with the aroma of chocolate chip cookies, a pumpkin-scented candle, or fresh-baked bread? If nothing else, you'll enjoy watching your learners' eyes light up when they walk into the room.

One last thing: keep in mind that many kids have sensitivities to aromas. You must know your students well, and if there is any allergic sensitivity to an aroma, stop using it or move the source of it far from anyone who is allergic to it. The safest aromas are those that are mild or from real foods. (For further reputable scientific discussion of this topic, see Schnaubelt, 1995; and Davis, 1999.)

 **What This Means to You**

Smell is an important sense that is underutilized in the learning environment. An awareness of aromas can give you a very powerful edge in reaching learners and optimal learning states. Peppermint, basil, lemon, cinnamon, and rosemary enhance mental alertness, while lavender, chamomile, orange, and rose calm nerves and encourage relaxation.

Impact of Negative Ionization

Have you ever heard of negative air? In spite of its label, this is a desirable thing. The air around us is electrically charged by many environmental factors, including cosmic rays, friction caused by air movement, radioactive dust, ultraviolet radiation, and atmospheric pressure changes. In areas of higher population, the atmosphere's healthy balance of positive to negative ions can be disrupted. Human activity, it seems, destroys negative ions and ultimately reduces the amount of oxygen in the air. Smoke, dust, smog, pollutants, electrical emissions, heating systems, coolers, and traffic exhaust are all culprits. The air can become too highly electrified (i.e., contain too many positive ions), and the human reaction to it is counterproductive to learning.

When it comes to air, the more negatively charged it is, the better. When the electrical charge in the air is too positive, it can cause you to feel groggy, lethargic, sleepy, or depressed. Have you ever noticed that when you stand in front of a waterfall, step outdoors just after a rain, stand atop a mountain, or just get out of a shower, you feel fresh and energized? You may be enjoying the benefits of negative ionization.

Ion levels have been studied for their ability to speed recovery in burn and asthma patients, to stabilize alpha rhythms, to positively impact reactions to sensory stimuli, and to impact serotonin levels in the bloodstream. Higher levels of alertness and an improved sense of well-being are definite learning enhancers. Evidence pointing to air quality as an important factor should not be ignored.

THE ROLE OF ACOUSTICS IN LEARNING

Poor acoustics is a huge issue for schools. Poorly designed classrooms that fail to address and reduce ambient noise, echo effects, reverberation, and other acoustical problems cause a decrease in student attention and an increase in off-task behaviors, and discipline problems increase—issues that take a serious toll on learning. Why? Our amazing brains typically process up to 20,000 bits of auditory stimuli every second. This means that nearly every sound in the range of 20 to 15,000 cycles per second is fair game for processing. Getting students to hear what we want them to hear in the classroom, therefore, can be a problem. As an example, the most significant variable in predicting reading performance (even greater than being identified as a gifted student) is a loud ballast hum from poor lighting. It has a –19 percent influence, compared to the +16 percent effect of being gifted (Heschong Mahone Group, 2007).

Asbjornsen, Hugdahl, and Hynd (1990) conducted a study with 40 right-handed females undergoing 36 trials with four different instructions to determine if hearing side mattered in direction following. The researchers varied head and eye turns (together and separate) for both left and right sides, and varied directions toward and away from the source of the voice. The results indicated a significant and clear right-ear advantage in all groups during all conditions.

Tomatis (1983), one of the pioneers of sound, acoustics, and hearing, says that the right ear is the best ear for listening, learning, and language. In fact, his studies show that normal readers became dyslexic when they can listen only with their left ear. Conversely, he has successfully treated thousands of dyslexic people by using sound therapy to improve their ability to hear high frequencies.

Campbell (2001), a music pioneer, claims that half the people in the world change their voice response depending on which ear receives the information. He adds that if you have sequential, detailed information for your learners, position yourself so that you can address their right ear and the superior path to the left side of the brain.

 **What This Means to You**

Watch your learners. You may notice that some of them consistently turn their head to one side or the other in an effort to hear better. They may be unconsciously appealing to the side of their brain that will provide them with the best understanding. Just as there is right- and left-handedness, there are also ear dominances—however, this characteristic is unrelated to handedness. Some listeners will do better by changing positions or cupping their dominant listening ear. As you present material, ensure that you reach all learners effectively by frequently changing your position in the room. Move around the room as you speak, and consider redefining the "front" of the room. Have students move into groups each day, and allow them to sit in different locations each week so that no one is consistently disadvantaged.

Music's Effects on the Mind-Body

Teachers who use music appropriately have a tremendous advantage; it's like having a second instructor in the class to manage the emotional state of students. We all know that music is a common experience for students. Amazingly, it seems that our responses to music may even be hardwired into our brains. In *The Origins of Music,* Wallin, Merker, and Brown (1999) say that music may be a universal form of communication that has influenced species preservation and played a role in mate attraction, bonding, and harmony. Weinberger (2004), a neuroscientist at the University of California at Irvine, points out that recent findings support the theory that the brain is specialized for the building blocks of music. His research suggests that the auditory cortex responds to pitch and tones rather than simply raw sound frequencies and that individual brain cells process melodic contour. Other specific correlates regarding the brain and music are illustrated in Figure 11.1.

Music's impact can also be felt on heart rate, as measured by the pulse, which tends to synchronize with the beat of the music we're hearing—the faster the music, the faster our pulse. The body resonates at a stable molecular wavelength; music has its own frequencies, which either resonate or conflict with the body's own rhythms. When both are resonating on the same frequency, we feel in sync, we learn better, and we're more aware and alert.

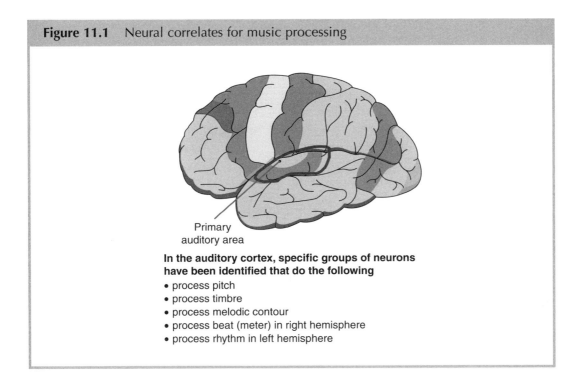

Figure 11.1 Neural correlates for music processing

Primary
auditory area

In the auditory cortex, specific groups of neurons have been identified that do the following
- process pitch
- process timbre
- process melodic contour
- process beat (meter) in right hemisphere
- process rhythm in left hemisphere

Music's potential effects on the mind and body include the following:

- increases muscular energy
- increases molecular energy
- influences heartbeat
- alters metabolism
- reduces pain and stress
- speeds healing and recovery in surgery patients
- relieves fatigue
- aids in the release of emotions
- stimulates creativity, sensitivity, and thinking

Music elicits emotional responses, encourages receptive or aggressive states, and stimulates the limbic system. The limbic system and the subcortical region of the brain are involved in engaging musical and emotional responses, as well as mediating long-term memory. This means that when information is imbued with music, there's a greater likelihood that the brain will encode it in long-term memory.

Some neuroimaging studies have compared activity and blood flow in the brains of professional musicians and nonmusicians as they listened to music. In one study, when the musical novice listened, the right hemisphere lit up, while the left hemisphere and amygdala were more activated when the professional musician listened (Bangert & Altenmüller, 2003).

Activations occur in various parts of the brain depending on the specific learning task involved. The brain responds differently depending on whether you are learning music by hearing it, playing it, reading it, or being told about it; visualizing a score; recalling a concert; or experiencing strong emotions involving music. Each of these events is registered and processed differently in the brain. For example, melody activates the right brain, while harmony and rhythm activate more of the left brain and measuring beats activates the cerebellum.

It is deplorable that in some public schools music is considered a right-brain frill. According to Peretz and Zatorre (2005), there is little doubt that the entire brain is engaged when a person listens to music. Reading or composing music particularly engages both sides of the brain. Music in the curriculum, both as a subject of study and as accompaniment to the learning process, may be a valuable tool for the integration of thinking across both hemispheres of the brain.

Incorporating Music in the Classroom

We may be underutilizing music in the context of learning. We rely so much on our own voices to deliver meaning, yet music is a terrific carrier of information to the brain. In fact, recent research suggests that music may be a powerful tool in building reasoning power, memory, and intelligence.

There are numerous ways to incorporate music purposefully. Depending on the type of music played, you can also use it to help learners cool down, warm up, relax, mark an important moment or occasion, or get energized. Beyond influencing mood, some educators use music to carry positive messages and content to learners unconsciously. At its most elemental, frequent music playing will increase the pleasure of learners and give them the feeling that their classroom is a happy, pleasant place to be.

Learner preference is an important consideration when incorporating music in your lesson plans. As with room temperature, there are significant differences among learners with regard to music preference. For some, low-level background music (e.g., Baroque, in a major key) will be ideal, while others will get a better response from nature sounds or popular tunes with inspirational lyrics. Variables include learners' cultural background, learning-style preference, personality type, and prior exposure. Volume level, music type, and instruments featured are other important factors. The best results will be achieved by experimenting with your particular group of learners (see Figure 11.2).

 ## What This Means to You

Provide a variety of lighting and music choices, maintain a quiet corner with earplugs available for students who prefer silence, and encourage cooperative as well as individual learning.

Figure 11.2 Tips for incorporating music in the classroom

- Discuss the value of music with learners. Explain the various benefits and approaches (e.g., stress reduction, memory enhancement, concentration, creativity, energy).
- Listen to music selections carefully before playing in class, choose them purposefully, and exclude any that are not gentle on the nerves. Do not use selections whose lyrics are questionable or not easily interpreted.
- Involve learners in the choice and control of the music. Ask for a volunteer to be the DJ for the day, and be open to student suggestions for selections that will complement the learning goals.
- Customize music selections based on activity type.
- Involve students in a classroom study that focuses on determining what learning benefits might be derived from music.
- In dealing with differences, preferences, and complaints, do not disregard anyone's opinion. It is very important to accommodate the needs of all learners as much as possible.
- Be careful not to overuse or saturate the environment with too much music. A basic rule is to limit its use to 30 percent of total class time.

Consider this: each of the countries with the highest science and math results in the world has strong music and arts programs. The relationship between SAT scores (college entrance) and music participation is strong. Compared with honors students (570), average SAT scores for students who take music are 538 for verbal and 537 for math (National Association for Music Education, n.d.). This is not a causal relationship, but the correlations are glaring. In fact, almost all of the past winners in the prestigious Siemens Westinghouse Competition in Math, Science and Technology (for high school students) play one or more musical instruments.

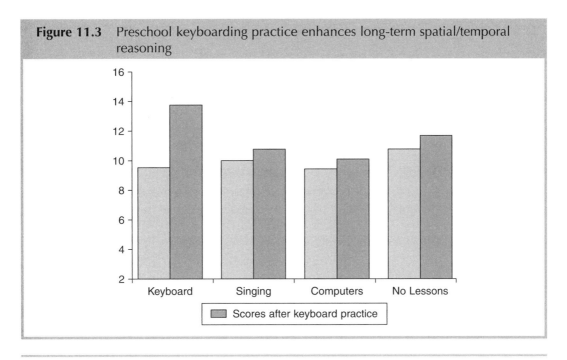

Figure 11.3 Preschool keyboarding practice enhances long-term spatial/temporal reasoning

Note: N = 78 children, ages 3–4 years; object assembly task, 60–75 minute sessions; study done over 2 years. Mean score for age groupings.

Source: Rauscher et al., 1997.

Brown, Martinez, and Parsons (2006) discovered that while Mozart beat the control group in spatial reasoning enhancement, the other simple subsets of music actually helped the experimental subjects do far better than did listening to Mozart. What this suggests is that it may be rhythms, tones, or patterns of music that enhance learning. Discretion is important when interpreting and applying these results. There are appropriate times for music in the learning process, just as there are appropriate times for quiet. The degree to which learning may be enhanced and the specific learning tasks impacted remain the focus of current research.

> Significant positive effects of music during learning have been reported, especially with music from the baroque and classical periods; however, positive effects of music played during testing are not consistently supported.
>
> —Uschi Felix

Robert Monroe, engineer and founder of the Monroe Institute, has produced audiotapes that use specific beat frequencies to create synchronized rhythmic patterns of concentration. He calls them *Hemi-Sync*. They are designed to help the left and right hemispheres of the brain work together for increased concentration, learning, and memory. He reports a multitude of success stories with a wide range of learners from first graders to seniors.

The following learning benefits are attributed to music:

- relaxation and stress reduction (stress inhibits learning)
- fostering of creativity through brain-wave activation
- stimulation of imagination and thinking
- stimulation of motor skills, speaking, and vocabulary
- reduction in discipline problems
- focusing and alignment of group energy
- conscious and subconscious information transmission

 **What This Means to You**

Music should be used purposefully and judiciously for best results. Too much can saturate the listener, reducing its effectiveness. As a general rule, music should be used for no more than 30 percent of total class time (unless, of course, it's a music class). How the music is used is as important as the type of music used. Many educators have claimed success using reggae, Latin, pop, jazz, new age, big band, waltz, hip-hop, rock, and soul. Don't get caught up in using only Mozart just because that's what we've heard the most about. Mozart is great, but it is just one piece of the larger puzzle. Other types of sound are beneficial as well. Even clapping games, singing, nature sounds, and simple rhythms alter physiological states and create more receptivity for learning.

Beneficial Music Selections

What music is most beneficial? The answer to this question depends on the individual and what the intended state is. We know that the brain's attention is drawn by variations rather than predictable patterns; thus, if you want to increase writing focus, for example, Baroque on low in the background is great. Since Baroque, unlike most other types of music, is highly predictable, it poses a lesser distraction problem. If you want to increase your class's energy level, use energizing selections that have high beats per minute. If you want learners to relax, nature sounds or soft piano music is ideal.

What This Means to You

Because different types of music elicit different psychophysiological states, incorporate a variety of music types. For example, as learners are arriving, play music that creates a state of anticipation or excitement (e.g., epic movie themes, Olympic fanfare, the andante movements in major keys of Vivaldi's *Four Seasons,* Bach's *Brandenburg Concertos* in major keys). For storytelling, use music that has built-in peaks and valleys and that engages fantasy and emotion (classical or romantic). To deliver content with a musical accompaniment, use classical or romantic music. For closed-eye review or background accompaniment, low-volume Baroque is optimal. Many other forms of expression also work—from world beat, folk, jazz, or country to gospel, marches, pop, positive rap, or new age. Experiment and use what works for your particular circumstances. Have learners rewrite well-known songs with words that reflect what they're currently learning. Give them the opportunity to experiment (in a structured way) with music in the classroom.

Music as a Carrier to the Nonconscious

Music carries with it more than just feelings; the melody can act as a vehicle for the words as well. This powerful communication transfer can happen on either a conscious or nonconscious level. You may have noticed how easily children pick up the words to new songs. It's the melody that helps them learn the words. For example, consider how you learned the alphabet. If you're like most of us, you absorbed this fundamental information to the tune of "Twinkle, Twinkle, Little Star." As infants, we hear the melody over and over, and when it's time to learn the alphabet, we simply apply the letters to the tune. This is done so unconsciously that most of us don't even realize that the "Alphabet Song" and "Twinkle, Twinkle, Little Star" are sung to the same tune.

What This Means to You

There are many ways we can use music to carry messages into the minds of receptive learners. One is to use learner-generated songs. Have students select five songs that they already know well (e.g., "Jingle Bells," "Happy Birthday," simple and traditional folk songs). Then rewrite the song's lyrics with new words from the lesson. Sing the song several times. The new lyrics will bind easily to the minds of learners.

The Best Uses of Recorded Music

Entertainment

We often synchronize our body's pacing with common rhythms and beats.

Socialization

Music can bring people together.

Better Cognitive States Elicited

Manage learner states since specific music can enhance precise states for learning.

Emotions

Music—sung, heard, or performed—can trigger the release of the brain's natural opiates and hormones.

Delivery System for Content

Words can be embedded in music.

Memories Triggered

Elicit prior events, places, and people to trigger strong states.

Calming

Music can slow and calm the mind and body.

Priming

Activate precise, specific neural pathways for learning content, performing a task, or encouraging creativity.

Binding Learning and Meaning

Create a memory link between concept and state, making recall more likely.

Movement

Get people up and moving: dance, work, transit, talk, or take action.

12 The Role of Emotions in Learning

Traditionally, Western educators have separated thinking and feeling. Those days should be long gone; the two are inseparable. When we feel right, we can think better. Teachers commonly refer to the "feel" of their classes. This reference to the emotional state is critical. The ability to think is highly dependent on mood and emotional state. In the current test-taking climate, some seem to believe that thinking is cognitive and does not involve emotions. But brain research shows us that any disconnect between thinking and feeling is dead wrong. Renowned University of Southern California neuroscientist Antonio Damasio (1994) argues that the brain is a natural extension of the body, not the reverse.

In fact, while the brain feels like an isolated, lumpy, temperamental computer sitting on top of your neck, it's actually just a smarter part of your body. The new virtual reality games demonstrate that even visceral and proprioceptive inputs can also be simulated. It's all one huge, connected sensory map. How you feel directly influences your ability to think and solve problems.

> **The essential understanding here is that** our brains are highly sensitive to each of our emotional states, and they run our thinking ability in several important ways. Anyone interested in improving thinking skills had better understand the complex interplay between emotional states and cognition. Just as important, educators ought to know how they can influence the emotional states of their students.

THE NEW PARADIGM: "EMOTIONAL LOGIC"

The old way of thinking about the brain is that mind, body, and feelings are separate entities, but there's actually no division between these functions. Our emotions help us focus our reason and logic. Our logical side may help us set goals, but it is our emotional side that provides the passion to persevere through trying times. Certainly excessive or undisciplined emotions can harm our rational thinking, but a lack of emotion can make for equally flawed thinking (Damasio, 1994).

Holistic learning means that we as teachers acknowledge learners' emotions, feelings, beliefs, cravings, problems, attitudes, and skills, and include them in the learning process. While the outdated academic model addressed primarily the explicit aspects of the learner and learning (e.g., facts and figures, things we can touch and see), the prevailing model contends that students learn best when their minds, hearts, and bodies are engaged. The more aspects of self that we can tap into for learners, the more effective we'll be as educators.

> All learning involves the body, emotions, attitudes, and physical well-being. Brain-based learning advocates that we address these multiple variables more often and more comprehensively.

The influence of emotions on our behavior is immense. Because they give us a "live" report at all times on the body's response, they receive priority status. Scientists believe the critical networks that process emotions link the limbic system, the prefrontal cortices, and perhaps most important, the brain areas that map and integrate signals from the body (see Figure 12.2 later in this chapter). We know that damage to the limbic system (primarily the amygdala and anterior cingulate) impairs primary emotions (e.g., innate fear, surprise). But damage to the prefrontal cortices compromises the processing of secondary emotion—that is, our feelings about our thoughts (Damasio, 1994). Emotions let us mind the body's physical reaction to the world.

When the body experiences primary emotions, the brain reads them as part of the critical information that ensures our survival. The body serves as a critical frame of reference for the internal creation of our reality. In other words, the body generates the sensory data, feeds it to the brain, and then integrates it with emotions and intellect to form a *thinking triumvirate* for optimal performance and decision making. An over- or underreliance on any one of these elements can impair our quality of thinking.

Our thinking is not "contaminated" by emotions. Rather, our emotions are an integral aspect of the neural operating system. Emotions speed our thinking by providing an immediate physical response to circumstances. When a result makes us feel good, naturally we're going to select it over a result that makes us feel bad. And when we value something strongly—whether a principle, a person, or a thing—that relationship becomes emotionally charged. If our emotions have been badly neglected by others (especially early in life), this can result in emotional problems fortified by an overproduction of some neurotransmitters. However, such intense reactions to our emotions are a survival benefit and allow us to preserve what is important, including our lives.

What This Means to You

Develop a greater awareness of all the factors influencing your learners, and take the time to influence as many of these variables as you can. Although we clearly cannot control all of them, we can surely influence many more than has traditionally been expected. Your learners' emotional state is at least as important as the intellectual–cognitive content of your presentation. Never avoid emotions; deal with them gently and personally. Allow negatives ones to be processed and positive ones to be celebrated. Elicit positive emotional states from learners with enjoyable activities, games, humor, personal attention, and acts of caring. Modeling these states will teach learners indirectly how to better manage their own optimal states for learning. Give learners time to destress before you present new information. Reflect on your priorities as a teacher. Do you put learners' emotions and feelings on par with the mastery of content and skill learning? Remember, the two are directly biologically linked.

The Chemistry of Emotion

From the desire to learn to the etiquette we employ in the cafeteria, how we act usually reflects how we feel. Brain chemicals (neurotransmitters and neuropeptides) are released from neurons and transmitted to many areas of the brain and body. From excitement to calm, from depression to euphoria, these chemicals influence our thinking and behaviors. They are responsible for the lift we get from a cup or two of coffee, the thrill of a roller-coaster ride, and the common experience of having a gut feeling—as when neuropeptides released in your brain land at receptor sites in the gastrointestinal tract. Some of the most influential chemical inputs on feelings and behavior include serotonin, acetylcholine, dopamine, and norepineph-rine, which are released from areas such as the brain stem. These chemicals linger in our system, and once an emotion occurs, it is hard for the cortex to shut it off.

Are Feelings and Emotions the Same?

Neuroscientists usually separate emotions and feelings. Emotions are gener-ated from biologically automated pathways and are experienced by people uni-versally across cultures. The six universal emotions are joy, fear, surprise, disgust, anger, and sadness. Feelings, on the other hand, are culturally and environmen-tally developed responses to circumstances. Examples include worry, anticipation, frustration, cynicism, and optimism.

Although analyzing feelings is problematic, we have a vast array of highly specific and scientific ways to measure emotions. These measurements include electrodermal (skin) responses, heart rate, blood pressure, electroencephalogram activity, and brain-imaging techniques. With these common medical procedures, it is fairly easy to get readings on a student's response to fear; however, we have yet to find a way to measure the more elusive experience of feelings (e.g., a stu-dent's level of sympathy for a fellow classmate).

Feelings and emotions travel along separate biological pathways in the brain. While feelings may take a slower, more circuitous route, emotions always access the brain's superhighways, which are reserved for information that takes emo-tional priority over measured thinking—a survival mechanism that ensures intense, emotionally laden events get attended to immediately.

In an emergency situation, stopping to weigh and judge our feelings could cost us our life. When a lion is chasing you, this is not the time for reflection and contemplation. As Goleman (1995) points out, this priority status (although it has a critical purpose) also allows us to become "emotionally hijacked" by our responses. Simultaneously, our emotional system is acting independently as well as cooperatively with our cortex. A student who is getting threatening looks from another student, for example, may strike out at the other student before even thinking about it. The teacher's behavior-improvement lecture in response to the event will likely do little to change such automated responses. Rather, students need to learn emotional intelligence skills in a way that acknowledges what's hap-pening in their own bodies and reinforces more positive responses over time.

DISSECTING AN EMOTION

Your emotional state is composed of an emotion, a specific posture, your thoughts, your bodily sensations, your breathing rate, and the chemical balance in your body. We might call it the *moment* in the sense that it comes and goes. Damasio (1994) argues that the brain, mind, body, and emotions form a linked system and that "certain aspects of the process of emotion and feeling are indispensable for rationality" (p. xiii). He criticizes the typical neurologist's narrow-minded view of emotions: "uncontrolled or misdirected emotion can be a major source of irrational behavior . . . [but a] reduction in emotion may constitute an equally important source of irrational behavior" (pp. 52–53). Emotions are not separate, but rather enmeshed in the neural networks of reason. Damasio's work, based mostly on animal and human studies of subjects with brain damage, established that damage to particular areas of the brain—especially to the prefrontal lobe (bilaterally) and the amygdala—eliminate the ability to feel emotion, and as a result, faulty cognition occurs.

Joseph LeDoux (1996), of New York University, analyzes the anatomy of an emotion. Basing his work on a meta-analysis of previous research (including his own), LeDoux argues that emotions, or arousal, is important in all mental functions and "contributes significantly to attention, perception, memory, emotion, and problem solving" (p. 289). In fact, "without arousal, we fail to notice what is going on—we don't attend to the details. But too much arousal is not good either" (p. 289). If we are overaroused, we become tense, anxious, and unproductive. LeDoux subscribes to the theory that various systems contribute to arousal, with four of them located in the brain stem. Each area contains different neurotransmitters that are released by their axon terminals when the cells are activated by the presence of novel or otherwise significant stimuli. While the old model linked only the midbrain (the limbic system) to emotions, other areas are now also implicated, including the orbitofrontal cortex and the ventral frontal lobes. But there's more. The brain structures involved in emotional processing influence cognition because of their role in the following:

- perceptual processing
- safety or threat evaluation
- motivational evaluation
- self-regulation of states
- memory modulation

Although some researchers cite the orbitofrontal cortex as the central processing area that orchestrates emotions and cognition, emotions are not the exclusive domain of the brain. Neuroscientist Candace Pert (1997), author of *Molecules of Emotion,* says that emotions aren't just in the brain; they operate throughout the body. It's all done with an elaborate network of hormones and peptides, which influence thinking, moving, feeling, and decision making. These chemicals are released from the adrenals (adrenaline), kidneys (glucose), peripheral nerve endings (norepinephrine), and other locations. The bottom line is that we are each a complex system of systems, and the communication network does not consist solely of the neural networks; it's the bloodstream that supplies the chemical cocktail for the moment.

The Amazing Amygdala

While other areas of the brain help process emotions, the amygdala—an almond-shaped mass of nuclei within the limbic system (see Figures 12.1 and 12.2)—is highly involved. It is nearly mature at birth and stores intense emotions, both negative and positive.

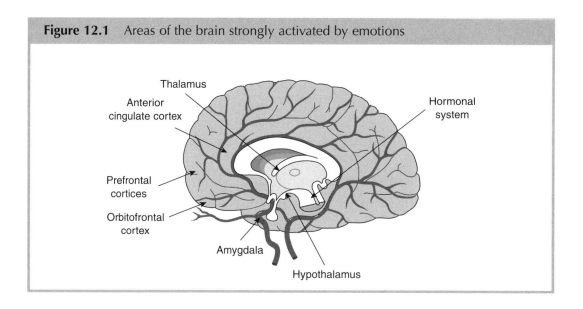

Figure 12.1 Areas of the brain strongly activated by emotions

The amygdala exerts a tremendous influence over the cortex. The cortex has more inputs from the amygdala than the reverse, yet the information flows both ways. By far, the amygdala is more reactive, while the frontal lobes are reflective. Although the amygdala seems to contain 12 to 15 distinct emotive regions, so far only two (those linked to fear) have been specifically identified. Other emotions, such as intense pleasure, may be linked to other areas.

The amygdala's primary task may be its responsibility for linking emotional content to memory. Because the amygdala connects to the hippocampus, it has long been believed to play a role in memory. While most now believe the amygdala does not itself process memory, it is thought to be a source of emotions that imbue memory with meaning. It is most concerned with our survival and the emotional flavoring or interpretation of feelings in a situation. If we can make one generalization about what activates the amygdala, it is *uncertainty*. Anytime we don't know what's going on and the likelihood is that it's not good, the amygdala becomes activated. It is activated not only by fear but also by an overall sense that something isn't right at the moment.

Hot Buttons and the Amygdala

Have you ever had a "hot button" triggered by a student, family member, or colleague? Most of us have. This automatic response (usually considered negative) to a perceived threat of some kind is probably the reactivation of an old pattern triggered by your amygdala. The perceived threat might only be a put-down, withdrawal of attention, or a sarcastic comment, but it feels on a very deep level like a threat to your emotional or physical safety. Whether you're 6 or 60, when your amygdala says, "Hey! Survival is at stake—strike back!" you usually do. Fortunately, unproductive patterns of behavior resulting from early neglect or trauma can be altered with awareness and practice.

Figure 12.2 Amygdala location

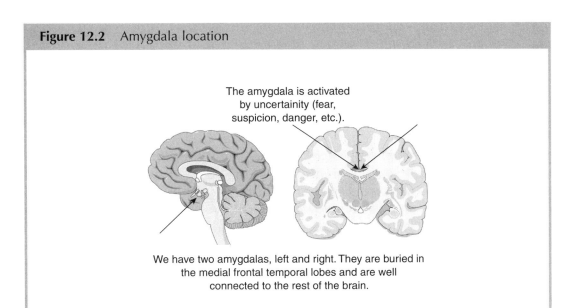

The amygdala is activated by uncertainity (fear, suspicion, danger, etc.).

We have two amygdalas, left and right. They are buried in the medial frontal temporal lobes and are well connected to the rest of the brain.

We rarely ever get angry for the reasons we think. Rather, each time we react, it's the retriggering of an earlier, stored reaction. The trigger may be nearly insignificant; nevertheless, the brain says, "React! This is horrible!" Over time, the body can become a storehouse of defensive postures. When a hot button is pushed, we (or our students) may not be able to stop our immediate reaction. But we can pause for a moment (if the threat is, in fact, insignificant) and then take a slow, deep breath to relax. After we've allowed ourselves to get past the reactive behavior, we can then choose to act more appropriately.

> Since survival is the most important function of the brain, the physiology involved most heavily in our emotional processing center dominates our everyday lives in more ways than we can imagine.

What This Means to You

Integrate emotions into the learning process. One simple way to do this is by encouraging learners to reflect on their feelings. In response to a reading assignment, for example, you might ask a question like "When you read what happened to Johnny after he told the truth, how did you feel?" Asking students how they feel about a topic will help cement the learning in their memory. Remember, the best thinking is integrated with emotions. Some behaviors are going to occur regardless of what you do, and many of them can feel destructive. Accept the need for them, and help learners move through the experience toward a more positive outcome.

(Continued)

(Continued)

Here are three immediate strategies for providing alternative, productive outlets for what are basically powerful, biological expressions:

- Establish new, positive, and productive rituals such as arrival handshakes, music fanfare, positive greetings, hugs, and high-fives.
- Set a tone of teamwork with class rituals such as team names, cheers, gestures, games, and friendly competition.
- Encourage participation rituals, such as class applause when learners contribute or present; closing rituals with songs, affirmations, discussion, journal writing, cheers, self-assessment, gestures, and so on; and your own personal ritual to celebrate a learner's achievement, such as a special student award, a note of praise sent home, or extra privileges.

These positive-feedback circuits capitalize on the value of emotions for cementing learning. It is, in fact, the emotional response that animates us, not the logical one. We are emotional beings. Even when we evaluate student performance, it's all about how we feel about what we've seen and heard. The feelings strongly flavor our evaluation. We call it a *professional opinion*, but to say there's no emotion involved would be a case of serious denial.

Our emotions are our personalities. When researchers examined subjects with most of their frontal lobe (the area of so-called highest intelligence) damaged or removed, a significant score reduction on standard intelligence tests was evident. When researchers examined subjects with damage or removal of their amygdala, there was even more profound personality change. Deficits in the amygdala result in a greatly reduced (if not completely absent) capacity for creative play, imagination, and emotional nuances that drive the arts, humor, imagination, love, music, and altruism. These are the very cornerstones of personality—the qualities of those who have made great contributions to our world, such as the genius of Quincy Jones, Martha Graham, Steven Hawking, Eddie Murphy, and Mother Teresa. Our emotions drive our creativity.

Emotions as Mind-Body States

Emotions impact student behavior by creating distinct mind-body states. A state is an exact frozen moment composed of a specific posture, breathing rate, and chemical balance in the body. The presence or absence of norepinephrine, vasopressin, testosterone, serotonin, progesterone, dopamine, and dozens of other chemicals dramatically alter a person's frame of mind and body. How important are states to us? They are all that we have. They are our feelings, desires, memories, and motivations. We are driven by our emotions. Everything we do is motivated by them. When students buy a new pair of Nikes, they are not likely in need of new shoes but are rather seeking more confidence or popularity. A state change is what they are after. Even buying drugs is evidence of the desire for a state change—perhaps to feel better, or to simply feel something, or nothing, as the case may be. We need to pay attention to this. Teachers who help their students feel good about themselves through learning success, quality friendships, and celebrations are doing the very things the learning brain craves.

While some believe the reverse, one could make a good case that the brain operates more like a gland than a computer. It triggers hormones, is bathed in them, and is partially run by them. Emotions are the catalyst that impacts the conversion of mind into physical matter in the body. They are distributed as white blood cells and peptide molecules. Emotions trigger the chemical changes that change our moods, behaviors, and eventually our lives. If people and activities are the content in our lives, emotions are both the contexts and the values we hold.

Outlets for Expression

Many behaviors, like flocking, dominating, and preening, are simply a carryover from ancient survival patterns. However, some of these common ritualistic behaviors can be counterproductive to learning unless positive outlets for them are provided. Some examples of these rituals are put-downs or taunting, compulsions, rigid routines, fads, cliques, peer pressure, arguing over meaningless subjects, competing for approval, trying on roles, nesting or personalizing a space, top-dog behaviors, flirting, and adhering to group mentality. Traditionally, teachers invest a great deal of energy combating these ever-evolving rituals, mostly to no avail. But there are alternatives.

Rituals can fulfill learners' needs without being counterproductive to learning. Brain-based learning environments acknowledge the anthropology of such behaviors and recognize their value to the organism. These environments focus on understanding the brain and working with its natural tendencies instead of fighting them in an attempt to suppress them. A brain-based environment supports the expression of emotions in the following ways:

- creating a brain-affirming learning climate; acknowledging the role of chemicals in behavior
- not denying the importance and recognition of feelings and emotions
- providing more personally meaningful projects and more individual choice
- using productive rituals to adjust mind-body states
- maintaining an absence of threat, high stress, and artificial deadlines
- ensuring that the resources necessary for success are available to every learner
- creating multistatus groups of learners supported by peer review and feedback
- using self-assessment tools for nonthreatening feedback
- assigning large group-oriented projects that require learners to learn to work with others and problem solve for the greater good

The Thinking Tool of Emotions

For years we believed that thinking was the main domain of the frontal lobes. That is, we credited this area with our brilliant best-of-humanity thoughts. We know now that the frontal lobes may allow us to elaborate on the details of our goals and plans, but it's our emotions that drive the execution of these goals. That's why when we ask students to set their goals, it's just as important to ask them why they want to reach them as it is to ask what their goals are. You might say, "Write down three good reasons why reaching your goals is important to you." Then have students share their answers with others.

> Remember, it is the emotions behind the goals that provide the energy to accomplish them.

Some suggest that emotions are a form of intelligence—a distillation of learned wisdom that may even be hardwired into our DNA. In other words, we have been biologically shaped to be fearful, worried, surprised, suspicious, joyful, and relieved, almost on cue. Emotions are a critical source of information for learning, and they ought to be used to inform us rather than considered something to subdue and ignore. Students who feel tentative or afraid to speak in front of a group of their peers, for instance, may have a very legitimate and even logical reason for the fear: failing might cost them significant loss of social status.

Emotions help us make better and faster decisions. We make thousands of microdecisions daily that illuminate, for example, our character as either good or bad, dependable or not, honest or sleazy, gossipy or noble, creative or straight-laced, generous or stingy. Each of those decisions is made with a guiding hand—our values. All values are simply emotional states. If my value is honesty, then I feel bad when I'm dishonest. Conversely, I feel good when I do honest things. In a sense, character is shaped by the conscience of emotions. While too much or too little emotion is usually counterproductive, our everyday emotions play an important role in our lives and make us who we are.

What Is the Specific Role of Emotions in Learning?

- to bind the learning
- to help us determine what's real, what we believe and feel
- to activate long-term memory on an intense and widespread chemical basis in both amygdaloid and peptide structures
- to help us make faster decisions by using nonconscious and gut-level judgment
- to help us make better-quality decisions by engaging our values

In what ways can you help your learners stimulate appropriate and productive emotions for learning?

We remember that which is most emotionally laden because of the following:

- Emotional events receive preferential processing.
- The brain is overstimulated when strong emotions are present. Emotions give us a more activated and chemically stimulated brain, which helps us recall things better.
- The more intense the amygdala arousal, the stronger the imprint.

University of California, San Diego, neurobiologist and memory expert Larry Squire (1987, 1992) says emotions are so important that they have their own memory pathways. Hence, it is common for students to remember most events like the death of a friend, a field trip, or a hands-on science experiment far longer than they would a mere lecture. As teachers, we can purposely engage productive emotions.

We've come a long way! The old thinking was, "First get control of the students; then do the teaching." Today, neuroscientists would say, "First engage the emotions appropriately; then continue to engage them." Engaging emotions must be intrinsic to the curriculum rather than something done as an afterthought.

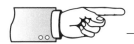

What This Means to You

We simply cannot run a good school without acknowledging emotions and integrating them into our daily operations. Many schools do this already; they have pep rallies, athletic competitions, guest speakers, poetry presentations, community projects, storytelling, debates, clubs, sports, drama performances, and comedy routines. Which forms of emotional expression are you orchestrating?

The following are strategies you can incorporate to help learners understand the importance of their own emotions in the learning process:

Role Model. Exhibit a love of learning. Bring something to class that you're in the process of learning about—something that really excites you. Build suspense, smile, tell a true emotional story, show off a new CD, bring in a favorite book or discuss a recently read one, bring a pet to school, or get involved in community work. But most important, show enthusiasm.

Celebrate. Throw parties. Provide acknowledgments. Incorporate high-fives, team cheers, food, music, decorations, and costumes. Show off student work. For example, when students are finished doing a group mind map, have them share it with at least two other groups. Tell the groups to find at least two things they like about each other's mind maps. Do this in an atmosphere of celebration; have background music, and provide some words of praise for a job well done.

Controversy. Set up a debate, a dialogue, an academic decathlon, a game show, or a panel discussion. Any time you vest two groups in competing interests, you'll get action! Theater and drama can create strong emotions as well. The bigger the production and the higher the stakes, the more emotions will be engaged. Event planning on this scale evokes stress, fun, anxiety, anticipation, suspense, excitement, and relief: What better way to engage a wide range of emotions?

Physical Rituals. There are innumerable examples of classroom rituals that can inspire and engage emotions. A few examples include clapping patterns, cheers, chants, movements, or theme songs. Incorporate arrival and departure rituals that are fun, quick, and frequent to prevent boredom. Obviously, rituals need to be age appropriate.

Introspection. Incorporate assignments that require journaling, small-group discussions, story swapping, surveys, interviews, and other reflection tasks. Use people and issues to engage students personally. Ask students to write or talk about a current event that has drawn attention. Help them make personal connections between current events, the current curriculum, and their own everyday lives.

Learning Has to Feel Right

Bandler (1988) reveals that the brain has three criteria that must be fulfilled in order for it to "know that it knows something"—also called the self-convincer state. Although the criteria vary from person to person, in general, the brain needs the following forms of verification in order to truly believe what it's learning:

1. **Modality:** The learning must be reinforced in the learner's dependent modality (i.e., visual, auditory, or kinesthetic). We must see it, hear it, or feel it. Examples include a written test score, a compliment, a trophy, a smile on another person's face, a positive peer assessment, or an audience's applause.

2. **Frequency:** The new learning must get reinforced with repetition. The number of repetitions necessary varies from one to 20 depending on the individual. Some learners may reinforce their learning by looking over prior tests and rereading the questions and answers numerous times. Some may want to watch a video about a subject they're studying, as well as read a couple of books about it and experience a related field trip. Others might feel they really know something only after teaching it to others.

3. **Duration:** The learning must be validated for a length of time—anywhere from two seconds to several days, depending, again, on the individual. Learners may learn something in their dependent modality and even get it reinforced for a few hours, but still not feel that they know it. An unspecified duration of time, however, may alter this feeling. This is another reason that review is such an important learning step.

Once learners have experienced learning in their preferred modality the right number of times and for the right length of time, they will feel that it is now true. When this happens, we believe it in our gut. Until then, it's only data with little meaning.

Think about how often you've questioned your own sense of knowing something. Have you ever left the house and then suddenly wondered, "Did I lock the door? Did I unplug the iron? Did I turn on my answering machine?" Or perhaps you look at a word you've just spelled out and wonder, "Is this right?" This is not a memory problem. It is a case of not believing yourself. If you do believe yourself, you've achieved the self-convincer state.

We've all heard people say, "I'll believe it when I see it." This is clearly a case of the visual learner who has to see something to believe it. Others may need to get a neighbor's opinion before they feel they know. And yet others may say, "If I can touch it, hold it, or be there firsthand, I'll believe it." These three responses represent the major modality variables: visual, auditory, and kinesthetic.

Self-convincers are especially critical when it comes to changing beliefs. If students already believe that they are going to succeed, only maintenance reinforcement is required to preserve that belief. But if students believe that they are failures and you want to convince them otherwise, all three of the criteria must be met. Otherwise, the students' internal belief will remain the same.

In general, at-risk, slow, discouraged, or low-level learners don't possess strong self-convincing strategies. They may either self-convince too easily, meaning they think they know something before they really do, or not self-convince easily enough, meaning their learning self-confidence is very low. Gifted learners, on the other hand, may merely possess more accurate self-convincing skills and, as a result, exhibit more self-confidence.

 ## What This Means to You

Many learners access the self-convincer state on their own. They simply know how to convince themselves of what they know or want to know. They tend to have more self-confidence, perhaps even arrogance. But others aren't so easily convinced. We've all heard children remark to their parents that they learned nothing at school. Although they may have actually learned a lot, brain-based learning says we must elicit the self-convincer state to ensure that the learners *feel* they know it.

To ensure that all learners leave your class in a state of "knowing what they know," provide activities that give them a chance to validate their learning. The activities should cross all three modalities, be repeated numerous times, and last for several hours or days. Some examples of approaches that meet these criteria include setting up peer-assessment opportunities, conducting role-plays, assigning journal writing, creating self-assessment instruments, assigning tasks that require teamwork, and peer teaching. When enough of these activities are conducted, students will leave your class feeling that they've really learned something.

For those who self-convince too easily and think they know it all long before they really do, there's another solution. These are usually the more contextual-global learners. Give them a checklist of criteria for learning, and ask them to assess themselves based on the specific measures. This will help them acquire a more realistic view of their mastery level.

At the end of an activity, listen for expressions that confirm learners are processing the veracity of an experience, such as "It just doesn't feel right" or "I'll believe it when I see

Learners not only need to learn; they need to know that they learned what was taught.

it" or "Wait until my friend hears about this." These phrases indicate an attempt to feel convinced about something; only then will there be actual belief.

Once students are sucked into the self-confidence/intrinsic-motivation loop, future learning is easy. Rituals that celebrate learning go a long way toward moving learners into that success loop. Even beyond making the learning more fun, they seal the new learning as real and worth remembering.

Part 4

Neuroscientific Perspective on Teaching and Learning

13 Teacher Communication

There's quite a bit of irony in teaching. One of the ironies stems from the fact that most teachers go into the profession because they want to help others. The result of helping others is that you feel needed and valued. But if you're not very skillful or experienced, you may not feel that you make much of a difference yet. Or if you're very experienced and have not upgraded your skill set or atti-tudes lately, you may struggle in your class. What does this have to do with you? The better you get as a teacher, the stronger you'll see, feel, and know that you make a profound difference in the lives of your students. This chapter focuses on the "how" of making a difference. When students are treated well, their brains produce feel-good chemicals and commonly make decisive statements such as "I like learning." It's a given that quality teaching makes a difference. But what are the intangibles and less measured qualities that also affect student outcomes?

The essential understanding here is that teachers are a huge part of the environment. The 30 or so other brains in the room filter what the teacher says and how he or she acts. It may not be fair to put all of this on a teacher, but it's true. Teachers are the mobile, shifting environment for learning. If you had to send your child to a school and the choice was either a great classroom and an average teacher or an average (even run-down) classroom and a great teacher, it's an easy call. Take the great teacher!

A TEACHER'S INFLUENCE ON A CLASSROOM

Teachers are not merely influenced by the overall school climate; they create their own microclimates in the classroom. Learners in a positive, joyful environment are likely to experience enhanced learning, memory, and self-esteem. How does this happen? What is it about the brains of students that makes them so suscepti-ble to teacher actions, emotions, and beliefs?

The primary way in which teachers affect students is through student observa-tion of the teacher. This activates the brain's *mirror neuron* system. Two Italian researchers named Iaccomo Rizzolati and Vittorio Gallasse discovered these amaz-ing subsets of brain cells by accident. They found that neurons in the ventral pre-motor area of a macaque will fire anytime the monkey performs a complex action, such as reaching for a treat, pulling a handle, or pushing a small door (different neurons fire for different actions). Amazingly, however, a small subset of neurons will fire even when the monkey watches another monkey perform the same action, but it has to be an action that interests the monkey (Iacoboni, Molnar-Szakacs, Gallese, Buccino, & Mazziotta, 2005). In essence, the mirror neuron is part of a net-work that allows you to see the world from another person's point of view, hence the name. All of us have these mirror neurons, though there is evidence that they are significantly impaired in people with autism (Iacoboni & Dapretto, 2006).

The significance of this system is profound. It is likely the basis for imitation learning, contagious yawning, social learning, mob behaviors, copycat crimes, and why kids pick up on the teacher's emotions. In short, it helps us understand why we are affected by the behaviors of people around us. But are these mirror neurons always on and working? Assuming that they are healthy, they are always on. But our frontal lobes, as they mature, can dampen down the effects of the mir-ror neurons. So instead of copying another person's negative or dumb behavior, you might say to yourself that the action is crazy, irrelevant, or dangerous and choose to avoid it. However, many younger kids, and even teens, have not yet reached this point and thus will still copy the bad behavior. In fact, many adults with compromised frontal lobes (e.g., from brain injury, drugs, or depression) still make poor choices based on seeing others in action.

In a classroom, because of the mirror neuron system, students may, to some degree, pick up on the teacher's mood, facial expressions, and actions far more than previously thought. When teachers are happy, some of it can rub off on students (and vice versa), and a teacher's frown, scowl, or sarcastic comment may be more hurtful than we might think. But how do teacher attitudes impact learning? Learners pick up on the emotional state of the instructor, which either enhances or interferes with cognition. Teachers who smile, use humor, have a joyful demeanor, and take genuine pleasure in their work generally have high-performing learners. This may help explain why when you're in a good mood, your learners seem to mirror it back to you.

> The fact that negative comments may pose a health risk to students is stunning new evidence that speaks to the importance of positive teacher attitude.

We know that teacher expectations influence student learning. But how? Expectations increase the likelihood of certain behaviors, which in turn may influence the outcome. Beliefs can and do lead to specific outcomes. An experiment carried out by Rosenthal and Jacobson (1968) at an elementary school tested the hypothesis that in any given classroom there is a correlation between teachers' expectations and students' achievement. All students at the school were given an intelligence test at the beginning of the school year. Then the researchers randomly selected 20 percent of the students—without any relation to their test results—and reported to the teachers that these students showed "unusual potential for intellectual growth" (p. 181) and could be expected to bloom in their academic performance by the end of the year.

Eight months later, at the end of the academic year, all the students were retested. Those previously labeled as "intelligent" showed significantly greater increases in scores on the new tests than the children who had not been singled out for teachers' attention. Because the teachers' expectations about the intellectual performance of the so-called special children had changed, so had the intellectual performance of these students (Rosenthal, 1991). For ethical reasons, Rosenthal and Jacobson's experiment focused only on favorable or positive expectations and their impact on intellectual competence, but it is reasonable to infer that unfavorable expectations could also lead to a corresponding decrease in performance. In fact, nearly half of the teachers in Zohar and Vaaknin's (2001) study considered higher-order thinking inappropriate for poor or low-achieving students. Yes, expectations do matter, but how much?

A good deal of research has been devoted to this topic, which is surprisingly controversial. The questions revolve around three core issues:

1. Is this effect genuine and has it been reliably reproduced? (yes)

2. To the extent that there is an effect, how great is it? (2–10 percent)

3. Is the effect size significant? (depends on what you compare it to)

Historically, the quoted estimate of the significance of teachers' *expectancy effects* on student achievement was about 5–10 percent (Brophy, 1983). More recently, average expectancy-effect sizes from 0.1 to 0.3 have been reported, although it is "likely that under certain conditions expectancy effects may be larger or smaller" (Jussim, Madon, & Chatman, 1994, p. 324). An effect size of 1.0 means that there is a 100 percent correlation between the action taken and the behavior produced.

Yet a small EE can result in larger cumulative effects over time, particularly for more vulnerable and at-risk students (Jussim et al., 1994). A small act, a choice word, a choice affirmation, and a positive act—and now the effect is snowballing. If the effect size seems small to you, use the following examples for comparison: Reducing the risk of dying from a heart attack by taking aspirin is 0.02 (not 0.2, but 0.02!), and the impact of chemotherapy on breast cancer survival is 0.03. That's far less than the expectancy effect. While there is some controversy about the size of the effects, there is an effect—and it's free to teachers!

> Learners in positive, joyful environments are likely to experience enhanced learning, memory, and self-esteem.

Our beliefs and attitudes as teachers, are inextricably intertwined with how we teach. Moment by moment, we offer suggestions about learning through our unconscious attitudes. We may, for example, suggest that learning is hard or easy, homework is valuable or not, schools are happy places that we enjoy or merely places we have to go. We may also suggest that a student might find a subject easy, fun, and challenging or hard, boring, and frustrating. Our smiles, or lack thereof, communicates more to students than the words we verbalize. The tone of our conversations, appearance, organization, and effort all contribute to the collective whole.

What This Means to You

Your attitude each day is as important to learning as the material you present. Take the time to get centered and positive. Do whatever ritual or activity is necessary for you to be at your best. More important than *how* a positive attitude works is that we know it works. Teachers who are happier and more pleasant to be around bring out the best in their learners. Take a few minutes each day to destress and regroup. Listen to music that enhances your mood, eat well, exercise if that grounds you, and post affirming or humorous reminders around your home and teaching area. Making the conscious effort to get into a good teaching state before you start the day will go a long way toward creating a successful learning environment.

Teacher Authority and Credibility

Some schools have lost the magic middle ground between being an authority and being authoritarian. Some of the defining characteristics of a strong educational leader are strength of character, integrity, purpose, presence, charisma, confidence, and competency. Teachers should be authority figures, not because of their job title but because of their words and actions in the classroom. Traditional authority based on using a heavy hand may have worked in the past, but the more appropriate approach for today's students involves recognizing their rights, offering them some choices, and instilling in them the desire to cooperate. The defining question educational leaders of today are asking is, "Is my approach to teaching worthy of respect?"

As a teacher, you often don't have the luxury of gaining immediate respect by virtue of donning a uniform. Rather, your credibility is determined by your ability to win learners' respect. They will judge your actions as well as your content message. If you're successful, they will want to do what you ask of them because they believe and trust you.

What This Means to You

Become more aware of the things you do, or can do, to increase your credibility. Here are some specific examples:

- Model respect. Respect your learners, and they will be more respectful of you.
- Share your experience. How long have you been in the profession? How did you develop your specialty knowledge or area of expertise? What are some personal experiences that have been instrumental in your growth?
- Talk about your mentors and role models.
- Volunteer to work on district, state, or national projects or committees.
- Become known as your organization's spokesperson on a particular subject—preferably your area of expertise.
- Attend continuing education courses, conferences, and workshops. Present at them if possible.
- Keep your promises and commitments.
- Use positive language—never vulgarity or profanity. Interrupt all racist or sexist remarks made by anyone in your presence.
- Contribute articles to periodicals, anthologies, or scholarly journals for publication consideration.

Teacher Congruency

Although we are only able to consciously process one incoming sensory message at a time, the subconscious works overtime translating all the other sensory data. For example, while you watch a movie, what you hear is being registered on a subconscious level, and while you listen to a concert, what you see takes a back seat to the music. Thus, it is critical to ensure that what you're saying is congruent with your body language. Your learners are aware of both your verbal and nonverbal communication. They are influenced by messages that you may not even be aware you are sending.

Let's say, for example, that you verbalize to your students the following: "I'm very happy to be here today." But actually, your head is shaking from side to side as if to say, "I'd rather be elsewhere." Although both messages are received, the second one has the most impact.

What This Means to You

We all convey mixed messages at times, which can undermine the goal of our communication and reduce our credibility. You may want to practice your nonverbals. Videotape yourself for review. Identify two or three areas in which you might improve your congruency and delivery. Seek feedback from others. And be sure that what you're trying to convey is accurate and true to your real position on the matter.

Teacher Appearance

As we learned from the Pygmalion experiment (Rosenthal & Jacobsen, 1968), teacher expectations of a learner's ability affect learning outcomes, but does this theory work in reverse? Do students' expectations of teachers affect performance? According to clothing consultant John Molloy (1988), yes. He conducted a study to determine the impact of teacher dress on student learning. Malloy reports that better-dressed teachers experienced fewer student discipline problems and better work habits. He also found that socioeconomic background influenced the type of clothing students best responded to. Some critics attribute the results of Malloy's study to the placebo effect—that is, teacher credibility positively influences believability, which positively influences the treatment results. Once again though, expectations, beliefs, and results are all connected.

Let's say, for example, that you attend a conference and the presenter is wearing something very outdated or sloppy. Your first impression will be different from what it would be if he or she is wearing a suit or other business apparel. Like the patient who believes the doctor knows best, the student who believes the teacher knows best will likely have better results. Whatever credibility edge one can obtain by dressing presentably is one that should not be overlooked.

What This Means to You

Your clothing conveys powerful messages about your attitude, values, and personality. Make the effort to dress professionally. Take pride in your appearance, as you would want your students to do. We may not like it, but human nature is to judge others—whether unconsciously or consciously—based on their appearance. When it comes to credibility, image plays a key role.

Tight Teacher Control

Excessive control by teachers may reduce learning by increasing the stress or threat level. If students are to be predominantly self-motivated, they must be given the opportunity to focus on their own areas of interest and to participate in activities they find interesting. Unless learners are stakeholders in the learning process (i.e., they have some influence over it), the learning will be forced, rote, mechanical, short-lived, and eventually distasteful. As Glasser (1999) notes, the more learners feel controlled, the more resentful they get. And resentment, whether expressed (and manifested as frustration, rebellion, and anger) or suppressed (and manifested as detachment, sabotage, and apathy), detracts from learning. Students who lack perceived control on an assigned task will hold back and give less than their best efforts. It makes sense: if you feel that you lack control over your own destiny, why would you want to invest in someone else's?

The brain's most important work is thinking and problem solving. Learning is an interactive process that occurs on many levels. The learning has to be input, filtered, associated, processed, evaluated, and stored to be useful. Learning to think is an evolutionary process. The more learning is generalized, contextualized, and reframed, the more the learner owns it. Deep learning requires usage and feedback. Over time, the meaning of the material expands, and eventually the learner develops a level of expertise. The new model of teaching, analogous to offering substance for the learner to fill his or her own container, reframes the teacher as more of a learning coach.

> Highly controlling motivational strategies such as real or implied threats, strong punishments, compelling rewards, and forced competition are sometimes effective. However, they are likely to produce negative developmental consequences if they are repeated across many different behavioral episodes.

Although teachers have a tendency to establish conformity when dealing with a large group, this approach almost always backfires. By consistently using controlling means on your learners, you'll undermine their overall success. People lose interest in activities when they feel coerced or manipulated to engage in those activities, even when the motivational strategies used are intended to be positive and motivating.

In most cases, school starts off being fun and motivating with high initial interest. But that enthusiasm is typically replaced with resentment, complacency, and avoidance as controlling strategies are used, creativity is discouraged, choice is reduced, and parental pressure intensifies. Sadly, intrinsic motivation is sidelined for another year.

 ## What This Means to You

We may have much more to do with the behaviors of our learners than we previously thought. Hold a staff meeting. Get everyone aligned on this issue. Develop a policy that everyone can buy into. Eliminate rewards; replace them with the alternatives of choice, creativity, enthusiasm, multicontext learning, and celebration.

LEARNER EXPECTATIONS

The results of Chang's (2001) study suggest that an important factor in processing new data is whether learners think the material is going to be useful to them. The key determiner of how successfully learners responded was their expectation about the information's relative utility.

Just as we don't conduct research in a vacuum, we don't learn or teach in a vacuum either. Rather, our expectancy of the future must be acknowledged as a factor if we are to move toward the goal of objectivity. Philosopher Karl Popper points out that the supposed science of scientific reasoning is staged against a backdrop of prior beliefs, presuppositions, and prejudices, which can certainly influence what is, or is not, discovered. In lectures, he made the point beautifully by asking the audience to please "observe." Their reply was typically, "Observe what?" To which he said, "Exactly my point." Observation does not occur in a vacuum; it is strongly influenced by what we are looking for. Perhaps the teaching tip here is to acknowledge that our predictions and projections indeed influence results.

What This Means to You

Because your so-called top learners often expect to get the most out of a class, they usually do. The proverbial snowball effect seems to apply here: the more often students practice learning, the more they learn. You can positively influence your learners' expectations regarding your class by consciously embedding positive suggestions into materials, your presentation, and the learning environment. How much learners get may be affected profoundly by how motivated they become, how much relevance the material has for them, and how much they think they will learn. Some suggestions for generating positive expectancy include sending home positive notes about the course content; asking students to describe their hopes, expectations, and desires for the class; encouraging excitement and celebration over new learning; and providing learners with a time for "showing off" to peers and parents.

Altering Learner Behavior

Teachers can affect student behaviors in many ways. One powerful way is in the words that teachers choose. Overall, there are seven primary forms that are universally used to alter a learner's behavior. Your role as a teacher is to determine which is the best approach for particular learners as a means of motivating without manipulating or controlling them.

Generally More Effective Communication Methods

Suggest. Make a request that illuminates the preferred options. For example, "You might like to use your colored pens for taking notes." This approach provides a strong perceived choice. If students like the options, they're likely to choose one.

Ask. Make the request in a way that encourages students to follow. For example, "Would you please use your colored pens for taking notes?" This approach provides some perceived choice.

Tell. This option is primarily used to provide instructional directions. Simply give learners a directed statement in an expectant tone. For example, "Using your colored pens, please write this down . . . ." This approach provides minimal perceived choice.

Generally Less Effective Communication Methods

Hope. This request is not verbalized; rather it is simply assumed that learners will comply. The thought is actually outside their awareness. Since the learners don't know about it, there is no perceived choice.

Imply. This request is never made; rather it is talked around in the hope that learners will infer from the implication. Because no overt recommendation is made, there is minimal perceived choice.

Demand/Threaten. This is an order, delivered in a way that learners have minimal or no perceived choice. This method should be reserved for occasions when a person's safety is in danger.

Force. This approach is to be used only in an emergency. Learners have no perceived choice; no other option is available to them. This is unacceptable unless lives or property are at stake.

Forced Silence and Class Inactivity

Teachers who believe that a controlled and quiet environment is best for learning ask learners to remain in their seats and stay quiet. But research by Valle (1990) suggests that this may not be a good idea. Among adolescents studied, 50 percent needed extensive mobility while learning. Of the remaining 50 percent, half (25 percent of the total) needed occasional mobility and the remaining subjects needed minimal movement opportunities. We've all been in the situation of addressing a group and some of the listeners appear to be tired, drowsy, or listless. Is this your fault or the audience's? It doesn't matter; let them get up and move around!

 **What This Means to You**

If learners seem lacking in attention, energy, or curiosity, they may need more permission to move around. Provide more active-learning opportunities and kinesthetic/tactile stimulation. What may seem like a boring topic or a bad time of day may simply be a product of learners who are restless and need some activity. Schedule a stand-up-and-stretch break every 20 minutes or so. Include cross-lateral movements and deep breathing. Provide a diversity of activities so that learners can choose what appeals to them. Offer team and partner learning, excursions outside the classroom, frequent water breaks, and simple movement activities that get the circulation going and keep active learners happy.

The Climate Can Be Highly Active

To millions of teachers around the world who plead with students to please sit down and be quiet, James Asher is a rebel. A pioneer in second language learning and the developer of the Total Physical Response (TPR) approach, Asher maintains that learning on an immediate, physical, and gut level speeds acquisition dramatically. Asher's (1966) hypothesis is still true today: teach the body; it learns as well as the mind. This approach to learning reminds us that actions and movement can play a powerful role in the learning and recall of new information.

While it's true that much learning can occur without anyone's ever leaving a seat, it's also true that most of what you think is important in your life that you "really know," you have learned through experience, from doing something, not from a chalkboard or textbook. In addition, the research on the power of physiological states is conclusive: the body remembers as well as the mind. In many cases, it remembers better. To use the TPR approach successfully, the following conditions are recommended:

- The teacher creates strong rapport and a relationship with students.
- The learning climate is cooperative, playful, active, and fun.
- The teacher establishes an environment of mutual respect.
- The teacher gives imperative instructions to students in a commanding but gentle manner.
- The students respond rapidly without analyzing the input.

The TPR approach associates a body movement with new learning. In teaching Spanish, for example, you might simply stand up and verbalize the Spanish word for *stand*. Then you might touch your knee and say the word for it in Spanish, or tell students to follow you in walking around the room and repeat the Spanish word for *walk*. The approach is very natural, much like how a parent teaches an infant. Although Asher created the approach for teaching languages, it is transferable to other subjects as well. For example, it can help learners remember vocabulary words, spelling, geography, science concepts, social studies, collaboration skills, and math formulas.

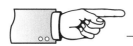 ## What This Means to You

Associate new learning with various physical movements. Draw from the dramatic arts, fine arts, music/band, and sports. Engage your class in regular role-playing, charades, games, and movement activities. Students can organize extemporaneous pantomimes to dramatize a key point. Incorporate overviews of future learning or reviews of past learning in one-minute commercials adapted from popular television advertisements.

14

The Nonconscious Learning Climate

As revealed in previous chapters, so much of what impacts learning is not in a teacher's lesson plan at all. Rather, it is the hundreds of microvariables present in every learning environment. From instructor appearance to personal belief systems, the brain is bombarded by stimuli from all directions, and there is no way anyone can be conscious of it all. In fact, we are designed to pay attention to just one sensory input at a time. Nevertheless, the brain has mechanisms that allow information to be taken in without our conscious awareness. Consequently, things influence us beyond our will moment by moment, day by day. This chapter explores the nature of that influence. You'll learn what it is, how it works, and how you can use this idea in your teaching.

SOME LEARNING IS AUTOMATIC

Your nonconscious mind acts before your conscious one does. In fact, as early as two seconds prior to an actual activity or movement, the brain has already decided what body parts to activate and which side of the brain to use. This means that we are already acting on a thought before we're even aware of it. To illustrate this perspective, consider that you have just driven from one city to another. You arrive safely and check into a motel or stay with a friend. Someone asks you about something, and you can't quite recall it. But then they mention a company's name, and suddenly a light goes on. "Yes," you say, "I have heard of that company. I think I saw its billboard somewhere on the road. Oh, yes, now I remember." You actually learned this information hours ago, but you were not conscious of it at the time.

Researchers say that more than 99 percent of all learning is nonconscious. This means that the majority of what you and your students are learning—a quantity of stimuli that far exceeds that derived from traditionally delivered content or what's outlined in a lesson plan—was never consciously intended. From visual cues, sounds, experiences, aromas, and feelings, you are a walking, talking sponge. For example, let's say your students are working on a group project in cooperative teams. In their view, they are learning the content, but they are also learning about each other and acquiring collaboration skills. In fact, this may constitute the majority of their learning. Simply absorbing an experience is valuable to the learning process as the brain expands its perceptual maps. We are all learning all the time. The question really is, what are we learning, and are we consciously aware of it?

The Power of Nonconscious Learning

Nonconscious simply refers to something that we do not pay attention to in the moment. A few key principles outline this type of learning:

1. **Acknowledge the mind's enormous capacity for reception.**

    We say that everything suggests something to our complex minds, and we cannot *not* suggest. What a teacher wears, what the environment is like, how the material is presented, and hundreds of other simple factors are all couched in suggestion. While conscious, directed content learning drops off over time, the use of suggestion actually increases learning over time.

    All communications and activities occur on conscious and nonconscious levels at the same time. It is critical, therefore, to train teachers to make the most of nonverbal messages and replace negative implications with affirming impressions.

2. **Categorize the value of visuals, music, stories, myth, metaphor, and movement.**

   All stimuli to the brain are coded, symbolized, generalized, and multi-processed in ways we have yet to fully understand.

3. **Address perceptions, biases, and barriers before learning.**

   Once we recognize our strengths and weaknesses, we can achieve dramatic results.

> Every sensory impression suggests something—good, bad, or neutral. Every environment suggests something to a learner's brain. The question is, what are you now suggesting to learners? And is this what you want to suggest?

Because of the nearly unlimited capacity of the human brain, and its natural predisposition to sort, label, and code things, all the so-called unimportant influences turn out to be very important.

What This Means to You

Create a learning environment that is rich with positive suggestions. Set high standards for yourself and the environment in which you teach. Involve learners in setting and achieving agreed-upon standards as well. Remember that even though you may be focusing on content, learners are absorbing much more than just what you're saying. For example, while you're putting up an overhead transparency, they are also listening to your utterings and observing your facial expressions. In fact, they may be hearing more of what you're not saying than what you are saying. Thus, it is important that you be aware of your nonverbal messages and that they be congruent with what you intend to impart. Practice your presentation in front of a mirror or with a colleague to ensure that your words are congruent with your body language. Or videotape your presentation and critique yourself. Most important, check your attitude; you can be sure that your learners have, and it does influence them.

More on "Suggestion"

Since suggestions affect the biases, beliefs, limiting thoughts, and attitudes of the learner, there can be no suggestion without desuggestion. All positive suggestions are simply a counter to negative beliefs. In that sense, we are continually countering prior negative conditioning with current positive conditioning. If negative suggestions suddenly stopped existing tomorrow, there would be no need to pump learners back up with positive suggestions.

Consider how the following destructive suggestions (a) can easily be made more constructive and positive, as exhibited by the second sentence (b):

> The brain is designed to make meaning out of experiences. As a teacher, you should assume that everything you say, do, or design will create some kind of meaning—good or bad—for your students. Now take advantage of that to enhance learning.

a. If the instructions are not clear to you, start paying attention.

b. Let me repeat the instructions; then I'll check back with you to make sure I've presented them clearly.

a. What part of the word *no* do you not understand?

b. Let's check for meaning. Tell me what you heard.

a. While I don't expect to make scientists out of you, I do expect to provide you with the basics.

b. You might be surprised by how interesting science can be; many students ask me to give them more resources.

a. Don't forget to do your homework.

b. Be sure to remember to do the word problems tonight at home. We'll go over your answers tomorrow.

a. Have a Merry Christmas everyone!

b. Happy holidays everyone! (Always be inclusive and consider diversity.)

a. Forget about Spanish, and enjoy your holiday break.

b. Be sure to use your Spanish on your break—especially when you eat out at a Mexican restaurant. Adios and buena suerte!

a. Hey, guess what? There are only 45 days left until school's out!

b. Bummer, only 45 days are left for us to be together in this classroom. The good news, though, is there are only 153 days until school starts again, and you'll be a grade higher.

a. If you do not complete any of the four basic requirements, you can expect to fail this course. There are no exceptions.

b. Complete all four requirements for this course, and you can expect to pass. Anything less, however, means a no-pass grade.

a. I know you feel nervous about the upcoming test, but don't worry, you won't fail.

b. Relax. If you've prepared well, you'll do well.

a. I hope you will gain an appreciation for the power, simplicity, and elegance of this material.

b. What do you think? Is a change needed here?

Suggestion is operating at both the conscious and the nonconscious levels. It is also the single greatest untapped influence you have with your learners:

- If the learner is confident, learning increases.
- If the learner believes in the teacher, learning increases.
- If the learner thinks the subject is important, learning increases.
- If the learner believes it will be fun and valuable, learning increases!

How do you get the learner to believe these things? Use the power to influence through the artful application of positive suggestion. You can influence (but not control) what students believe about themselves, you, the topic, learning, and so on. In fact, you already influence them in those areas; you simply may have underestimated the power of that influence. You could say, "This upcoming chapter is the hardest in the book, so everyone bear down!" or "This upcoming chapter is my favorite, so get ready for a great experience."

As an authority figure, the teacher carries the potential for vast influence. It is common to have had a teacher tell us that we were "bad" in math or spelling or writing. Naturally, that subject became nearly impossible to master. Students can carry such a bias with them for the rest of their learning lives.

All learning is affected by our personal history. We have a lifetime of experiences, beliefs, values, and attitudes about each subject and our probability of learning it. We call these *biases*. If all learning is heavily influenced by our biases, should we try to change these or simply teach? You may have guessed the answer: the overwhelming evidence is that teachers who influence learner biases are much more successful. We can change the behaviors in the classroom, or we can change the biases, or we can do both.

> The shortest route to learner success is not simply to change learner biases but to change the behaviors and biases simultaneously. Changing biases will eventually and automatically change learner behavior.

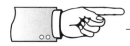

What This Means to You

Positive suggestion is a powerful and ethical method for motivating learners. Post affirming messages on doors and bulletin boards that read, for example, "My success is absolutely assured." Suggest to learners how interesting they might find the material. Communicate to them that learning is fun, easy, and creative. Suggest that they might enjoy further study on their own. Suggest that new ideas might start popping into their mind as their learning increases. Aim for orchestrating at least 20 positive messages per hour.

Teaching Tips for Optimizing Nonconscious Learning

We absorb so much information nonconsciously that downtime is absolutely necessary to process it all. If it seems that students have stopped paying attention, consider that they may be doing something just as important to their learning process: reflecting. Downtime, in fact, is absolutely necessary for the learning to become imbued with personal meaning. The amount of information individuals can take in before they become overwhelmed varies from person to person, but everyone eventually must look internally if the new learning is to become imprinted on the brain. In our roles as educators, we can offset problems by paying more attention to this basic need. Plan downtime activities after each new learning session. Such activities might include a partner walk, a music session, ball-toss time, a stretching session, or a few minutes to make a mind map.

The bottom line is this: your students learn much more than you teach. How you treat them, what you say, how you say it, what you don't say, your sensitivity to their needs, your attitude about your own work, your feelings about your environment and life, how well you listen or don't—all of these assorted impressions influence your students, whether they (and you) realize it consciously or not.

The teachers who have the toughest time with discipline or motivation are consistently the ones who are out of balance in using the *suggest, ask, and tell* (SAT) method. Too much telling creates resentment in students. If you are always telling learners what to do or hoping they do what you want them to, they will begin to resist your leadership. Too much asking or suggesting creates confusion.

The following strategies reflect an indirect or softer way to reach students. Such techniques can go a long way toward reversing the paralyzing of learner beliefs and attitudes:

- Model a positive attitude and your enjoyment of learning.
- Post affirming posters and peripherals in the room.
- Highlight positive role models, idols, guest speakers, and so on.
- Cite experts in a subject area.
- Incorporate videos, CDs, slides, and photographs on topics students are learning.
- Tell stories about prior students who have persevered and succeeded.
- Create a contemporary spin on the topic or subject so that it is perceived as "cool" and relevant.
- Counter negative stereotypes and myths with positive ideas.
- Focus on skill building and problem solving so that learners who want to succeed can learn how to do so.
- Open a new subject or topic with a celebration.
- Hold student discussions, and encourage students to talk about their fears, feelings, and concerns about learning.
- Provide sufficient resources, and enable students to learn in the style that is most natural to them.
- Encourage learners to find personal meaning in their studies and projects. Always be receptive to students' questions and comments.
- Provide an atmosphere of physical and emotional safety, where students feel accepted, respected, and welcome.

What This Means to You

Even the best lesson plans can fail if you are too controlling. Control strategies may seem effective in the short run, but inevitably they will backfire. Learners who feel controlled and manipulated will eventually begin performing below their abilities. They will feel resentful and begin to associate learning with work. It is far more effective to elicit learner cooperation and personal responsibility. Involve students in decisions about the classroom environment, music, goals, assessment approaches, and learning activities. Provide choices whenever possible. Facilitate discussion groups about classroom rules and performance expectations. Encourage student input. Utilize suggestion boxes, teams, group work, and expression areas. Students buy into and take pride in doing activities that they have helped define and over which they have some control. There is a time to be in charge and a time to allow others to lead. Find the balance, and learning will flourish.

15 Motivation and Rewards

Acommon question asked by teachers is "How do I motivate my students?" It's a legitimate question, yet there's a better one to ask. Since the brain is designed to learn, you could ask, "What am I accidentally doing that is demotivating my students?" or "How can I undo the damage that was done to this student in his or her past?"

The human brain loves to learn. Our very survival, in fact, is dependent upon learning. If you believe your job is to be a learning catalyst (one who lights a fire for learning), rather than someone who simply delivers information once you have students' attention, then motivating your learners will likely be a nonissue. After all, in a brain-based learning environment, the learners are already motivated (just the way they were, ideally, when they walked in your door).

LEARNED HELPLESSNESS

Under ordinary circumstances, most good learning environments encourage active student learning. Healthy brains usually make good choices, but unhealthy brains often make poor choices. Learners who have acquired a condition called *learned helplessness* generally fall into the second category. The good news is that you can do something about it, but you have to be informed so that you can recognize and act on your awareness.

Helplessness can devastate even the brightest learners. Since being active is our natural state, what causes a student to feel helpless? What causes learners to sit in class like a lump on a log and not participate? Temporary helplessness is one thing; what we're talking about here is a chronic condition or disorder that develops over time. The symptoms in Figure 15.1 often accompany learned helplessness.

Students who suffer from learned helplessness are not necessarily hostile or argumentative. They simply don't want to take action because they truly believe there is no dependable cause-and-effect relationship between their efforts and the outcome. When you believe you don't have any control over

Figure 15.1 Symptoms of learned helplessness

- not caring what happens
- giving up before starting, or sabotaging positive outcomes
- motivational and emotional deficits; depression, anxiety
- not acting on a request, or not following directions
- increased attraction to hostile humor
- cognitive impairment
- belief that the outcome of an event is independent of input
- passivity instead of activity
- self-imposed limitations that exacerbate passivity

your environment, why try? The following are some of the probable causes of learned helplessness:

- It can be developed over time from repeated exposure to trauma and high stress. It is most likely to occur when one feels both out of control and lacking influence.
- It can be influenced by society. In many cultures, the prevailing attitude is that whatever happens, good or bad, "it is God's will." This is a different point of view from "God gave us the power to choose our destiny."
- It can be learned in a specific context through repeated uncontrollable experiences. For example, one might be otherwise capable but feel helpless in math class due to multiple prior failures.
- It can come about through observation of others who encounter uncontrollable events. For example, viewing global disasters on television day after day may be a contributing factor, as may growing up in a welfare-supported family in which a vicious cycle of poverty prevails over a long period of time.
- It can be strengthened by well-intended but overly controlling relationships. Parents who do their children's homework, or teachers who take over when students seek help, can both be culprits.

Changes in the Brain

There can be no change in student behavior without a corresponding change in the brain. Body-mind, mind-body: There is no separation. Depending on the population sample, only 5–25 percent of kids may have learned helplessness. Here are some of the changes we see in the brain when a robust condition of learned helplessness is evident:

- decreased amounts of norepinephrine—an important compound that contributes to the arousal system
- lowered amounts of GABA (a common neurotransmitter), with links to anxiety
- decreased amounts of available serotonin and dopamine—the "feel-good" neurotransmitter
- increased activation in the amygdala—the structure that is involved in intense emotions
- increases in both the autonomic nervous system and the sympathetic nervous system—both of which are involved in stimulation of the stress-related hormone cortisol

Conditions and Constraints

Although the characteristics listed above are not causal, these biological markers are evident in many cases of learned helplessness. In other words, a decreased amount of serotonin or dopamine does not cause learned helplessness, but those who experience learned helplessness exhibit lower levels of these neurotransmitters in general.

There are varying levels of susceptibility to learned helplessness. It turns out that only about two-thirds of students are likely candidates. This is because many individuals are "immunized" against it by previous successful experiences in which they had a certain amount of control over their environment. There is greater susceptibility among those who are aggressive or dominant in a group. This is counter-intuitive: those who seem to be the most social, outgoing, assertive, strong, and in control are, in fact, the most likely to be victims of learned helplessness.

In addition, some links with depression have been identified. One of the few distinctions between learned helplessness and depression, in fact, is that depression triggers a generalized belief that responding will be ineffective, whereas those with learned helplessness believe that responding is independent of the outcome. This is a subtle but important difference.

Typically, the criterion for learned helplessness status is an inappropriate passivity, via mental or behavioral actions, to meet the demands of the situation. Can it be contextual? Yes, and an example would be students who are active in all classes but math. Perhaps these students learned through prior failures that there is no causal relationship between their behaviors and the outcome of their math studies. Learned helplessness can be evoked or triggered by a location, person, or event, and this transient quality makes it even more difficult to diagnose and treat.

Unlearning Learned Helplessness

It should be noted that most of the time when we see an unmotivated student, it is not a case of learned helplessness. It is more likely a temporary motivation deficit due to lack of clear goals, underarousal, malnutrition, value conflicts, inactivity, conflicting learning styles, prejudice, or lack of resources. Genuine learned helplessness is a serious and chronic condition. It is not treated by a few compliments and a smile. Teachers who have students who fit the description should know that they are in for a challenging test of their patience and skill. The good news is that there are steps you can take to facilitate hope and contribute to healing. All of these steps have one important thing in common: they increase the students' perception of their ability to control the outcome of an event. You'll see improvement from the following types of experiences:

- teaching *Learned Optimism* (Seligman, 1998)
- extending positive emotional states and redirecting negative states in class
- engaging in community service (e.g., scouts, Red Cross, cross-age tutoring)
- taking activist roles (e.g., changing school or community policies)
- planning classroom activities with some choice involved (e.g., field trips, teamwork, ball toss)
- enhancing personal skills (e.g., CPR, martial arts, academic competitions)
- engaging in physical immersion events (e.g., Outward Bound, camping, SuperCamp, boot camp)
- taking part in active hobbies (e.g., caring for animals, skating, sports)
- making family contributions (e.g., meals, cleanup, yard work, car work)
- enjoying sports, theater, and music programs

Giving learners more control over their environment is the first step toward boosting confidence. In *Choice Theory*, Glasser (1999) says that confidence increases whether the control is real or illusory. In an experiment on noise and control, two groups were put into a noisy room. One group had no control over the noise, and the other had a placebo control knob that they thought gave them control over the noise; neither group actually had control. The subjects reported their moods before and after each equally administered 100-decibel session. After the group that knew it had no control ended its sessions, the subjects reported increases in depression, anxiety, helplessness, stress, and tension, while the other group reported being affected very little by these factors.

Helplessness is a common state for students who do poorly in school. It is common for students in schools where the administration or teaching staff is controlling, manipulative, and coercive. Since the natural state of the brain is curiosity and motivation, schools and staff have to ask themselves hard questions such as "What are we doing that makes learners feel powerless?" and "In what ways might our behavior create helplessness, and how can we change this?"

 **What This Means to You**

Participation and motivation are boosted by inclusion, ownership, and choice and are impaired by autocratic insistence and tight control. Make a list of choices you provide to learners. Do they have control of their environment? For example, who maintains the temperature, volume, lights, and other physical elements in your room? Do students feel free to get up and walk around when they need to move? Can they get water when they are thirsty? Can they take a break from one type of learning if they feel the need to so? As you provide more learner control, you will find that participation and motivation increase quite naturally.

Excessive Praise Is Detrimental

According to Kohn (1993), children can become negatively dependent on praise, just as they can on any other external reward. This dependency can lead to lower self-confidence, loss of intrinsic joy in the learning process, and decreased self-esteem. When the reward is withdrawn, learners feel let down. Praise is also interpreted by some as manipulative, and relying on it can easily backfire. Learners may feel controlled and resent the scrutiny, or they may feel self-conscious and inadequate if they sense any insincerity on the part of the praiser.

Overly heavy praise given to a learner can be detrimental to learning. While intermittent praise can be positive, too much praise from authority figures can increase the pressure to perform and result in performance anxiety. Subjects who were given praise right before a skills test consistently performed worse than those who did not receive praise. Students who were heavily praised became more tentative in their answers and gave up on their own ideas more quickly than those who were not.

If a teacher continually praises students for doing their homework or for sitting quietly in class, soon they discover that it is the praise that they seek, not the behavior that the teacher is attempting to reinforce. The following are characteristics of ideal feedback:

Frequent is better than infrequent.

Both positive and negative can be effective.

Task oriented (not personal) is more effective.

Localized negative ("Put the A function on the left side of the equation, not on the right.") is most effective.

Global negative ("You're not trying.") is the least effective.

Positive feedback ("Great job!") falls in the middle.

Personal positive specific is effective ("Your choice of descriptive words was highly effective in establishing the emotional tone.").

 **What This Means to You**

The most striking and permanent aspect of a positive judgment is that it's still a judgment. Reduce your praise, and increase peer feedback and support, which is more motivating to the learner. Encourage rather than praise. Say, "You're on the right track" or "Give it your best effort." Give praise that is not contingent on performance. Encourage learners to take risks. Provide affirmation, not back slapping. When the task is completed, ask learners what their assessment is. In this way, learners begin to develop a sense of quality about the learning, instead of feeling pressure to perform the right way. Teach learners how to provide supportive feedback to each other.

MOTIVATION AND REWARDS

All of us have two different sources of motivation acting upon us: that which arises from within (intrinsic) and that which is externally reinforced (extrinsic). The intrinsic source for learning motivation is ideal for many reasons, the most obvious of which is that even without the artificial controls of a classroom environment, students will continue to achieve.

Remember, all human beings are born with intrinsic motivation; we don't need someone to monitor it unless a brain-antagonistic environment has been set up. Yet if you are operating under the assumption that more teacher control is better, learner motivation is always going to be a problem. Why? Control creates resentment, which undermines natural curiosity and intrinsic motivation. The more fundamental question is, what is your responsibility as a teacher? The answer is both simple and complex: create environments in which learning is as natural as breathing.

The essential understanding here is that we are all biologically driven to seek out new learning. The human brain loves to learn; our very survival, in fact, is dependent on learning. Usually our motivation looks as if it is the pursuit of curiosity, novelty, social contact, food sources, shelter, and enjoyment. Learners have a built-in motivation mechanism that does not require a teacher's input or manipulation to work. Our brains have hungrily absorbed information, integrated it, made meaning out of it, remembered it, and used it at the appropriate times for eons. At school, if we use our natural motivations and curiosity, we can expect students to learn better and enjoy more.

We've all seen apathetic students. But if they made it to school, there's hope. Either the specific classroom environment demotivated them or they brought negative baggage from prior school experiences. In either case, "the unmotivated learner" is a myth. The root of the problem is not so much the learner as the conditions for learning that are less than ideal in most school contexts. A great number of kids have been labeled "underachievers," yet when we stop to consider the amount of motivation it takes for some undersupported children to simply get to school, we tend to rethink our labels. Once learners are in their seats, the teacher's role is to elicit their natural motivation. If learners are severely stressed, they may not be able to process information as efficiently as other learners can, but you can bet their motivation to solve problems is strong. Negative behaviors are commonly reinforced in the artificial and unresponsive school environment. And the problem is perpetuated when we identify, classify, group, label, evaluate, compare, and assess learners.

> There is no such thing as an unmotivated learner. There are, however, temporary unmotivated states in which learners are either reinforced and supported or neglected and labeled.

The following techniques demotivate learners and drive away intrinsic motivation:

- coercion, control, and manipulation
- weak, critical, or negatively competitive relationships
- infrequent or vague feedback
- racism, sexism, or prejudice of any kind
- outcome-based education (unless learners help generate the outcomes)
- inconsistent policies and rules
- top-down management and policy making
- repetitive, rote learning
- inappropriate or limited learning styles
- sarcasm, put-downs, and criticism
- perception of irrelevant content
- boring, single-medium presentation
- reward systems of any kind
- teaching in just one or two of the multiple intelligences
- systems that limit achievement of personal goals
- responsibility without authority

Rewards and the Human Brain

To the brain, a reward is simply a strong positive feeling. It is generated by the release of the neurotransmitter dopamine, which can be triggered by many experiences. To an educator, a reward is a compensation or consequence that (1) is predictable by students and (2) has market value, meaning that it is valued by most students.

In a never-ending effort to control, manipulate, manage, and influence learners, some educators have become accustomed to using rewards; however, considering the brain's natural operational principles, this technique is not productive. To understand this irony, first let's define *reward*.

If it is only predictable but has no market value (e.g., smile, hug, compliment, random gift or token, awards assembly, public approval), then it is simply an acknowledgment, not a reward. If it has market value but absolutely no predictability (e.g., spontaneous party, pizza, cookies, gift certificates, small gifts, trips, tickets), then it is a celebration, not a reward. However, if students know that by behaving a certain way they might get a prize, that's enough predictability to be called a *reward*. The determining criterion is simple:

Did the learners change their behavior in the hopes of getting the favor?

If you offer learners something that meets this criterion, you are, in fact, bribing the learner. A reward system, regardless of what you call it, carries an implicit and covert threat: if learners don't meet the criteria, they will not receive the reward or some opportunities will be withdrawn. As you can tell, the issue has a great deal to do with intent, which can sometimes be tough to read.

What do rewards do to the brain? The brain, which has its own built-in reward system (see Figure 15.2), is highly customized to each individual. This system can be tracked and observed with tracers injected into the blood that measure the release of the chemical dopamine—the "feel-good" neurotransmitter.

This customized reward system develops over time based on each person's unique experiences and perceptions. And each person's system responds to rewards differently. What is a reward to one person may not be much of a reward to another. Events and thoughts can change the system by altering the receptivity of the receptor sites to the brain's endogenous opiates.

The reward system habituates easily, which means that although a reward may be motivational at first, soon thereafter the ante must be increased for the pleasure to remain stable, much as an addict who needs ever-greater amounts of a drug to get the same high. The first time a person uses cocaine, the rush of pleasure may be 500 times that of his or her normal experience, but by the second time, it may drop to 200 times, and by the third, the brain may release only 100 times the amount of dopamine in response. You can imagine what a predicament this puts the brain in. The promise of pleasure entices, but each time the drug is used, the pleasure is less. The brain has habituated. In school, this means that what worked the first time might be insufficient the next time, and the need for an ever-increasing value of reward is sought. The gold stars that worked for first graders become

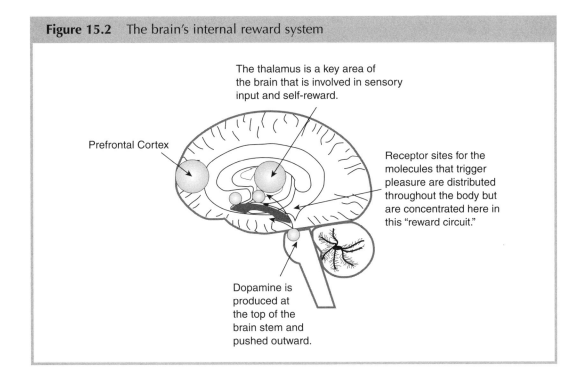

Figure 15.2 The brain's internal reward system

The thalamus is a key area of the brain that is involved in sensory input and self-reward.

Prefrontal Cortex

Receptor sites for the molecules that trigger pleasure are distributed throughout the body but are concentrated here in this "reward circuit."

Dopamine is produced at the top of the brain stem and pushed outward.

cookies for third graders and pizza for fifth graders. Before you know it, you can't provide what the students desire. It's a vicious cycle! Thus, rewards in the learning process must be used judiciously, if at all, to accomplish increased learning.

The Detrimental Effects of Rewards

A student's ability to be creative appears to be linked to intrinsic motivation, since it gives the brain greater freedom of intellectual expression, which in turn seems to inspire even more creativity. A reward system prevents the establishment of intrinsic motivation because there's rarely an incentive to be creative—only to exhibit the requested behavior. Creativity is rarely measured in relation to a reward system; in fact, the two are usually at opposite ends of the spectrum. You either get intrinsically motivated creative thinking or extrinsically motivated repetitive, rote, predictable behaviors. Amabile (1989) found that reward systems lower the quality of the work produced. She conducted more than a dozen studies over nearly 20 years with the same results: in the long run, rewards didn't work. Among artists, creativity (as judged by their peers) dropped subsequent to signing a contract to sell their work upon completion. The fact that financial rewards were pending lessened their fullest expression.

Most behavior-oriented threats and anxiety, coupled with a lack of learner input and

> A system of rewards and punishments can be selectively demotivating in the long term, especially when others have control over the system.
>
> —Geoffrey and Renate Caine

control, will shut down learner thinking and cause learners to prefer repeated, predictable responses to lower their anxiety. This may make teachers think the reward system is working, but initiating changes within this system becomes more difficult because any change increases threat and anxiety to students and teachers alike. Learners who have been bribed for either good work or good behavior find that soon the previous reward wasn't good enough. They want a bigger and better one. Soon, all intrinsic motivation has been killed off, and learners are labeled "unmotivated." Like a rat in a cage pushing a food bar, the learner behavior becomes just good enough to get the reward.

Rewards conflict with learners' goals under the following circumstances:

1. **The learner feels manipulated by the reward.** "You just want me to dress your way."

2. **The reward interferes with the real reason for the learning.** "Now that I'm getting rewarded for receiving good grades, I care only about what's on the test."

3. **The reward devalues the task, and the learner feels bribed.** "This class must be pretty bad if they're giving us a bribe just to attend."

Consider, for example, a school that is having problems with truancy and low attendance. The administrative staff decides, as an incentive, to reward those who come every day. Now each student gets a reward for having 100 percent attendance during the month. The school has worked out an arrangement with local businesses so that the reward is a free meal at McDonald's or Pizza Hut. Students immediately feel bribed for coming to school. They think, "The situation must be really bad for them to bribe us." But learners still respond to the rewarded behavior. "It's stupid, but we'll play the game," they say. Now school is about working the system instead of learning.

Strategies for Eliciting Intrinsic Motivation

1. **Meet learners' needs and goals.** The brain is designed biologically to survive: it will learn what it needs to learn in order to survive. Make it a top priority to discover your learners' needs, and engage those needs. If students need what you have, they're interested. If the content relates to the students' personal lives, they're interested. For example, 6-year-olds have a greater need for security, predictability, and teacher acceptance than 14-year-olds do; the teens' needs are more likely to be about peer acceptance, a sense of importance, and hope for the future. And an 18-year-old is likely more interested in autonomy and independence. Use what's appropriate for the age level of your students.

2. **Provide a sense of control and choice.** Creativity and choice allow learners to express themselves and feel valued. The opposite of this is manipulation, coercion, and control.

3. **Encourage and provide for positive social bonding.** This can come in many forms—a likable teacher, classmate, situation, or group. Encourage teamwork, collaboration, and group activities.

4. **Support a sense of curiosity.** Inquiring minds want to know; this is the nature of the human brain. Keep engaging curiosity—it works! Newspaper tabloids and electronic tabloids have played off our curiosity for years. Just witness all the stories about Elvis, aliens, Princess Diana, Hollywood celebrities, and UFOs.

5. **Engage strong emotions.** Engage emotions productively with compelling stories, games, personal examples, celebration, role-plays, debates, rituals, and music. We are driven to act on our emotions because they are compelling decision makers.

6. **Encourage adequate nutrition.** Better nutrition means more mental alertness. Learn about how diet influences the thinking and learning process. Write up a list of suggestions to give to your students and their parents. Suggest specific brain foods—eggs, fish, nuts, leafy dark green vegetables, apples, bananas, and others known to increase mental alertness.

7. **Incorporate multiple intelligences.** Draw learners in through their strengths, which may range from spatial, bodily-kinesthetic, interpersonal, and verbal-linguistic to intrapersonal, musical-rhythmic, and mathematical-logical. We are particularly motivated when we can demonstrate our strengths and proclivities.

8. **Share success stories.** Tell inspiring stories about other learners who have surmounted obstacles in order to succeed. Develop a mythology and a culture of success. Consider how just walking on a college campus can elicit feelings of motivation.

9. **Provide acknowledgments.** These include assemblies, certificates, group notices, team reports, compliments, and appropriate praise. Positive associations fuel further action.

10. **Increase frequency of feedback.** Make it your part-time job to see that learners get a lot of feedback during each class. Use charts, discussion, peer teaching, projects, and role-plays. Feedback needs to be nonjudgmental and immediate.

11. **Manage physiological states.** Learn to read and manage states. There is no such thing as an unmotivated learner, only unmotivated states. Elicit anticipation and challenge states in your learners and in yourself.

12. **Provide the hope of success.** Learners need to know that it's possible for them to succeed. Regardless of the obstacles or how far behind they may be, hope is essential. Frank (1985) strongly believes that hope works like a powerful drug and is essential to restoring demoralization. Every learning context must provide some kind of hope.

13. **Model the joy of learning.** Since more than 99 percent of all learning is nonconscious, the more excited you are about learning, the more motivated your learners will likely be.

14. **Mark successes and achievements with celebrations.** These include peer acknowledgment, parties, food, high-fives, and cheers. These create the atmosphere of success and can trigger the release of endorphins that further boost learning and motivation.

15. **Maintain a physically and emotionally safe learning environment.** An environment in which it is safe to make mistakes, ask questions, and offer contributions is essential. Meet learners' physical needs for adequate lighting, water, food, movement, and comfortable seating. Also ensure that learners are physically safe from building hazards. Make sure they know you are always available to discuss any concerns about their safety, including concerns about other students.

16. **Incorporate learners' individual learning styles.** Provide both choice in how students learn and diversity in what they learn so that they can use their preferred learning styles.

17. **Instill positive beliefs about capability and context.** Reinforce learners as they meet difficult challenges. Tell them that you know they can succeed and accomplish their goals. Discover what beliefs individual may hold about themselves that might be holding them back, and work to affect them positively.

None of these strategies cost anything (no rewards or bribes are necessary), and they work. They certainly involve more initial preparation and work to create a climate of intrinsic motivation, but it pays off in the long run. Teachers who rely on extrinsic motivation may be vastly underestimating three things: (1) the power and limitations of their influence, (2) learners' desire to be intrinsically motivated, and (3) the long-term ease of reinforcing intrinsic rewards.

Rewards . . .

reduce the learner's ability to solve complex problems without extrinsic motivators
reduce learner responsiveness to the environment
result in increased stereotypical, low-risk, low-creativity behavior
increase learner attentiveness to, and reliance on, external systems of rewards and punishments

---

Deci and Ryan (1987) say there is evidence linking extrinsic motivation to positive outcomes in work involving noncreative tasks, memorized skills, and repetitive tasks. However, in order to get learners to be creative and have greater subject interest, higher self-esteem, and the ability to be reflective, there must be intrinsic motivation. Reward systems prevent this, but make no mistake about it, some learners will respond to rewards in the short term.

Paradoxically, the more demotivating the environment is, the more learners seek rewards. Stressed and anxious learners are more likely to look to others for safe, predictable role modeling; to listen to others for goals; and to increase their own stereotyped, lower-order thinking. But this creates a catch-22. At a low level, rewards work. The teacher continues their usage, and learners are now victims of the glass ceiling principle: they learn to perform to the lowest level needed to get the reward. I often have teachers say to me, "My students seem to like the reward system. They complain when it is dropped, and their performance goes down." Teachers use this as evidence to say, "I know I shouldn't bribe them, but the system works!"

> Learners who experience stress and anxiety in their environment will prefer external motivation, meaning a system of reliable rewards.

The problem is that the system does work—too well. Rewards lead to learners who become preoccupied with "playing the game" and not really doing quality learning. Why? Quite simply, the ability to alter perceptual maps, to do higher-order thinking, and to create complex thematic relationships with the subject is not available to the brain when it experiences the anxiety of a reward system.

> In the long run, rewards do more damage than good toward motivating the so-called underachiever.

The more you use a reward system, the more you evoke the two-headed dichotomous dragon: (1) the psychological anxiety of performance increases, and (2) every reward carries with it an implied certainty of success or failure. But which will learners achieve: success or failure? They want to reduce the uncertainty, so they pick tasks that have a high degree of predictability (often boring, repetitive skills). Learners are also more likely to pick goals set by others instead of themselves (even the goals they do pick are often the basic, overworked, media-reinforced, cliché types).

 ## What This Means to You

Replace rewards with positive alternatives, including meeting learner goals, peer support, positive rituals, self-assessment, acknowledgments, love of learning, enthusiasm, privileges, increased feedback, more options for creativity, and more student control. Rewards do more harm than good; they encourage results other than those originally intended. Phase out reward systems. It makes more sense to make school or work a worthwhile place to be, rather than trying to bribe people to attend or perform. When you incorporate the brain-based strategies in this book, rewards will become unnecessary.

Rewarded Actions Lose Appeal

Following a decade of postreward analysis, Kazdin (1977) concluded that when the goodies stop, the behavior stops, too. At first, he was excited about the behavior changes. In an earlier publication, Kazdin (1976) talked about how much patient behavior had changed. And that's what people remembered the most. Once a proponent of rewards, he set up a token economy system in a health care institution. But by 1977 he had determined that although the rewards worked temporarily, they did not maintain the desirable outcomes.

> Removal of token reinforcement results in decrements in desirable responses and a return to baseline or near-baseline levels of performance.
>
> —Alfie Kohn

All learners have their own biases that they bring to a particular context. The biases constitute personal beliefs, hopes, expectations, fears, values, and emotions. These are what hold a behavior in place. Rewards are designed to change the behavior, not the biases. Hence, any reward-driven activity is likely to fail in the long run.

We all know teachers often offer rewards for attendance, homework, or good behavior. Pizza Hut had a program designed to reward students for reading by offering pizzas. The follow-up, however, would likely confirm that those who read the most were those who had been reading already; they just decided to play the game. And learners who had not ordinarily read before the promotion likely returned to their prior habits afterward. If that program was as successful in the long run as it was in the short run, we would have a nation of ravenous readers right now.

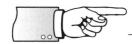 ## What This Means to You

Many learners would become more intrinsically motivated if given a chance, but as long as a reward system is in place, they'll play the game and undermine their own progress in the long term. Reduce or eliminate all rewards. Phase out slowly any rewards you are now using. Incorporate positive alternatives: celebrations, variety, novelty, and feedback.

Should You Ever Use Rewards?

According to Kohn (1993), "if your objective is to get people to obey an order, to show up on time and do what they're told" (p. 41), rewards can work. But, he adds emphatically, rewards simply change the specific, in-the-moment behavior and not the person. If your objective is to help learners authentically achieve, rewards simply don't work.

Rewards don't help learners . . .

achieve long-term quality performance
become self-directed learners
develop values of caring, respect, and friendliness
develop creativity and higher-order thinking skills
increase integrity and self-confidence
develop inner drive and intrinsic motivation

Here's an example of when a reward might be used: You have a bunch of chairs to move to another room. It's the end of the day; you're tired and hungry. You ask a couple of students if they'd be willing to help you move them after class. They say, "No, not really." But you're desperate, so you say, "How about if I get you both a Coke?" They change their minds and decide it's worth it. The chairs get moved. Everybody's happy. The reward was appropriate.

ALTERNATIVES FOR BRIBERY AND REWARDS

There are many positive alternatives to bribing students for better behaviors. The first and most powerful one is to make school more meaningful, relevant, and fun. Then you won't have to bribe students. If you are using any kind of reward system, let it run its course and end it as soon as you reasonably can. If you stop it abruptly, you may get a rebellion. The learners will need to detox from the reward drug. Remember, the research says that learners who have been on a reward system will become conditioned to prefer it over free choice.

But replacing rewards with alternatives gets a bit tricky for two reasons. First, the entire system of marking and grading is a reward-and-punishment system. The rewards are good grades, which lead to teacher approval, scholarships, and university entry. How can an instructional leader work properly (without bribes and rewards) within a system that is so thoroughly entrenched? What if other teachers use rewards but you don't? You will have your work cut out for you, but if you provide learners with the reasoning behind your approach, they will eventually prefer your methods. Be patient.

Second, there are many gray areas. A certificate may be just an acknowledgment when you give it to students, but what if parents reward learners with money when it is taken home? Then it becomes a reward in spite of your best intentions. The solution is to try to make parents aware of the destructive effects of rewards at an open house night or by letter. You don't have to bribe learners to learn. The human brain loves to learn! Simply follow the "rules" for brain-compatible learning, and learners' thirst and hunger to learn will return.

What the Reward Proponents Say

Behaviorists treat learners as empty vessels that need to be filled. In this paradigm, the way you get learners to learn is to first gain control, then control what and how they learn; if they aren't interested, you simply bribe them. Those who are steadfast in their insistence on rewards usually defend themselves on the following grounds:

Proponents of reward systems often claim that . . .

rewards are necessary ("After all, what's the intrinsic reward for computing the problem 4 + 4?")
the studies on intrinsic rewards are theoretical only
rewards are harmless
the real world uses rewards
rewards are effective

Those who have discovered the power of alternatives know the answers already. But for the others, here are some comments about the five points raised above:

1. "Rewards are necessary." This is false. In the control paradigm, students have been so conditioned that even simple learning begs for a motivating cue. This is because their natural love of learning has been manipulated out of them. Millions of students learn based on curiosity, joy, and their natural love of learning. Learners who say they want rewards have simply been conditioned to want them.

2. "The studies on intrinsic rewards are theoretical only." This is false. Hundreds of studies on the follies of rewards have been done with real people in everyday situations. One of the most innovative programs for almost 30 years, SuperCamp, uses no rewards, and its results have been reported worldwide. It has more than 50,000,000 graduates, and one-, five-, and ten-year studies demonstrate that its methods work.

3. "Rewards are harmless." Once again, false. Consistent studies have documented that, under the context of a reward, the brain operates differently. Behaviors become more predictable, stereotyped, rigid, and narrow. You can get a desired behavior with rewards, but you won't get intrinsically motivated students with a passion for learning.

4. "The real world uses rewards." In some cases, yes; in many other cases, no. Critics say that everyone gets rewards for their work, but that's not true. Many people work because they love what they do. The majority of teachers went into their profession because they liked the satisfaction of helping others grow and succeed, even though other jobs pay better.

5. "Rewards are effective." For rote, repetitive tasks, yes, rewards enhance performance for a while. But then the novelty of the reward wears off, and the performance drops. Someone can hold a gun to your head and get you to do almost anything. It's effective, isn't it? But this doesn't make it right. Rewarded behaviors rarely continue after the rewards are removed, unless the learner did not depend on the rewards to begin with.

Replacing Rewards With Learning

When you begin to remove rewards from your learning environment, don't expect a standing ovation. Research has shown that many learners prefer rewards even though they are counterproductive to their learning. Why? It's predictable. Take your time phasing out rewards. Allow existing programs to expire on their own. Then ask students for their partnership in replacing extrinsic rewards with intrinsic rewards. Teachers who make unilateral decisions about classroom operations while ignoring student input reinforce a sense of powerlessness. Rather, engage students in active discussion about the real cost of rewards and the real rewards of learning.

If you replace rewards with more student choice, feedback, and empowerment, learners begin to choose to learn for their own reasons. This transition to learning for learning's sake will not happen overnight. Students will need time and support in directing their focus inward—on their own needs, values, goals, belief systems, and emotions. Thus, the removal of external rewards is only the first step. Next, students need to be supported while their locus of control shifts from external to internal. When you stop hearing "Is this going to be on the test?" you'll know you have achieved the goal. What this question tells you about learners is that they've had the love of learning bribed out of them by unknowing teachers. Since they don't think learning is any fun, they need a bribe for their effort. The goal of brain-based teaching is to let the brain reward itself for its own growth, just as it is naturally equipped to do.

GOAL SETTING INCREASES PERFORMANCE

Teachers maintain many types of goals for their students. Some are directed by a governmental entity (e.g., standards for outcome-based learning). Others may be your own goals (e.g., "I want them to develop a real love of learning"). And yet others may be determined by a particular learner's situation (e.g., "Johnny's going to learn to read this year"). But most critical to a brain-based learning approach are the learners' goals for themselves. The best goals are student-generated goals.

Locke and Latham (1990) reviewed 400 studies examining goals for motivation, and the results were definitive. They found that specific, difficult goals lead to better performance than easy, vague ones. The results, based on studies conducted in the United States and seven other countries, included more than 40,000 subjects, 88 different tasks, time spans ranging from one minute to three years, and numerous performance criteria, including behavior change, quantity and quality outcomes, and costs.

A few other criteria are also important for effective goal setting (Ford, 1992). The target has to be at an optimal level of difficulty—challenging, but attainable. In addition, learners need to have (1) ample feedback to make corrections, (2) capability beliefs to help them persevere in the face of negative feedback, (3) the actual skills needed to complete the task, and (4) an environment conducive to success. The three keys to learner goal acquisition, says Ford, are the learners' beliefs, the emotions, and goals.

But if goals are given too much attention, they can be counterproductive. When the pressure is too great, learners report feelings of self-consciousness and the tendency to make simple mistakes and "choke" on material they know that they know but can't remember in the pressure of the moment.

Personal Agency Beliefs

Personal agency beliefs (PABs) is a term used to describe people's capability beliefs about themselves. These are activated once a goal is set and are influenced by the context of the moment. For example, a student's belief upon being accepted to a university might be, "Wow, I think I can do well and graduate from this university in four years." However, once the student is attending classes, he or she may begin thinking, "Gee, with a full load at school and working part time, getting good grades is harder than I thought."

In a long-term study of 250 students, ages 12 to 15, Meece, Wigfield, and Eccles (1990) found that the single best predictor of success in mathematics was the students' expectancy of future math success. Once these students were in the classes, the best predictor of their likelihood of continuing in math classes was its importance to them.

Although an instructional leader isn't always privy to learners' ever-evolving PABs, when it is obvious that students lack strong capability beliefs, there is a solution. With significant student input, establish controllable short-term goals (Barden & Ford, 1990). If you do that, the long-term outcomes may still be in doubt, but the short-term successes can positively impact the PABs of underconfident learners.

Goals are best when they . . .

are created by the learner
are concrete and specific
have a specific due date
can be measured through self-assessment
are reviewed and adjusted periodically by the learner

The beliefs or PABs that teachers have about their students—both individually and collectively—impact the learners in powerful ways as well. Rosenthal (1991) and Rosenthal and Jacobsen (1968, 1996) present a compelling argument for why teachers and trainers should maintain high expectations of learners. As previously mentioned, results of their study suggest that students will perform (not coincidentally) as well as you expect them to. Some learners may get sufficiently engaged with simple goals, such as "Here's what we can get done today," while others may require more challenging goals, such as "Let's design a better health care system and see if we can get it picked up by the local news."

 ## What This Means to You

Goal setting is an important aspect of the learning process. Let students generate their own goals. Let them discover whether their own beliefs can support these goals. Ask them about the learning environment: Do they feel it supports them in achieving their goals? Do they have the resources they need to reach their goals? Most learners who want to succeed are capable of succeeding, though they often lack the beliefs necessary to do so. Ask learners to set immediate short-term goals for the day in addition to longer-term goals. Make sure the goals are positive, measurable, and obtainable. For example, a goal could be as simple as wanting to learn two new interesting things today. You then need to provide the necessary resources, learning climate, and feedback to help learners reach their goals. Hold them accountable. Check back later to assess results and celebrate, if appropriate. If necessary, help learners reassess their goals or their approach to achieving them. Celebrate each step on the road to success.

Previsualization Boosts Learning

A study at Oxford University found that visualization before a learning activity improved learning (Drake, 1996). A group of elementary school children were asked to practice visualization, imagery, and make-believe before being tested, whereas the control group simply took the test. The group that did the visualization first scored higher on the test.

Before you went to your last job interview, chances are you rehearsed the interview in your mind a few times over. This kind of practicing help you access important information and, in a sense, pre-exposes your mind to pertinent data.

 ## What This Means to You

In some cases, learners may not be unmotivated; they may just need mental warm-ups. A few minutes invested early in the class can produce a big payoff later. Create a daily routine for learners. Before you start, have them do some physical stretching and mental warm-ups, such as role-playing, generating questions, visualizing a scene, solving a problem, or brainstorming.

Inspiring Optimal Motivation

Ford (1992) researched optimal environments for motivation and found that four factors were critical to what he calls *context beliefs,* the functional elements that are in vitro, or embedded within a learner's situation:

- The environment must be consistent with each individual's personal goals. This means that the learning environment must be a place in which learners can reach their own personal goals.
- The environment must be congruent with learners' biosocial and cognitive styles. If abstract learning is taking place in a crowded, competitive room with fluorescent lighting, it will be a problem for a concrete learner who needs space and prefers to work cooperatively.
- The environment must offer learners the resources they need. In addition to materials, advice, tools, transportation, and supplies, learners need to have adequate time, support, and access.
- The environment must provide a supportive and positive emotional climate. A sense of trust, warmth, safety, and peer acceptance is critical.

As a child, did you find yourself naturally and effortlessly engaged in learning? Why or why not? Were the qualities described above inherent in your learning environment? How inherent are they in the learning environment you provide for your learners today?

What This Means to You

Many students you consider to be unmotivated may be very motivated under the right conditions. Make a big poster featuring the conditions for optimal learning, and post it in your classroom and/or office. Let it be your guide for how to motivate learners and yourself.

16 Attention and Survival Value

The wording in the phrase *to pay attention* is appropriate. We are giving to another person a precious commodity: our attentional resources. Strong attention requires that we orient, engage, and maintain each appropriate neural network. In addition, we must exclude or suppress both external and internal distracters. And although not every type of learning requires attention and engagement, explicit learning (of facts, names, and faces) actually does require attention. Even when we go for a walk, our brain "learns" a great deal. But it's not an in-depth type of learning; it's known as *priming*. In the typical word-based, semantic-style classroom learning, more focused and engaged attention is better than less of it. That's no news flash to most teachers, yet most struggle to maintain attention. Why?

Biologically relevant school stimuli include opportunities to make friends, quench thirst or hunger, and learn safety considerations such as a change in weather or bullying. The student's brain is also concerned with avoiding danger of embarrassment, failure, or harm. Yet some teachers ask students to orient and sustain attention until instructed otherwise (even if it means listening, reading, or focusing for up to an hour) and to do so daily in a gossip-ridden, physically inactive, and emotionally insensitive environment. It rarely works out the way the teachers would like.

The level of attention we are able to apply to a learning situation is limited by our perception of the value of doing so. Remember that our brains are most alert to information that helps ensure our survival. This is the state that elicits maximum attention—a state that thankfully isn't often experienced in a classroom or training environment. Since the survival state is reserved for issues of life and limb, we as teachers can't hope for our students' complete attention in the classroom; nor would it even be healthy. We can, however, create an environment where learners have the flexibility to focus on aspects of learning that are personally meaningful to them. This chapter explores the mechanisms and boundaries of the brain's attentional system and how we can best manage students' attention for optimal learning.

MAKING MEANING

Humans are natural meaning-seeking organisms. But while the search is innate, the end result is not automatic. Since meaning is generated internally, excessive input can conflict with the process. An important principle to remember is that either you can have your learners' attention or they can be making meaning, but never both at the same time. Facilitate a small-group discussion after new material is introduced to sort it out, generate questions, and play "what if" scenarios. Encourage learners to find personal meaning in their new learning. Explain to them how the brain naturally prioritizes information moment by moment.

During this necessary period of incubation, the brain filters out new incoming stimuli. It begins to sift through its full plate of information, looking for links, associations, uses, and procedures as it sorts and stores. This is a process that can occur only during downtime. Some kind of reflection time—writing in journals or having small-group discussion—makes good sense for the brain after new material is presented.

 ## What This Means to You

Provide settling time. Just as a cake needs to settle after baking, the brain's neural connections need time to solidify and settle after learning. The best type of settling time is not doing seatwork or homework, but rather taking a walk, stretching, performing rote classroom chores (e.g., clearing the bulletin board, hanging art), doodling, or merely resting. Breaks, recess, lunch, and going home can also be considered downtime. Ideally, "brain breaks" ought to be built into your lesson plans every 20 minutes or so. The more intense the new learning, the more reflection time is necessary.

Attention Shifts

The brain's E-I (external-internal) shift is frequent and automatic. This shifting of focus seems to be a critical element in (1) maintaining understanding, (2) updating long-term memories, and (3) strengthening our neural networks. The brain needs time to "go inside" and link up the present with the past and the future. Without it, learning drops dramatically.

> When we consider current findings in brain research, it becomes clear that the whole concept of on task or off task is irrelevant.

The two critical factors for determining the amount of processing time a person needs are the learner's background in the subject or how much prior knowledge and skill the learner has, and the intensity or complexity of the new material. High novelty and complexity with low learner background means more processing time will be necessary. The reverse is also true: high learner background with low novelty and complexity (e.g., a review) means less learner settling time is necessary.

Some students need equal external and internal time, while others may need a 5-to-1 ratio—meaning they have a longer attention span. When you see good students in class who are not paying attention, it is a mistake to automatically assume they are goofing around. It may be that something has triggered their memory or shifted their focus inward.

 ## What This Means to You

It may be that our notion of staying on task is really inappropriate and, in fact, a counterproductive way to measure learning. Keeping students' attention 100 percent of the time is a bad idea. The learner who you are assuming is not focused may simply be rethinking things in light of new information. Build into each day sufficient reflection time and group or partner processing time. Avoid long lectures, give frequent breaks, and pay attention to the individual and collective states of learners.

Optimal State for Learning

Very little learning happens when students are stressed out, despondent, or otherwise distracted. But when they are prompted into a positive state for learning, they naturally do better. Csikszentmihalyi (1990) reports in his book *Flow: The Psychology of Optimal Experience* that a state of consciousness (flow) is the primary criterion for optimal learning. Although it is impossible to merely will this uninterrupted state of concentration into existence, it happens when people lose themselves in an activity. That is, all self-consciousness and awareness of time fades, and what is left is a pure pleasure-producing absorption into the experience. Children, teenagers, and athletes find themselves in this state more often than the average adult.

Intelligence-Building States

Intelligence building is enhanced by maximizing complexity of states
↓
Continuity
(strength and persistence of previous states)
Flexibility
(capacity for variability and the responsiveness to context demands)

Csikszentmihalyi (1990) defines *flow* as a pattern of activity in which individual or group goals emerge (as opposed to being mandated) as a result of a pleasurable activity and interaction with the environment. When your skills, attention, environment, and will are aligned, flow is more likely to occur. Creativity and learning emerge in an accelerated fashion when learners are encouraged to go with the flow while enjoying themselves and defining and refining their own learning challenges. This philosophy allows learners to take responsibility for their learning in a relaxed state.

Flow is most likely to emerge when the balance of challenge and mastery is equal. Let's say, for example, that you've decided to learn to play the saxophone (or speak a foreign language, ice skate, golf, jog, surf the Web, etc.). At first, the practice takes a lot of effort, but over time it mysteriously gets easier, and before you know it, you're actually having fun! Time passes without your awareness, your skills improve, and you seem to be improving without struggle. You have reached the perfect balance. Your skill level matches the challenge.

The Best State for Learning

- intrinsically challenged with material that is not too easy, not too hard (best if the learner chooses it, so that it is personally relevant)
- low-to-moderate stress, general relaxation (this does not mean no stress)
- immersed flow state in which attention is focused on learning and doing (rather than being self-conscious or evaluative)
- curiosity and anticipation (when a learner discovers an interest in a particular subject, build on it)
- confusion (can be a motivator if it's brief and doesn't continue)

Matching Challenge and Mastery

As viewed by sophisticated imaging devices, brain activity increases when mental tasks are increased in complexity and difficulty. Even when learners are unsuccessful at very challenging experiments, their brains continue to be actively engaged. You play much better tennis, for example, when your opponent provides a good challenge for you. If, however, your opponent is at a different skill level than you (either better or worse), you will likely lose interest quite quickly.

Csikszentmihalyi (1990) further contends that we can get into the magical state of flow every day. When the challenge is greater than your skills, that's anxiety; when your skills exceed the challenge, that's boredom. But when the challenge and skill level are matched up, whammo! You've hit the jackpot! It is fairly easy to get learners into optimal learning states if you remember what gets you into that state.

 ## What This Means to You

Teaching in a way that encourages students to reach the flow state may be one of the most important roles you have. In this state, learners are highly internally motivated, and learning becomes enjoyable. Help learners reach flow by setting up favorable conditions for it. Mandated, step-by-step instruction can work well in the initial stages of learning (by instilling focus, confidence, and motivation), but once you're beyond this, learners will likely be stifled by a rigid structure. Keep challenge high but stress low. Let learners set the pace while you provide the support. Have them design a complex project that is personally relevant, and then vary the resources to keep the task appropriate to their ability levels. Make it exciting; use teams, simulations, technology, and deadlines while maintaining appropriate levels of guidance and control.

What Brain Waves Can Tell Us

Another way to view states is by considering brain-wave patterns. EEG readings provide a measure of brain activity for identified categories by observing chemical reactions, which produce electrical fields that have a quantifiable number of cycles per second. Brain-wave patterns are defined by the following categories:

Delta	0 to 4Hz	Deep sleep/no outer awareness
Theta	4 to 8Hz	Twilight/light sleep/meditative
Alpha	8 to 12Hz	Aware/relaxed/calm/attentive
Beta	12 to 16Hz	Normal waking consciousness
High Beta	16 to 30Hz	Intense outer-directed focus
K Complex	30 to 35Hz	The "Aha!" experience
Super Beta	35 to 150Hz	Extreme states (e.g., psychic, out of body)

So which state is best for learning? It all depends on what type of learning and for how long, but here's a general synopsis: Delta is useless for any type of learning, as far as researchers know. Theta is the state that we all go into and out of right before falling asleep and waking up. It can be great for sleep learning and free association of creative ideas; however, it's too passive for direct instruction. Alpha is an alert state for listening and watching, but it is still fairly passive. Beta is great for typical thinking, asking questions, and problem solving, but High Beta is ideal for intense states such as debating and performing. K Complex is difficult to orchestrate, but you can set up the circumstances for it, and if it happens, great. And finally, Super Beta is such an intense state that it isn't appropriate for schools, classrooms, and formal education. Obviously, you can't use an EEG to measure brain-wave activity in the classroom, but some simple observations about states can still be made. Here are a few examples of corresponding emotions and body language that may reflect a learner's state:

What the Learner Feels	*What You Might See*
Fear	Restricted breathing, tightened muscles, and closed body posture
Anticipation	Eyes wide open, body leaning forward, and breath held
Curiosity	Hand to head, bright facial expression, and head turned or tilted
Apathy	Relaxed shoulders/posture, slow breathing, and no eye contact
Frustration	Fidgeting and anxious movements, tightened muscles, and shortened breaths
Self-convincer	Breathing shifts, and body rocks, tilts, or rolls

If you observe a student struggling with an unproductive learning state, you have a decision to make: Either let it go or facilitate a change. Since all behaviors are dependent on a state, if you help move the learner into an optimal state, you'll get optimal results. But if you allow the learner to linger in an unproductive state, a negative association may develop and eventually impact learning on a very deep level.

For example, if a learner's state is curiosity but the task at hand is overly challenging, the learner can quickly move into confusion. At this point, if the confusion is not resolved, frustration is likely to follow. An aware educator may catch the confusion before it turns to frustration or, worse, anger or apathy. The stages of confusion and frustration last only a short time, so timing is important. You may have only a few minutes to observe the problem and react. If you ignore it, a bigger problem is sure to follow.

Most Common Student States

Fear
Anxiety
Boredom
Apathy
Frustration
Confusion

Most Desirable Student States

Anticipation
Self-convincer
Excitement
Curiosity
Celebration
Enlightenment

Students go in and out of countless states every day, just as you do. Learning is not all in our heads: it's a mind-body experience. How you feel and how they feel is important. It influences every single learning experience. Here are some strategies for managing learning states:

1. Activities. Facilitate a change from one to another, intensify learner involvement, lead a stretching session or an energizing game, shift from individual to group work, move locations, or do something novel.

2. Environment. Create an energy shift with a lighting, seating, or temperature change; use aromas, sound, ionizers, plants, or color. Provide an emotionally safe environment.

3. Multimedia sources. Incorporate a video, a computer program, an overhead projection system, music, or slides.

4. People. Change speakers, or shift learners' visual focus; have the students teach each other. Shift to groups or buddy-study.

5. Tone. Provide a shift in theme, schedule, time frame, goals, resources, rules, or opinions.

6. Focusing. Facilitate breathing exercises (inhale and exhale slowly through the nose); incorporate visualization and imagery.

7. Choice. Provide learners with choices; ask for their input. Student motivation increases as you increase their control and accountability. Provide a safe environment, frequent feedback, positive social bonding opportunities, and adequate nutrition and water. Engage multiple learning styles.

Every day, you'll get more adept at reading states and managing them productively. Always ask yourself: What's the target state for this learning activity? If the answer is a reflective state, facilitate a stress-reducing exercise; then play some slow music. If the activity calls for an active state, have students stand up and take a few deep breaths; then play some fast music. In any case, be respectful of your learners' processes. Sometimes a student's state may be reflective of a deep-seated problem that shouldn't be dismissed. If a problematic state continues for more than a couple of days with an individual student, it may be a good idea to seek additional help from a school psychologist or another mental health professional.

What This Means to You

The most effective instructional leaders know how to recognize and manage learning states and ultimately teach others how to do this for themselves. As learners begin to recognize their own attentional rhythms, the reward is fewer classroom disturbances and more empowered learners. To move learners from nonproductive states to productive learning states, provide them with some choice, suggest a change of activities, shift your voice or your approach to a problem, provide a change of location, alter lighting, facilitate a movement game or activity, play some music, or construct a class art project. Hundreds of other possibilities exist, of course; the bottom line is to give learners some control over their environment and facilitate a shift from a mental or cognitive activity to a physical, creative, or reflection activity.

17 Teaching How to Think

The brain is a natural at many things. It creates simple association effortlessly, without any conscious thinking processes. If we always have a good time in a restaurant with a certain friend or family member, we associate that restaurant with good feelings, even though there are no feelings in the physical building.

We also generalize without any conscious thought. If we are wronged several times in one week by red-haired people, we tend to generalize that to all red-haired people (false assumption!). But aside from a few exceptions, we as teachers have to actively teach thinking skills to our students.

Examples of the types of skills that must be taught explicitly include logic, cause and effect, correlations, the use of analogies, risk analysis, prediction skills, decision making, and a host of others. While in a perfect world each of these and others would be included or embedded in an everyday lesson at school, this doesn't happen very often. We have to choose the types of critical-thinking programs we use and be rigorous about implementing them.

WHAT EXACTLY IS THINKING, ANYWAY?

When we say, "I am thinking," what we are really saying is, "I am trying to manipulate internal symbols in a meaningful way." Thinking is a process whereby the brain accesses prior representations for understanding or creates a new model if one does not exist. The following categories represent some of these modes of representational thinking.

1. **Symbolic language.** Includes pictures, symbols, sounds, words, or "internal movies." This also includes verbal expression, music, or technological communications, such as computer-programming languages.

2. **Indirect knowledge.** Includes mental models, procedural thinking, physical patterns, and other implicit knowledge, such as feelings. How you feel about something or whether you have a sense about something plays a large role in the decision-making process.

3. **Direct sensations.** Includes touch, natural sounds, scenes, and the experience of nature.

When we break thinking down into the above three categories, we see how difficult it is to measure it. The mind, body, and feelings are all involved; there is no separation. Knowing this, it should be no surprise to hear that how we are thinking can be discerned by observing the body. When we are tense or happy, nothing necessarily has to be said for another person to interpret our thinking.

Factors That Influence Thinking

Critical thinking means that effective and reliable mental processes are used in the pursuit of relevant and correct knowledge about the world. Reasonable, reflective, and responsible mental processes help us decide what to believe or do. A person who thinks critically can ask appropriate questions, gather relevant information, efficiently and creatively sort through this information, reason logically from this information, and come to reliable and trustworthy conclusions about the world that enable one to live and act successfully in it.

Critical thinking is, in fact, a survival imperative in the twenty-first century. Children are not born with the power to think critically, nor do they develop this ability naturally beyond survival-level thinking, which is more innate. Throughout history, those most skilled in thinking and problem solving flourished, while the less skilled perished. Teachers can capitalize on this natural aptitude to survive by explicitly focusing on the related attributes of good problem solvers—primarily, critical-thinking skills. Fortunately, nature does some of the work for us, but there is still a great deal we can do in the classroom to ensure that learners develop high-level thinking skills. Let's start with a review of some of the primary factors that influence thinking or cognition (see Figure 17.1).

Environment

A challenging environment forces the brain to flex its thinking muscles. Intrinsic motivation kicks in to reverse the uncomfortable biochemical state called *stress*. On the other hand, when the body reaches the biochemical state of balance called *homeostasis*, motivation classically drops. When an environment provides an equal amount of challenge and stress with empowerment and support, you get an ideal learning situation whereby progress proceeds most rapidly.

The underchallenged learner may relieve boredom with disruptive behavior, while the overly challenged learner is likely to feel defeated and withdraw unless some resolution or success is achieved. Resting precariously between these two critical points is the magic learning moment. Teachers who provide a safe and challenging environment, while staying attuned to learner states and responding appropriately to them, facilitate a great number of teachable moments.

Will/Volition

Riding closely on the heels of the environment factor is the motivation factor, also known as *will* or *volition*. In fact, the two are inseparable. When an environment is conducive to learning, positive motivation naturally follows. However, when daily life is unchallenging (or dysfunctional in some other way), even the brightest learners can end up squandering their intellectual potential. Until learners get motivated to use and enhance their cognitive skills, they are likely to remain ensconced and stagnant in their relative comfort. The best way to

Figure 17.1 What enhances intelligence building?

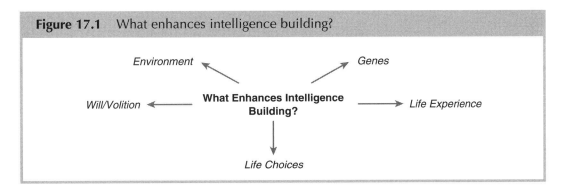

strengthen learner motivation is to provide meaningfulness, learner choices, and emotional support while affirming the individual.

Life Experience

Emerging brain research provides good evidence that the brain is biologically molded by life experiences—especially in infancy. At birth we immediately begin experiencing basic needs (or problems), which are either met or not. For example, the baby who wails with hunger and is promptly satisfied with feeding experiences a deep sense of success. The ignored baby, on the other hand, experiences a poignant sense of failure. Multiplied a thousand times in a few years, we soon start behaving in ways that reflect this fundamental programming. Influenced strongly by a sense of personal power or (all too often) a sense of powerlessness, our life experiences build on one another, usually reinforcing our early programming.

Genes

Although the nature-versus-nurture debate has reigned for years, the current cognitive science and neuroscience research suggests that both positions are correct. Although life experiences most certainly impact cognitive responses, genes influence such things as alertness, memory, and sensory acuity as well—all significant intelligence factors. Consider, for example, how rare it is for parents with very low IQs to produce offspring with very high IQs. Nevertheless, genes alone do not account for genius-level IQs. Thus, we begin to see the interrelated nature of these influences.

Life Choices

Cognitive-enrichment possibilities are ever inherent in our daily decisions, from the foods we eat and people we socialize with to the amount of physical and mental exercise and sleep we get. The brain, like the body, is either nurtured or neglected by our actions. Factors such as poor nutrition, lack of mental or physical challenge, abuse of drugs and alcohol, repeated blows to the head, and extreme stress kill you cognitively. Although we lose brain cells every day, recent brain research suggests that we also generate new cells throughout our lives.

Although the developmental stages highlighted in Figure 17.2 vary from individual to individual depending on the related factors previously mentioned, in general our cognitive development proceeds along a predictable time line. At birth, we possess only reflexes, but babies are quick learners. The development of basic reflexes generally takes place within 3 to 11 weeks, and in 3 to 13 months, infants become capable of basic actions, such as putting food in their mouths or taking a blanket off of themselves. Until this time, however, babies have only the basic cognitive capabilities exhibited by nonhuman primates.

Figure 17.2   Cognitive-development time line

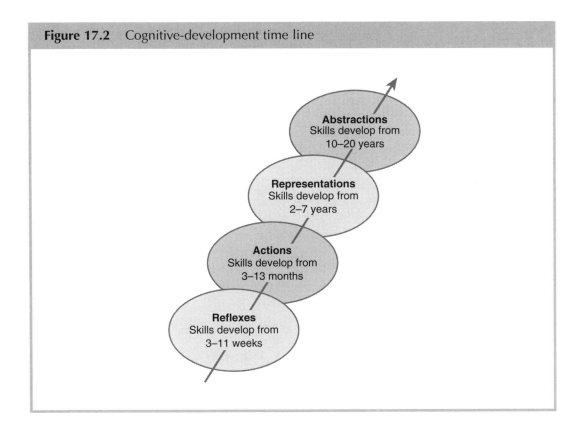

The toddler soon develops the basic representational framework that accompanies language development and sets humans apart in the primate world. Skills accompanying this stage include identifying objects and locations, consciously using body language to make a point, drawing cause-and-effect conclusions, imagining scenarios, and verbalizing needs and feelings with words.

The peak of the cognitive path—abstract thinking—is not reached until the later elementary to high school grade levels. Abstract thinking is reflected in such tasks as identifying universal truths, beauty, ethical dilemmas, and cultural frameworks. By adulthood most of us possess fully matured frontal lobes, the area of the brain thought to be largely responsible for this highest form of cognition.

> Being especially good at problem solving does not guarantee success in life, but being especially poor at it practically guarantees failure.

TEACHING THINKING

Can intelligent thinking be taught? Absolutely. Not only can it be taught, but it is also a fundamental part of the essential skills package necessary for success in today's world. A primary focus on creativity, life skills, and problem solving makes the teaching of thinking meaningful and productive for learners. These aspects of intelligence, though long undervalued in the traditional school setting, play an important role in intelligence. The following are some of the skills that ought to be emphasized at the abstractions level of development in the teaching of problem solving and critical thinking:

- gathering information and utilizing resources
- developing flexibility in form and style
- predicting
- asking high-quality questions
- weighing evidence before drawing conclusions
- using metaphors and models
- analyzing and predicting information
- conceptualizing strategies (e.g., mind mapping, lists of pros and cons, outlines)
- dealing productively with ambiguity, differences, and novelty
- generating possibilities and probabilities (e.g., brainstorming, formulas, surveys, cause and effect)
- developing debate and discussion skills
- identifying mistakes, discrepancies, and illogic
- examining alternative approaches (e.g., shifting frame of reference, thinking out of the box)
- developing hypothesis-testing strategies
- analyzing risks
- developing objectivity
- detecting generalizations and patterns (e.g., identifying and organizing information, translating information, crossover applications)
- sequencing events

It would be extraordinary if we could get all school-age kids to strengthen their own skills from this list. But realistically, it won't happen unless thinking skills are a full-time pursuit. The four skills most critical for achievement (if you had to choose just four) would be (1) memory capacity, (2) attentional capacity, (3) processing speed, and (4) sequencing. The good news is that critical thinking can be taught, and it can be taught within the context of other processes in a classroom, such as the following:

Summary and term papers. The best way to teach critical thinking is to require that students write. Writing forces students to organize their thoughts, contemplate their topic, evaluate their data in a logical fashion, and present their conclusions in a persuasive manner. Good writing is the epitome of good critical thinking.

Direct instruction. Teaching critical thinking during lecture is done by questioning students in ways that require that they not only understand the material but can analyze it and apply it to new situations as well.

Quantitative exercises. Mathematical exercises and quantitative word problems teach problem-solving skills that can be used in everyday life. This obviously enhances critical thinking.

Hands-on learning. Students inevitably practice critical thinking during lab activities in science class because they are learning the scientific method.

Homework. Both traditional reading homework and special written problem sets or questions can be used to enhance critical thinking. Homework presents many opportunities to encourage critical thinking.

Quizzes and tests. Exam questions can be devised to promote critical thinking rather than rote memorization. This is true for both essay and multiple-choice questions.

The intellect asks, "Is it possible?" Only intelligence asks the question, "Is it appropriate?"

If you are already using some of these techniques, then you don't have to change a thing.

 ## What This Means to You

From a brain-based perspective, the most effective way to teach thinking skills is to incorporate real-world problems under authentic (or simulated) conditions. With young children, simple games can produce a suitable environment for teaching thinking. With adolescents, sharing our own thinking processes, working through personal challenges with them, assigning complex group-oriented projects, and analyzing case studies are excellent ways to instill thinking skills. Most important, at any level, model high-level thinking. That is, verbalize your own thinking process as you weigh evidence, consider ramifications, and make decisions.

Brain Activated by Problem Solving

Some research suggests that problem solving is to the brain what aerobic exercise is to the body. It creates a virtual explosion of activity, causing synapses to form, neurotransmitters to activate, and blood flow to increase. A brain that is worked out with mental weights remains younger, smarter, and more creative longer in life. Especially good for the brain are challenging, novel, and complex tasks that require intense thinking and multitasking (i.e., doing more than one type of thinking at a time).

Boredom is a serious problem for the brain because the brain adapts from experience. If the experience is not stimulating, the brain reduces the connections, the strength of the connections, and expectations about learning. Diamond and

Hopson (1998) have shown in studies with rats that boredom does more harm to the brain than enrichment does good. Withdrawal from the world and reduction of stimulation most certainly contribute to senility and depression, while activity and challenge promote health and well-being.

What This Means to You

Our traditional educational system does not teach learners to think. Learners who spend all their free time "doing nothing" can get out of shape—not just physically, but mentally. Television is not exercise; active thinking and problem solving are. We, as instructional leaders, have to set the example and provide the climate that reinforces critical thinking and problem solving. There are many resources currently on the market that provide various types of mental workouts—from brainteasers to crossword puzzles. Make sure that you are not just teaching or training but that you are "growing" better brains. Use visualization, problem solving, debates, projects, and drama. Reduce lecture time, seatwork, and other rote activities. Challenge your students' brains, and be sure to give them the resources to meet the challenge.

Eye Movements and Thinking

As illustrated in Figure 17.3, there are six basic eye movements that relate to thinking. Determine the particular eye (and thinking) pattern for a learner by observing him or her in a real-life, no-stress situation. Controlled laboratory testing has yielded inconsistent results, but the real-world relationship between eye movements and cognitive functioning has been well documented. Cognitive activity occurring in one hemisphere triggers eye movements in the opposite hemisphere.

1. Visual recall. Looking up and to the left allows you to access stored pictures. Questions to ask yourself for verification: What car was parked next to yours in the parking lot? Describe your bedroom. Walk me through the clothes in your closet.

2. Visual conceptualization. Looking up and to the right allows you to create new images. Questions to ask yourself for verification: How would you look with a radically different haircut? What can you do to rearrange your living room? What would a dog look like with a cat's legs?

3. Auditory recall. Looking to the left allows you to access stored sounds (what was said or heard). Questions to ask yourself for verification: What did the other person say as you concluded your last phone conversation? What's the ninth word of the "Happy Birthday" song? When you were a child, how did your mother call your name when she was mad at you?

4. Auditory conceptualization. Looking to the right allows you to create new sounds. Questions to ask yourself for verification: How would a dog sound if it

Figure 17.3   Eyes movements and thinking

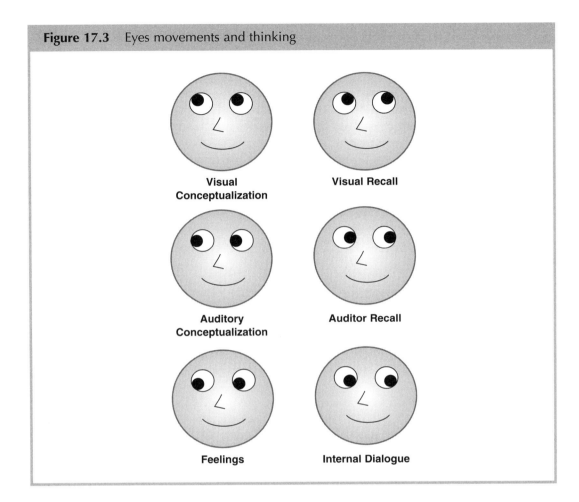

had a voice like a pig? What sound would you get if you heard a siren and a rooster at the same time?

5. Internal dialogue. Your eyes most commonly move down and to the left when you are engaging in internal dialogue. Notice others' eyes as they walk down the street alone.

6. Feelings. Your eyes go down and to the right when accessing feelings. Try it. Ask someone about something you know he or she has strong feelings about.

Eyes look straight ahead when no thinking is necessary, as when verbalizing an automatic response. For example, when someone asks how you are, your polite answer ("Fine, thank you") does not require you to search your brain for the answer.

> Eye movements facilitate the processing and retrieval of information to and from the brain.

With learners who are having trouble, for example, with spelling, the following strategies can better hook the brain:

1. Access feelings with regard to the word. Start with eyes looking down and to the right.

2. Visualize the image of the word. Move eyes up and to the right.

3. Cement a word in auditory memory. Say the letters while looking to the right.

4. Cement a word kinesthetically. Trace its letters with your finger.

5. Recall a stored image of the word. Close your eyes, and look up and to the left.

6. Write out the correct spelling on paper. Review it, and look up and to the left.

7. To cement the success and celebrate the feeling of empowerment, look down and to the right.

 **What This Means to You**

When you post students' work on bulletin boards, put it low if you want to access feelings, high if you want to facilitate discussion, or overhead if you want them to store the visual images in memory. When you present new material, stand to the right of learners (from their point of view). When you review, stand to the left of learners (from their point of view). This simple strategy enables learners to process and access the new information more efficiently. At test time, if you tell students to keep their eyes on their own paper, their ability to access information in their brain may be thwarted. As an alternative, have students spread out. This lowers everyone's stress levels.

The Use of Creative Problem Solving

The following account, from Leff and Nevin (1994), reflects a brain-based learning environment in which encouraging the use of thinking skills is one of the teacher's primary objectives. The teacher asks his high school science class to brainstorm a list of world problems. Working in small study groups, they narrow the list to 10. Then they brainstorm how the science topic of the week (weather) could impact, illuminate, or solve the problems. For example, overpopulation would be impacted by a natural weather disaster, or flooding could slow down tanks in a war. The class discusses these impacts. Then other academic areas are discussed in terms of their relationship to the topic of the week. Does physical education relate to an army at war?

> Forward thinking educators of today realize that any problem or situation can be turned into a creative-growth experience.
>
> —Herbert L. Leff and Ann Levin

How about home economics or math? Finally, students are asked to take these concepts home to discuss with their families and assess the personal impact.

Problem-Solving Strategies

The following specific strategies are flexible enough to be modified for various age groups and learning environments:

- Reframe a problem so that it is not a problem.
- Discover the source of the problem so as to prevent recurrence.
- Adjust your attitude to deal with life's difficulties.
- Consider how process impacts results.
- Analyze and discuss thinking (metacognition).
- Use various styles and models of thinking.
- Exhibit how your thinking skills add value and joy to your life.
- Apply your thinking skills so as to enhance the lives of others.
- Assign or read stories imbued with personal meaning—literally the oldest strategy in the book.
- Assign team projects, and incorporate a metacognition component (e.g., have team members keep a journal of the issues, challenges, and decisions faced and how they're resolved).
- Facilitate a group discussion in which you model (and/or comment on) higher-order thinking skills.
- Think out loud.
- Solve a problem or case study together using brainstorming, discussion, deduction, and decision-making skills.
- Set up debates between students or teams of students, and have them comment on the process.
- Put each learner in the role of teacher. Provide plenty of support and personal choice in the process.
- In groups of three, give learners the opportunity to play the role of listener, talker, and reviewer, respectively, while discussing a problem. The reviewer provides feedback to the talker and listener before exchanging roles.
- Assign projects that require reflection and personal expression.
- Take on class projects that benefit the school or community, and require students to use a wide range of real-life skills.
- Require learners to make mind maps or graphic organizers that reflect models or ways of thinking, patterns, sequences, and levels of detail.
- Honor the individual's feelings. Feelings are neither intangible nor elusive, but rather a very real and legitimate part of the thinking process.

The Role of Intuition in the Thinking Process

When we feel that something's true, that doesn't necessarily make it true. Nevertheless, nonconscious learning picked up along life's winding pathway often triggers what we call *intuition*. So how do we know when we really know something as opposed to when we just think we know something? The fact is, the majority of our knowledge is implicit—that is, there is no symbolic language attached to it. For example, we certainly know how to get up from a chair, but could you accurately write out the steps for doing so?

Two areas of the brain, the basal ganglia and the orbitofrontal cortex (see Figure 17.4), seem to be primarily responsible for intuition. The basal ganglia help us regulate, manage, and translate our emotions into thinking. Situated near the eye sockets and at the bottom (ventral) of the frontal lobes is the orbitofrontal cortex, which helps integrate our emotions and thinking. This is where values are weighed, emotions are mediated, and thinking is modulated. When these areas are healthy, then violent, immature, or inappropriate behaviors are inhibited, and we exhibit normal inhibition. If either of these two brain areas is malfunctioning, however, our intuition will be affected.

A third structure—the amygdala—also contributes to intuition. It processes and stores intense emotions, such as trauma, celebration, violence, and phobia. Since there is no connection directly from the amygdala to the language areas of the brain, we store these experiences but usually have inadequate language to verbalize them. For example, a child abandoned by a parent may exhibit a pattern later in life whereby he or she leaves relationships before the partner can leave first. In spite of the repeated pattern, the adult whom the abandoned child develops into does not make the connection: he or she has no language for it. Normally we have no memory of early traumas (the amygdala is mature at birth, but the frontal lobes are not developed enough to make logical sense of a traumatic incident). Later on, our well-meaning intuition guides us in ways that may no longer be relevant because the emotion is deeply embedded in the amygdala.

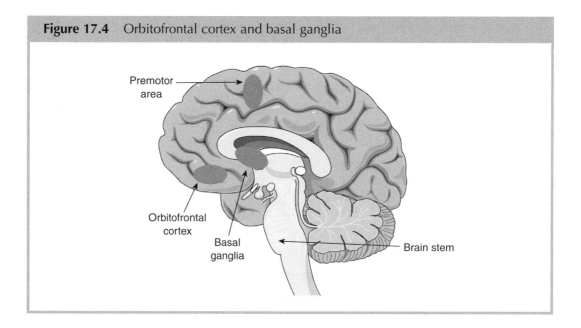

Figure 17.4   Orbitofrontal cortex and basal ganglia

 ## What This Means to You

We can help learners understand the role of intuition and emotions in learning and thinking by validating them. Ask students how an aspect of a lesson makes them feel. Encourage them to venture a guess when they are unsure of an answer. Realize that when learners act out illogically, a biological response may have been triggered that they don't have the awareness to stop. Learners who have sustained damage to key areas of the brain may exhibit inappropriate behaviors, which they cannot be expected to control. The most effective response is to effect a change in the students' state. Redirect them. Play some relaxing music, or take a break for stretching and deep breathing. Model solid problem-solving skills, and your learners will follow.

18

Memory and Creating Patterns of Meaning

Stages of Optimal Learning
Acquisition
Elaboration
Memory Formation
New Learning Maps

Most of us like to complain about our memory or that of our students. But nature has given us a very good memory for certain things. If you get food poisoning from a restaurant, do you remember to avoid that restaurant? Do you remember the names of your children, your parents, or your spouse? When was the last time you forgot your way home? Have you ever forgotten how to eat? When someone is rude to you, do you remember it? If someone did you a favor, do you remember him or her? Do you remember a divorce, an accident, a celebration, a honeymoon, or the birth of a child? These questions may seem laughable, but a second look at the kinds of things you consistently recall is quite revealing. If something is highly relevant, intense, or used often, it gets remembered. Our memories are not as bad as we might think. In fact, we are very good at certain, very specific types of memory. The good news is that the brain has the capacity to do that. This chapter, which focuses on both science and strategies, is about the brain's memory systems that help students remember things better in the classroom.

HOW MEMORY WORKS

How do students store and recall what they've learned? Current neuroscience describes memories as dynamic and not fixed. We can define our memories as the process of creating a persistent change in the brain by a transient stimulus. Surprisingly, there's no single master filing cabinet residing in our brains, nor do our brains archive our memories by number or some other linear system. It seems that the process is much more complex and holistic. It is important to think process, rather than location, when discussing the memory system. The current understanding is that multiple memory locations and systems are responsible for our learning and recall (see Figure 18.1).

Researchers emphasize that the retrieval process activates dormant neurons to trigger memories. The idea is that you cannot separate memory and retrieval—memory is determined by what kind of retrieval process is activated. Each type of learning requires its own type of triggering. When enough of the right type of

Figure 18.1 How memories are formed

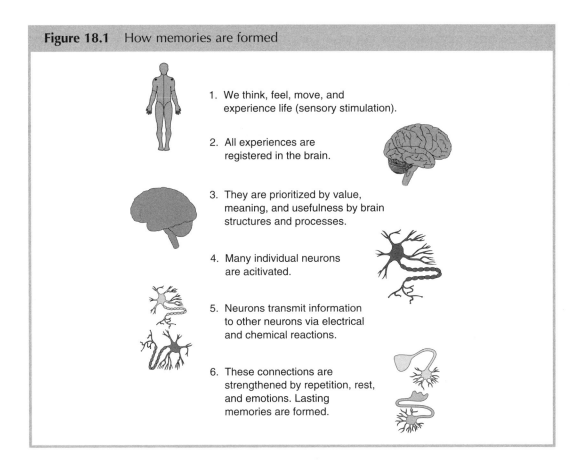

1. We think, feel, move, and experience life (sensory stimulation).

2. All experiences are registered in the brain.

3. They are prioritized by value, meaning, and usefulness by brain structures and processes.

4. Many individual neurons are acitivated.

5. Neurons transmit information to other neurons via electrical and chemical reactions.

6. These connections are strengthened by repetition, rest, and emotions. Lasting memories are formed.

neurons, firing in the right way, are stimulated, you get successful retrieval. In larger patterns, whole neuronal fields can be activated. For example, at hearing the word *school*, hundreds of neuronal circuits may be activated, triggering a cerebral "thunderstorm." This is due to the many associations and experiences most of us have with the subject. The how and where of memories are linked, so let's explore both of those issues.

Where Memories Live

There is no one area of the brain that is solely responsible for memory. Most of our memories are well distributed throughout the cortex. This spread-the-risk strategy explains why a person can lose 20 percent of the cortex and still have a "good memory." It also helps explain why a student can have great recall for one subject, like sports statistics, and poor recall for another, like names and faces.

Memories are generated from all over the brain (see Figure 18.2). Memories of sound are stored in the auditory cortex; memories of names, nouns, and pronouns are traced to the temporal lobe. The amygdala is quite active for implicit, usually negative, emotional events. Learned skills involve the basal ganglia structures. The cerebellum is critical for associative memory formation, particularly when precise timing is involved, as in the learning of motor skills. Researchers have found that the hippocampus becomes quite active for the formation of spatial and other explicit memories, such as memory for speaking, reading, and even recall about an emotional event.

When you think of an idea, hear your internal voice, get an image, recall music, or see a color in your mind's eye, you are reconstructing the original memory. Your brain creates a composite of the various elements of the experience on the spot. This means that you remember something only once; after that, you're remembering the memory. And as time goes by, your versions change. And your memories get more and more re-created, and less and less true to the event. Your instant re-creation of the original takes a split second (usually) and operates a bit like a volunteer fire department: there's no building, office, or central system, but when a fire breaks out, the volunteers quickly unite from various locals to (everyone hopes) extinguish the blaze. Your memory is on call at all times of the day and night.

The prevailing theory on how this miraculous process happens is that we have indexes that contain instructions (not content) for the brain on how to rekindle the

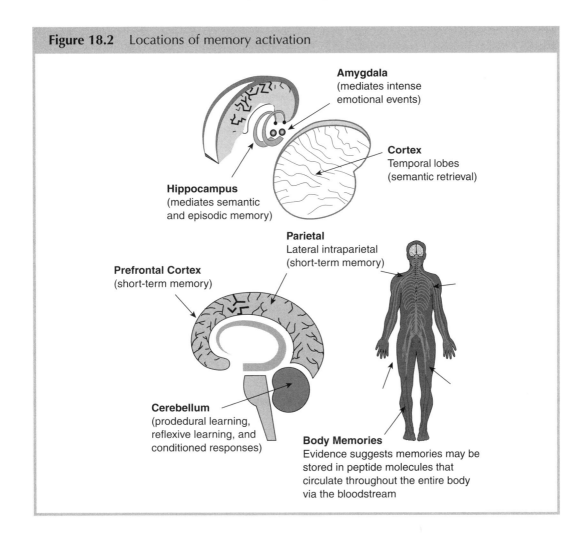

Figure 18.2 Locations of memory activation

Amygdala
(mediates intense emotional events)

Cortex
Temporal lobes
(semantic retrieval)

Hippocampus
(mediates semantic and episodic memory)

Parietal
Lateral intraparietal
(short-term memory)

Prefrontal Cortex
(short-term memory)

Cerebellum
(prodedural learning, reflexive learning, and conditioned responses)

Body Memories
Evidence suggests memories may be stored in peptide molecules that circulate throughout the entire body via the bloodstream

content. These convergence zones unite the pieces of a memory during the retrieval process. For the sake of analogy, consider that your semantic (words and pictures) memory works like just-in-time manufacturing: it creates a product on the spot, on demand, in its own store—an ingenious process considering that the parts are reusable on the next product or any other item you want to remember. For most word-based recall, we use mental indexes to help us find the word we want. A word like *classroom* is very likely linked to several related subjects like school, learning, kids, teacher, and principal. Our language is a classic example of having to pull hundreds of words off the shelf within seconds to assemble even the most common sentence. This theory explains why, when we are trying to say something, we often say a similar word (that is close, but still wrong).

Long-Term Potentiation: What Is It?

The term scientists have used to identify the actual molecular process involved in the formation of explicit memories is *long-term potentiation* (LTP). This process is a rapid alteration in the strength of synaptic connections as a result of stimulation. The classic study on LTP (Bliss & Lomo, 1973), which earned the researchers a Nobel Prize, was done in the early 1970s, and recent research has supported the initial study. Tonegawa (1995) discovered that LTP is actually mediated by genes, which trigger a series of complex cascading steps. Around the same time, Kandel and Hawkins (1992) and Kandel and Kandel (1994) identified a critical protein molecule known as CREB, which serves as a logic switch, signaling to nerve cells whether to store the information in short- or long-term memory. Yin and colleagues (1995) demonstrated that CREB activation gives fruit flies a photographic memory—the ability to remember after just one trial what ordinarily requires many trials. Researchers believe that the physical substrate of memory is stored as changes in neurons along specific pathways. Finally, after decades of speculation, the process of LTP was confirmed by Fedulov and colleagues (2007). This means that, in a sense, memory has been confirmed as a probability that neurons will fire in a particular way.

Chemicals Impact Memory

Many modulatory compounds can enhance or depress recall if given at the time of learning (see Figure 18.3). Researchers suspect that calcium deficiency may be one explanation for the memory loss often experienced by the elderly. Norepinephrine is a neurotransmitter that is linked to memories associated with stress. Recently, vitamin A has been found to assist in memory formation. Phenylalanine, found in dairy products, helps manufacture norepinephrine, which is also involved in alertness and attention. Adrenaline acts as a memory fixative, locking up memories of exciting or traumatic events. Acetylcholine is used in long-term memory formation, and increased levels of this neurotransmitter are linked to subjects with better recall. Lecithin, found in eggs, salmon, and lean beef, may raise levels of choline (which is converted to acetylcholine in the brain) and

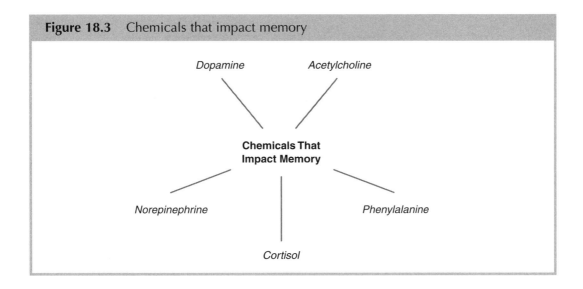

Figure 18.3 Chemicals that impact memory

has been shown to boost recall in repeated trials. Some studies even show that the presence of moderate levels of household sugar in the bloodstream can enhance memory, but too much impairs it.

Memory Is State Dependent

Amazingly, mental, physical, and emotional states "bind up" information within that particular state. In other words, anxiety, curiosity, depression, joy, and confidence also trigger information learned while in that state. It's as if the states constitute different libraries: a given memory record can be retrieved only by returning to that library, or physiological state, in which the event was first stored. The following are some practical applications of state-dependent learning:

- Facilitate reviews that engage all five senses.
- Encourage discussions about learners' feelings and emotions regarding new learning.
- Get learners to somehow incorporate the new learning in their personal lives.
- Use storyboards (e.g., oversized comic-strip panels) to present key ideas.
- Make a video or audiotape—the more complex, the better.
- Use peg words to link numbers or pictures to an idea for ease in recall.
- Create or redo a song with lyrics that represent the new learning.

How and where we learn may be as important to the brain as what we learn. Why? Because the success of memory retrieval is highly dependent on state, time, and context. In experiments with color, location, and movement, findings suggest that recency effects are enhanced by identifying the stimulus at the time of the state change. In other words, if you pause and take notice of the circumstances of your learning, it will subsequently be easier for you to trigger its recall.

Context is critical to the memory. Each physiological state is a moment in time that locks together two elements—the mind-body circumstances (e.g., feelings, emotions, arousal) and the contextual circumstances (e.g., sights, sounds, location). Thus, studying and cramming for a final exam may present a problem: if students study in a hyped-up state with coffee or other stimulants to keep them awake, unless they can match this state during test time, they may perform below their abilities.

Have you ever had the experience of hearing a favorite song or melody and suddenly were transported back to a different time and place? Have you ever decided you want something from another room, but once you were there, couldn't remember what it was you came for? So then you go back to the original place in order to remember your intention. These are examples of context-bound memory cues.

What This Means to You

Many learners may actually know the material they are being tested on but may not demonstrate it well during exam time. If they study under low stress but take the exam under high stress, for example, their brains may recall less efficiently than if the physiological states were matched. With so much subjectivity involved in the evaluation of learning, brain-based learning advocates that learners be evaluated with a wide range of methods and instruments, including portfolios, quizzes, projects, presentations, and tests that consider multiple learning objectives while emphasizing multiple intelligences.

Students who might be thought of as "lazy" learners may, in fact, be simply recalling only what they can. Just because particular students may be good at recalling names and dates doesn't necessarily mean they'll be good at recalling a poem, for instance. Learning is stored in distinctive pathways; if you can't retrieve it through one pathway, it may be accessible via another.

The fact that information is state-bound also lends credibility to the role of simulations, case studies, role-plays, and drama performances in the learning process. This may explain why the physical, concrete learning that happens when students act out new material better prepares them for real life. Pilots use simulators for training, the military creates mock war situations, and theater groups do rehearsals. In formalized learning situations, increased real-life simulation can also increase the applications of the learning. And, of course, this strategy is most productive when physiological, emotional, and mental states are matched as closely as possible between practice and reality. This is why popular self-defense courses that rely on mock attackers are so effective. And for this same reason, fire, safety, and health emergency drills are important and should be rehearsed periodically with some sense of urgency and an appropriate level of intensity.

Figure 18.4 What is memory?

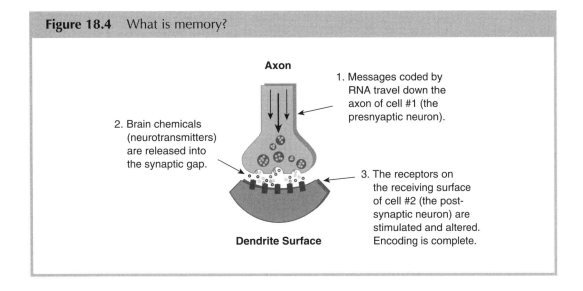

Axon

1. Messages coded by RNA travel down the axon of cell #1 (the presnyaptic neuron).

2. Brain chemicals (neurotransmitters) are released into the synaptic gap.

3. The receptors on the receiving surface of cell #2 (the post-synaptic neuron) are stimulated and altered. Encoding is complete.

Dendrite Surface

The Role of Glucose in Memory Formation

Some schools have overreacted and decided to ban all sugar products from the school. This may be a poor idea. Extensive evidence indicates that glucose plays an important role in learning and memory. In humans, doses of glucose that elevate blood glucose to moderate levels enhance memory in healthy adults, the elderly, and those suffering from a variety of neurological disorders (Benton, 2001). Although modest increases in glucose typically enhance memory, high concentrations of it have deleterious effects on memory.

A majority of findings suggest that high levels of glucose produce learning and memory deficits (e.g., Korol & Gold, 1998; McNay, McCarty, & Gold, 2001). The ideal is moderate, not low or high, glucose for memory formation. If students cannot have munchies or other snack foods to maintain those levels, there is an alternative. Physical activity stimulates the liver to produce glucose, which may support memory function. This gives you another reason to encourage sufficient movement in the classroom.

Sleep Time's Effect on Memory

Stickgold and Walker (2007) suggest that sleep time may affect the previous day's learning. Cutting nighttime sleep by as little as two hours may impair your ability to recall the next day. The more complicated and complex the material is, the more important sleep is to the learning of it. It is believed that sleep gives your brain time to do its "housekeeping"—to rearrange circuits, clean out extraneous mental debris, and process emotional events. Neural networks can become much more efficient when certain memories are "unlearned," much the way your computer cleans up the desktop. By eliminating unnecessary information (usually during sleep time), the brain becomes more efficient. The fact that you have trouble remembering dreams may indicate how effective your brain is at cleaning up your cerebral house.

What This Means to You

Many learners may need either more sleep or better-quality sleep. Discuss with learners the importance of physical rest and dreaming, and encourage them to get adequate rest at night. Also provide learners with some downtime during the day for optimal brain performance. Give them the opportunity to move around, stretch, drink some water, or change their focus periodically.

Based on what we currently know about the brain and learning, it is appropriate to ask a different set of questions. We used to ask, how can we make sure students learn what is expected of their grade level? Now we ask the following:

- What is the optimal environment for learning?
- What learning strategies have the highest impact at the lowest cost?
- How can we interest staff in making changes?
- How can we find the necessary resources to support these changes?
- What one simple step can I take immediately to improve learning?

In short, the answer to all of these questions is to get proactive and use more brain-based learning strategies. Although you don't have control of everything, it is important to remember that you do have control of a lot.

What This Means to You

Since it seems that literal memory declines throughout the day, rather than forcing learners to pay closer attention in the afternoon, relate learning at this time to their personal experience. Present new information in the morning, and integrate previously learned information in the afternoon. For example, schedule reading, listening, and watching activities in the morning, and role-playing, projects, and simulations in the afternoon.

May, Hasher, and Stoltzfus (1993) set out to determine how recall relates to age and time of day. Their findings suggest that young adults do best on memory recall in the afternoon or evenings, while older individuals perform significantly better in the morning. Given all of the variations in personality types, no matter when you present a particular topic, it is likely to be out of sync, or presented at the wrong time, for about one-third of your learners. However, as May and colleagues found, when adolescents were allowed to learn subjects at their preferred time of day, their motivation, behavior, and scores in mathematics improved.

Of course it is impossible to accommodate every learner's individual time clock; however, numerous practices help make the classroom more accommodating to learners' variations. For example, if a standardized test is always given after lunch, some students will consis-

The question then arises: If we know what time of day learning is optimized, what can we do about it?

tently underperform. And if test reviews are regularly scheduled early in the day, learners may better remember semantic material, such as names, places, dates, and facts, but more meaningful connections would be better grasped in the afternoon.

Memory Pathways

Why is it that learners tend to remember much more when learning is associated with a field trip, performance, disaster, guest speaker, complex project, or novel study location? Quite simply, when all of our senses are stimulated and our emotions aroused, multiple memory pathways are engaged. The two major mem-

ory pathways we'll focus on for our purposes here are *implicit* and *explicit*, meaning basically that information is automatically learned or learned by effort. These two memory types can be further divided into subgroups, as Figure 18.5 illustrates.

The brain sorts and stores information based on whether it is heavily embedded in context or in content.

The difference between the two primary ways the brain deals with explicit information is simple. Information embedded in context is *episodic* memory, which

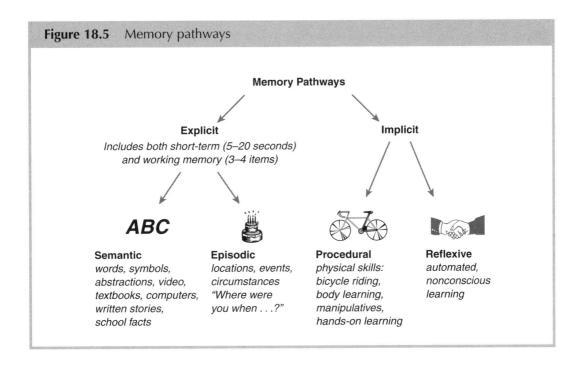

Figure 18.5 Memory pathways

means it is stored in relationship to a particular location, circumstance, or episode, and information embedded in content is *semantic* memory (facts), which is usually derived from reading and studying.

Episodic memory forms quickly, is easily updated, requires no practice, is effortless, and is used naturally by everyone. What did you have for dinner last night? This question triggers your episodic memory. Not only will context cues help you remember the answer, a body movement or posture, particular music, smell, sound, sight, taste, and so on can trigger your memory. The formation of this contextual memory pathway is motivated by curiosity, novelty, life experience, and expectations, and it is enhanced by intensified sensory input (sights, sounds, smells, taste, touch). The information can also be stored in a fabric or weave of *mental space,* which is a thematic map of the intellectual landscape, where learning occurs as a result of changes in location or circumstances.

Semantic memory, on the other hand, is usually formed (or attempted to be formed) through rote practice or memorization. It requires rehearsal, is resistant to change, is isolated from context, has strict limits, inherently lacks meaning, and is linked to extrinsic motivation. If I ask you, "Who was the author of that book we read last week in class?" your semantic memory is being tapped. This memory pathway is more difficult to establish; it is unnatural and requires practice and consistent rehearsal to encode. This is why we forget so much of the curriculum we are taught in school. Our episodic memory is absorbing knowledge all the time, which is what the brain attends to first.

> Semantic memory (facts and figures) may be a relatively new requirement in the history of humankind.

Engaging Multiple Memory Pathways

It is difficult for the brain to remember content when it is removed from context; yet this is the type of learning typified by traditional schoolwork and homework. How often have you heard or said, "Study for Friday's test by reviewing Chapter 6"? Although this is the least efficient way to learn, it is the way most teachers teach. With some imagination, however, we can create a more context-driven environment that makes learning more memorable—through real-life simulations, storytelling, ethnic celebrations, virtual learning, field trips, and so on. Also, when various cultural viewpoints are presented, the learning becomes more relevant to a greater number of students.

For most teachers, planning time is short, so simple alternatives have to suffice. Although it would be ideal to enmesh students in the places they're learning about, this is unrealistic in many cases. So although a trip to China to learn about the country's political system is out of the question, asking students to plan such a trip is not. Of course, to accomplish the task, they will have to learn something about the political climate, geography, money, language, passports, weather, foods, people, and customs. Students would have to problem-solve, organize, do research, discuss viewpoints, and discover what resources might help them in attending to the task.

Should we throw out book learning? No. Just because the brain is generally very poor at learning this way, the solution is not to discard the source. Semantic learning does have its place. When you ask for directions, for example, you want the shortest route from A to B. You don't want to drive all over the city to figure it out (although that would create a stronger contextual map). On the other hand, if you ask people what of significance have they learned in the past year, 90 percent of what they tell you will probably be contextually embedded information as opposed to rote or semantic learning.

 **What This Means to You**

Learners may seem to forget a great deal of what is taught, but the problem may stem from an over-reliance on a singular memory system. We may have accidentally created generations of "slow" learners who easily forget, and through no fault of their own. There are better ways to reach learners so that recall improves and self-confidence soars. First, do what you can to avoid excessive use of semantic memory strategies.

Through the use of real-life simulations, thematic instruction, interactive contextual learning, and a focus on multiple intelligences, we can activate multiple memory systems so that learning sticks. When you present a new topic, have learners read about it, listen to a relevant lecture about it, discuss it, and watch a related video. Then follow up with complex projects, role-playing, at-home assignments, and related music, discussion, field trips, games, and simulations.

Instead of putting most of the emphasis on memorization and recall, it may be smarter and more efficient to place more emphasis on the context in which something is learned. Contextual learning provides more spatial and locational "hooks" and allows learners more time to make personal connections. Reading, hearing, or experiencing the background on a topic aids understanding and recall. Placing the information being learned into a conceptual context (e.g., historical, comparative) boosts recall.

Other Influences on Recall

Research has verified that an easy way to remember something is to make it new, different, novel. This is because the brain has a high attentional bias toward something that does not fit a normal or expected pattern. When the brain perceives something as different, stress hormones are released, and the result is better attention. If it's perceived as a negative threat, the body may release cortisol, but if it's perceived as a positive stress (challenge), the body releases adrenaline.

The BEM Principle

BEM stands for *beginning, end, and middle*. When information is presented, it is most likely remembered in this sequence. What is presented at the beginning is the most memorable, followed by that which is presented at the end, and finally by that which is presented in the middle. Why does this happen? Researchers speculate that an attentional bias exists at the beginning and end. The novelty factor inherent in beginnings and the emotional release of endings foster chemical changes in the brain. These changes in our chemistry tag the learning and make it more memorable. Figure 18.6 illustrates this memory phenomenon.

There is a distinctly different mental set at the beginning and end of an experience (anticipation, suspense, novelty, and challenge) than there is at the middle, when the status quo (nothing new, boredom) mental state sets in. Thus, when reviewing a list of items, notes, or facts, or when presenting a lengthy lesson, remember to break up the middle part of the session with some surprise elements, a brain break, and/or some conscious strategies for remembering the material presented.

What This Means to You

Your students may be able to remember much more if you provide more novelty in the lesson plans and more beginnings and ends (with shortened middles). Introduce short modules of learning instead of long ones. Break up long sessions into several shorter ones.

All learning requires consistent review and updating. Even medical doctors are required by law to continue their education. Make time for reviews in class, and consistently draw from prior learning to reinforce connections. There are many ways to keep the memory of learned information alive in your learners. Have students participate in weekly peer-review sessions, or have them create a mind map representing their current understanding of a topic. Assign class murals, mindscapes, and student projects (see Figure 18.7 for more ideas). Continual revision, week after week, encodes the learning in more complex neural networks.

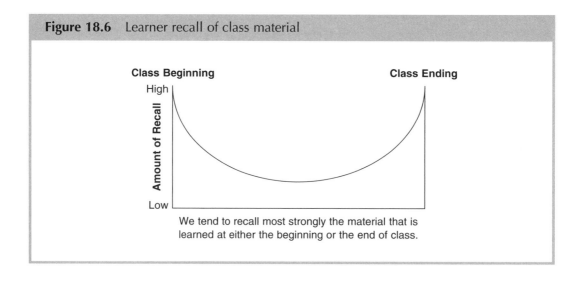

Figure 18.6 Learner recall of class material

We tend to recall most strongly the material that is learned at either the beginning or the end of class.

Figure 18.7   More memory, storage, and retrieval ideas

- Increase the use of storytelling, visualization, and metaphors in your presentations.
- Attach a strong emotion to new learning with a purposely designed intense activity.
- Review or repeat new learning within 10 minutes, then after 48 hours, and again after a week.
- Attach concrete reminders to new learning, like a token or an artifact.
- Act out new learning in a skit or role-play.
- Attach an acrostic to new learning (the first letter of each key word forms a new word) and other mnemonic techniques.
- Depict new learning on a large, colorful poster, and put it up in the classroom.
- Ask students to identify patterns and to look for connections with prior learning.
- Personalize the lesson by incorporating students' names, ethnic customs, and real-life issues.
- Ask learners to summarize new learning with a mind map.
- Give new learning strong context with field trips, guest speakers, and concrete objects to touch and feel.
- Have students identify "What's in it for me?" to increase meaningfulness and motivation.
- Start a new learning session with something exotic, then familiar, then unusual again.
- Increase accountability with frequent reviews and checkups.
- Incorporate real-life problems and situations to teach about content as well as process.
- Facilitate frequent group discussions on new material.
- Incorporate journal writing and other forms of personal reflection.
- Provide downtime and frequent short breaks to consolidate learning.

STUDY SKILLS MASTERY

Students who struggle are not lacking memory capacity but are more likely using a system of thinking and processing that cannot keep up. When learners are instructed in learning-to-learn skills, their ability to process new information can rise substantially. Better study skills upgrade the operating system in the brain instead of just flooding it with more content. New pathways, more efficient pathways, and better connections can boost student learning. If we fail to teach these skills to our students, who will prepare them for a fast-changing global society? What are the key ingredients for study skills mastery? Most sources suggest that learners do the following:

- get proper nutrition and enough sleep
- set goals and develop a purpose
- browse the material, learn how to identify key concepts, and build perceptual maps
- develop mind maps that reflect their thoughts, questions, concerns, and connections to prior learning
- read with a highlighter in hand and make notes in the margins
- summarize what has been learned, reflect on it, and ask questions
- act on the learning, build models, do projects, give PowerPoint presentations, and so on

What This Means to You

Among the many benefits of study-skills programs are that they (1) help students incorporate their preferred learning style; (2) improve students' confidence in learning, thus improving self esteem; and (3) encourage students to become more proactive—to take control of their learning. Ensuring that learners have the study skills necessary to succeed is a worthwhile investment of teaching time.

Importance of Pre-exposure

Pre-exposure to information (or exposure to information on a nonconscious level), sometimes called *preliming*, makes subsequent learning proceed more quickly. The greater the amount of priming stimulus, the more the brain extracts and compartmentalizes (lateralizes) the information (Gratton, Coles, & Donchin, 1992). The brain seems to have a way of putting information and ideas into a buffer zone, or cognitive waiting room, for rapid access. If the information is not utilized over time, it simply lays unconnected and random. But if the other parts of the puzzle are offered, the understanding and extraction of meaning are rapid.

There is a long history of studies suggesting that prior exposure to content (the *priming* effect) or even a simple presentation of questions leads to quicker responses. Learning and recall also increase when a pattern is provided prior to exposing learners to new material. Providing postorganizing clues is also useful as a framework for recall.

Mind Mapping

One of the key characteristics of the cortex is the ability to detect and create patterns of meaning. This process involves deciphering cues, recognizing relationships, and indexing information. The clues best assembled by the brain are those presented in a Gestalt format, rather than a sequential, linear format. Of course, the majority of teachers mistakenly learned that teaching must be sequential and linear to be effective. The result of this traditional approach is bored and frustrated learners.

> The brain's capacity to elicit patterns of meaning is one of the key principles of brain-based learning.

Pattern recognition depends heavily on what experience one brings to a situation. Our neural patterns are continually revised as new experiences provide us with additional information, insights, and corrections. In fact, learning is the extraction of meaningful patterns from confusion—in other words, figuring things out in your own way. For young children, cognitive understanding is limited by their ability (or lack thereof) to create personal metaphors or models for the information. This point is quite important with regard to the brain, so here it is again:

We never really cognitively understand something until we can create a model or metaphor that is derived from our unique personal world.

Many teachers know that comprehension increases when readers create a mental model for the material while reading it. Making connections between the characters' actions and a learner's own goals or values, for example, creates a mental marker in the learner's neural map. Activating these kinds of personal connections results in increased reader recall and comprehension.

Generally speaking, learning results from the operation of neural linkages between global mappings and value centers. Learning is achieved when behavior leads to synaptic changes in global mappings that satisfy set points. In other words, we are learning when we can relate the knowledge from one area to another, and then personalize it. Three essentials of higher brain functions are categorization, memory, and learning. The second depends on the first, and the last depends on the first two. Perceptual categorization is essential for memory, and the value centers for this function are located in the hypothalamus and the midbrain.

Consider this example: When you arrive in a new city, you need to know not only how to get where you want to go but also where you are in relation to your destination. The spatial, contextual relationships are the patterns that help you understand and get around in the world. You might link up information such as where the hotels, entertainment, and McDonald's are with personal meanings, such as why am I here or where should I eat dinner?

What This Means to You

Knowing facts may provide answers at test time, but it is pattern detection that helps learners become thinking adults. Before beginning a new topic, ask your students to discuss it orally or to represent it graphically in a mind map; then post it. This gives the brain an "address" or a visual storage space for the new information. Reduce the amount of piecemeal learning. During a course, continually have students make maps, storyboards, graphic organizers, paintings, models, or other artistic renderings of the material. At the end of the course, ask them to make a video, a play, or a larger, mural-sized map of their learning. The key is getting students to relate the learning to their own lives and increasing the contexts surrounding it.

How Mind Mapping Aids Learning

Did you know that hanging a poster-sized graphic organizer or a mind map on the wall in your classroom can improve learning? It's true! The process of creating a mind-map graphic visual display of a subject depicting key relationships with symbols, colors, and buzzwords creates meaning for the learner. Mapping ideas gives learners a way to conceptualize ideas, shape their thinking, and better understand what they do and don't know. But most important, when learners produce mind maps, it helps them feel as if the learning is really theirs.

Mind mapping is an excellent method for pre-exposing learners to a topic. Through the

Consistent pre-exposure encourages quicker and deeper learning.

use of color, movement, drawing, contrast, and organization decisions, information becomes encoded in learners' minds. Once the maps are created, learners can subsequently share them with others, thus further reinforcing the learning.

What This Means to You

Many students who seem like slow learners may simply need pre-exposure to lay the foundation for better comprehension and recall. Pre-expose learners to your topic before officially starting it. First expose them to the topic by mentioning the subject prior to exposure, then post mind maps two weeks before beginning the topic, then preview the texts to be used, and then provide handouts. You can also get learners ready with oral previews, music, personal examples, storytelling, and metaphors. Kinesthetically, you can facilitate role-plays, create simulation situations, or play games that expose learners to the new learning in a subconscious manner.

When prior learning is activated, the brain is much more likely to makes connections to the new material, therefore increasing comprehension and meaning. Let's say you're a student attending a new class and the instructor immediately starts in on the new material. You're lost and overwhelmed in the first 10 minutes. By the end of the first class, you're already worried about how you'll do. Wouldn't it have helped to first find out what you already know and then tie that into the course material?

What This Means to You

Many learners who should do well in a subject actually underperform because the new material seems irrelevant. If you don't make connections to students' prior learning, comprehension and meaning may be dramatically lessened. Before starting a new topic, ask students to discuss what they already know about the subject, do role-plays or skits, make mind maps, and brainstorm the topic's potential value.

Stages of Optimal Learning

Classroom learning for explicit material (content with text and/or pictures) occurs in a predictable sequence of five stages (see Figure 18.8). First, *preparation* provides a framework for the new learning and primes the learners' brain with possible connections. The more background learners have in the subject, the faster they will absorb and process the new information. Second, *acquisition* is achieved through either direct means (e.g., providing handouts) or indirect means (e.g., putting up related visuals). Both approaches can work, and they actually complement each other. Third, *elaboration* explores the interconnectedness of topics and encourages depth of understanding. Fourth, *memory formation* cements the learning

Figure 18.8   Five stages of optimal learning

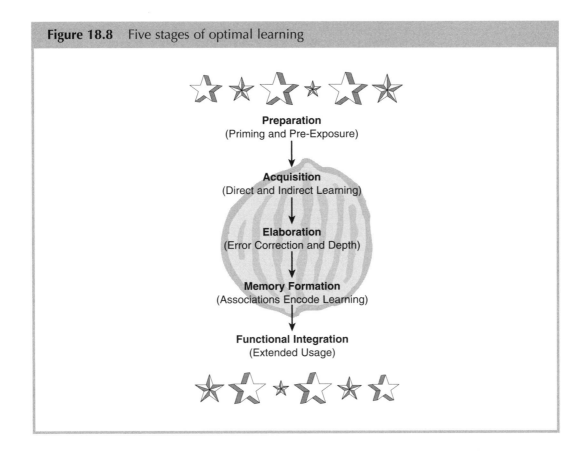

Preparation
(Priming and Pre-Exposure)

Acquisition
(Direct and Indirect Learning)

Elaboration
(Error Correction and Depth)

Memory Formation
(Associations Encode Learning)

Functional Integration
(Extended Usage)

so that what was learned on Monday is retrievable on Tuesday. Finally, *functional integration* reminds us to use the new learning so that it is further reinforced and expanded upon.

Ultimately, learning is the development of goal-oriented neural networks: Remember, single neurons aren't smart, but integrated groups of neurons that fire together, on cue, are very smart. This orchestrated neural symphony is what learning is all about. Elaborate neural networks are developed over time through the process of making connections, developing the right connections, and strengthening the connections. In a nutshell, the three most critical aspects of learning are acquisition, elaboration, and memory formation, which are described in detail below.

Acquisition

The neurological definition of *acquisition* is the formation of new synaptic connections. As described in earlier chapters, the cell body of a neuron has spindly branches (dendrites) and a single longer projection (axon). The cell's axon reaches out to connect with the dendrites on other cells. These connections are formed when the experiences are both novel and coherent. Quite simply, if the input is uninteresting and/or incoherent, only weak connections (if any) will be made. However, if the input is novel and/or coherent, existing connections get strengthened, and learning results.

The first stage of learning is receiving sensory input. A moment of insight does not necessarily translate to learning, but it is a vital step in the learning process. Making connections between cells is one thing; retaining them is quite another. And maintaining accurate connections is yet another. The point here is a critical one: never confuse a moment of insight with learning. *Ha ha* and *Ah ha* have the same impact on the brain, so to remember something, elaboration is necessary. As the Chinese saying reminds us, learning is not a singular event—it is the process of using it over time.

AH HA! HA HA! Both are the same type of neurological event from the point of view of how we learn and remember. Both are moments of insight, which trigger chemical releases, but unless processed for depth, meaning, and storage, these moments weaken.

Remember, making connections is not enough. We need to elaborate on them to make the right ones, strengthen them, and integrate them into other learning. Thus, the acquisition stage involves making connections, that is, getting neurons to "talk" to one another. The sources for acquisition are endless. They may include discussion, lecture, visual tools, environmental stimuli, hands-on experiences, role modeling, reading, manipulatives, videos, reflection, group projects, and pair-share activities. But remember that this first step of making a connection is highly dependent on prior knowledge.

 **What This Means to You**

Pre-exposure provides learners with a foundation on which to build connections. The more background you provide, the better and faster learning will occur. Let learners be surprised by the process rather than the content. Post a summary of what will be learned a month in advance, and suggest to learners that they start exploring the subject with video previews, museum visits, library exploration, TV viewing, and so on. The more they know before they get to you, the better off they'll be and the more fun you'll have together. Pre-exposure is a strategy that has been used at the college level for some time. University students often review the texts their professors will be using before the first day of class.

Elaboration

An enormous gap exists between what a teacher explains and what learners understand. To reduce this gap, teachers need to engage students for deeper understanding and feedback with implicit and explicit learning strategies (see Figure 18.9). If you don't know what students don't understand, how can you elaborate effectively? Making corrections as we go along is a critical approach for teaching with the brain in mind. Once a learner is lost, the brain somehow switches off. Experienced brain-based instructors adjust their course before this happens.

Figure 18.9   Explicit and implicit learning

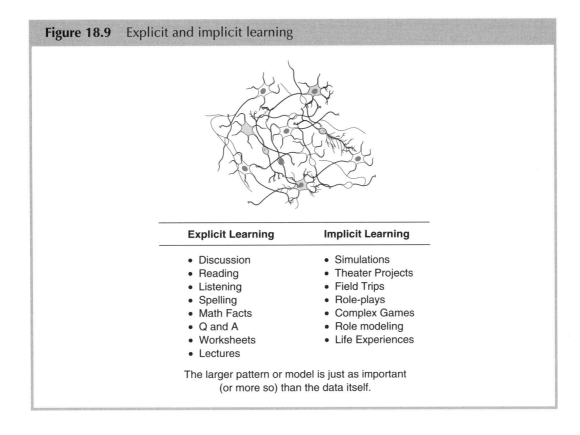

Explicit Learning	Implicit Learning
• Discussion	• Simulations
• Reading	• Theater Projects
• Listening	• Field Trips
• Spelling	• Role-plays
• Math Facts	• Complex Games
• Q and A	• Role modeling
• Worksheets	• Life Experiences
• Lectures	

The larger pattern or model is just as important
(or more so) than the data itself.

What This Means to You

Implicit and explicit approaches are useful in the elaboration stage. Explicit strategies, such as answer keys, peer editing, debriefing, or videotaping provide valuable student feedback, but this feedback can also be provided in a more subtle or nonconscious fashion with implicit strategies, such as simulations, role playing, role modeling, field trips, complex games, and real-life experiences. Elaboration gives the brain a chance to sort, sift, analyze, test, and deepen the learning. When multiple sources of feedback are engaged, not only do students learn more, and more accurately, but their intrinsic motivation is deepened as well.

In the elaboration process, students learn to review and evaluate their own and others' work and receive constructive feedback in a productive way. This is the step that ensures learners aren't merely regurgitating rote facts but are developing complex neural pathways that connect subjects in meaningful ways. This stage is a precursor of remembering.

Memory Formation

After incorporating the elaboration strategies described above, you'd think that learners' brains would have permanently encoded the day's learning.

Unfortunately, it's not quite this simple. Sometimes even after learners are provided with plenty of opportunity for experimentation and interaction, the memory trace is still not strong enough to be activated at test time. Additional factors that contribute to the issue of retrievability include adequate rest, emotional intensity, context, nutrition, quality and quantity of associations, stage of development, learner states, and prior learning. All of these encoding factors play a vital role in the depth of processing and learning that occurs. As you make your way through the following chapters, these factors will be addressed in more detail.

New Learning Maps

It wasn't long ago that we thought more learning simply "filled up" the brain with ideas and facts. But no responsible scientist 50 years ago would have thought that learning physically changes the quantity and size of cells and the connections as well the area they take up in the brain. Yet we now know that learning physically changes the brain. In fact, if a musician plays an instrument over time, the corresponding area of the brain (the motor cortex) actually gets larger as more and more cells become involved in the process (Pantev et al., 1998). Every new experience we encounter actually alters our electrochemical cellular and chemical maps. The more novel and challenging the stimuli (up to a point), the more likely it will be to activate a new pathway. The new learning happens like this:

- A new experience may trigger an electrical impulse from the cell body.
- It travels down the axon of a neuron and triggers the release of chemicals (neurotransmitters).
- Included with these chemicals are messenger ribonucleic acids (mRNA), which are the molecules that carry information.
- Simultaneously, a process known as *synaptic adhesion* takes place by using protein "strings" to help bind the two neurons at the synapse.
- The mRNAs and the other neurotransmitters dock into receptor sites on the surface of the receiving dendrite.
- When the electrochemical threshold is reached, long-term potentiation is created. This is a use-dependent alteration in the strength of the synaptic connections.
- This reaction stimulates new electrical activity in the dendrite, sending it toward the cell body of the receiving neuron.
- Many factors influence the efficacy of this connection, including chemicals known as *neuromodulators* (i.e., stress hormones).
- Learning is the result of the strengthening of the connection between two neurons.

If the stimuli are not considered meaningful to the brain, the information will be given less priority and will leave only a weak trace. If the brain deems something important enough to commit it to long-term memory, a memory potential occurs.

Bigger changes can happen when we compound our experiences over time. While one good day or one bad day won't usually change the brain, over the course of months and years, a new process can. The body has 50 trillion cells, and every cell has tulip-shaped receptors that receive information. Different cells have different receptor sites for different molecules. Things such as light or heat activate some receptors, whereas histamines, stress hormones, nutrition, or androgens active others. Amazingly, receptor sites don't just process this information, but they begin an electrochemical cascade of activity that can eventually affect our genes (Giancotti & Ruoslahti, 1999). So while there is a core of genes that maintain your basic functions, often called *housekeeping genes,* there are thousands of others that are responsive to environmental signals.

Gene expression has been known about for decades. This simply means that genetic material gets used strategically. How does gene expression turn into changes in behavior? It's a sequence of steps whereby the messaging from genes activates proteins, which influence our behavior. Remember that genes are blueprints, and just like blueprints for a house, they are useless without a contractor to turn them into a "home." For decades, the body and brain were thought of as a one-way street, unfolding from genes outward. The new science tells otherwise. It's actually a two-way street, where genes influence our lives and our lives influence our genes. The meaning of this is profound. The fact that the process goes *both* ways is a revolution in biology, and we now know that it is possible to influence gene expression purposefully, which has implications for educators.

At each stage of development, particular genes are affected by particular environmental factors. Recent research has focused on what has been called *windows of opportunity*: a period of heightened readiness for learning. It is thought that exposure to appropriate stimuli during these peak times can optimize a child's natural appetite for learning—especially learning related to language, music, and motor development. Genes are not templates for learning, but they do represent enhanced risk or opportunity. Thus if children are born with the genes of a genius but are raised in nonenriched environments, the chances of their actually becoming geniuses are low. On the other hand, children with average genes who are raised in supportive and intellectually stimulating environments may achieve greatness by virtue of their enriched environments.

Neural networks are developed through trial and error. The more experimentation and feedback, the better the quality of the neural networks. Smarter humans don't always get the answers first, and they don't always get them right. But they do eliminate wrong answers better than their peers. This ability to avoid bad choices is a result of trial and error, not of someone else telling us the right answer and then having us repeat it back to them. This type of rote learning may produce high scores on a standardized test, but it does not produce high-level thinking.

Typical learners arrive not with blank slates but with highly customized brain banks of experience. Their cognitive maps are already a reflection of much more than just previous grade coursework and test scores. This, in fact, is only a small sliver of the neural pie. Even by preschool age, learners' brains have already been shaped by a multitude of influences, including home environment, siblings, extended family, playmates, genes, trauma, stress, injuries, violence, cultural rituals and expectations, enrichment opportunities, primary attachments, diet, and lifestyle (see Figure 18.10). Even a seemingly trivial incident like a bump on the head can have a lifelong impact on learning ability. For example, if the fragile temporal lobes (or other key brain areas) are injured, a child may experience emotional, processing, and/or memory function problems. And it is likely that the association between the head injury to the learner's challenges will never be made. This example illustrates the complexity of issues that educators face.

Figure 18.10   Influences on learners

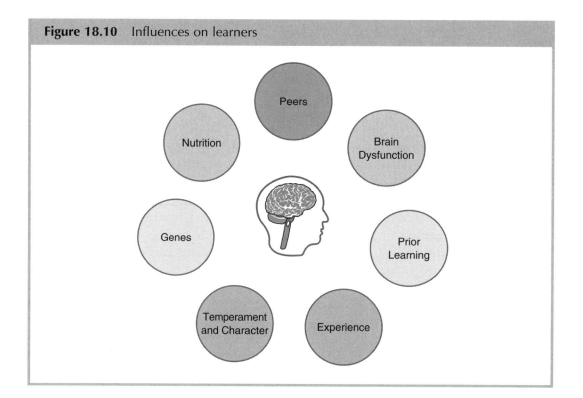

19 Meaning Making

There's an enormous difference between memorizing a few key facts and having an authentic grasp of a subject. It's the difference between doing well on a multiple-choice test and being able to hold a substantial discussion about a topic. It's the difference between reading about hospitals and being hospitalized for a week. It's the difference between eating at a Mexican restaurant and living in Mexico for a year. It's the difference between memorizing a few math facts and being able to tutor another student in mathematics.

Requiring students to learn lists of information has little to do with true learning. It's a throwback and a hangover from mid-twentieth-century schoolrooms. It's not that kids can't do it; it's simply a poor use of time. The brain is not very good at learning isolated information, especially when it is devoid of any joy or meaning. In fact, rote learning is the best way to turn kids off to nearly any topic. Most government estimates are that a school-age child today will have at least 10 jobs in his or her lifetime, many of which don't even exist today. This suggests that we must offer platforms for learning new things, not buckets of content that will become outdated quickly.

Authentic, meaningful learning requires that students process information in their own way, along their own time line, and in relation to their own perceptual maps. Sorting, analyzing, and drawing conclusions in the context of one's own life are what makes information stick.

There is no single place in the brain where meaning occurs. Brain scans reveal that different areas are activated depending on the nature of the event and the type of meaning derived from it. Events that trigger our so-called hot buttons are stored in the amygdala. When something is meaningful during reading, there's usually more activity (as measured by glucose consumption) in the left frontal, temporal, or parietal lobe (Posner & Badgaiyan, 1997). If it has a more spiritual meaning, there's probably parietal lobe activity (Ramachandran & Blakeslee, 1998). If it involves an emotionally felt meaning, there may be activity in the frontal, occipital, and mid-brain areas (Damasio, 1994). If it has an *Ah ha!* type of meaning, there is more likely activity in the left frontal lobe. These diverse areas of activation suggest that the concept of *meaning* may also be diverse.

> Our brains fully know something only when we represent the information in our own meaningful way.

In fact, research suggests that teachers who try to give learners as many facts as possible are doing both their students and themselves a disservice (Russell, Hendricson, & Herbert, 1984; Shaffer & Resnick, 1999). In the study by Russell and colleagues, students were randomly distributed into three groups. The professor prepared three different lectures on the same subject, one with 90 percent new information, another with 70 percent, and another with 50 percent. During the remaining class time, the professor added no additional information, but simply reinforced what was already presented. A pretest, one posttest, and another unannounced posttest 15 days later were given. The students with the 50 percent lecture density scored highest, even on the second posttest (see Figure 19.1).

TYPES OF MEANING

There are two types of meaning: *reference* and *sense*. Another way to think about it is *surface* or *deeply felt* meaning. Reference/surface meaning is a sort of pointer, a dictionary definition that refers to the lexical territory of the word. For example, *raincoat* is defined as an "oversized waterproof cloth or plastic garment." But the sense/deeply felt meaning of the word is different.

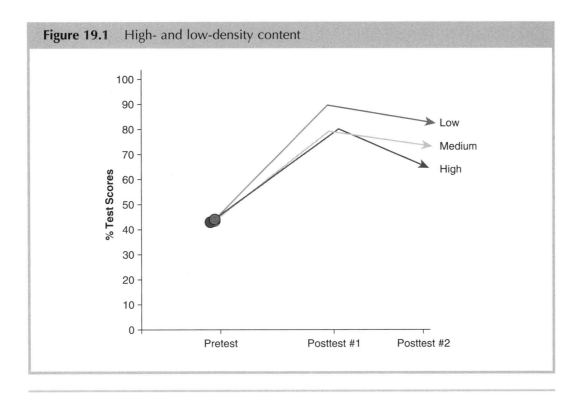

Figure 19.1   High- and low-density content

Source: Russell, Hendricson, & Herbert, 1984.

While I know what a raincoat is, it means little to me personally because I live in a climate where it rarely rains. The raincoat I own is used only rarely (when I travel) and seems like a waste of closet space most of the time. Contrast this to a very different sense/deeply felt meaning one might have about the word *raincoat* if one lives in a rainy climate. Perhaps your raincoat not only protects you from severe weather but is also a well-worn friend that preserves your health, protects your nice clothes, and elicits many compliments. Thus, your raincoat has sense meaning to you, which has developed over time and become meaningful through personal experience.

For a classroom example, consider the concept of the Iraq War. It can be explored either at the surface level or on the deeply felt level. The latter might happen if the teacher is a veteran who shares remembered experiences with the students. As we explore meaningful learning in this chapter, it is the sense meaning that we're after, rather than the dictionary-type reference meaning, which leaves emotions untouched.

Many of our deeply felt meanings in life are built in—sort of hardwired into our brains. An example would be the human response of sadness to sickness and death. We have learned over the centuries that life is valuable and to be protected. The meaning that is not hardwired is a bit trickier. The importance people give to attending college, for example, is derived from constructed meaning, which is influenced by people's culture, their personal experiences, and themselves.

What Triggers a Sense of Meaning?

Factors involved in meaning making are relevance, emotions, and context. Relevance is a function of the brain in making a connection from existing neural sites. Emotions are triggered by the brain's chemistry and tag the learning as important. Context triggers pattern making, which relates to the activation of larger neural fields. In other words, if the information is personal to us, if we feel deeply about it, and if it makes sense, chances are pretty good that we'll find it meaningful.

Anything meaningful has at least one of these three ingredients, but the reverse is not true. Something could be relevant and still be meaningless. For example, eating a nutritionally sound diet is very relevant, but doing so may hold little meaning to a teenager. Of the three items, the one most commonly associated with meaning making is relevance.

Relevance

Relevance actually happens on a cellular level. An existing neuron simply connects with a nearby neuron to make a connection. If the content is irrelevant (lacks understanding or emotional valence), it's unlikely that a connection will be made. While neurons are constantly firing, much of the time it's an inaudible chatter. The meaning we experience happens when a multitude of connections or the activation of a neural field takes place. In the brain, a nearby connection is often less than a centimeter away. The brain's nerve cells rarely move; they simply extend their axons to connect with other dendrites. If they can't make the connection, it's going to be harder to establish relevance. These connections are what form the basis of our personality, thinking, and consciousness.

Some thoughts activate entire neural fields that may cross cell and axon boundaries. The greater the number of links and associations that your brain creates, the more firmly the information is woven in neurologically. Unfortunately, many students find that classroom information lacks the personal relevance necessary for authentic learning.

 **What This Means to You**

Never assume that because something is relevant to you, it's relevant to your students. Help them discover their own connections rather than imposing your own. Give students time to link prior learning with current learning through explorations encouraged by special events, discussions, and introspection. Use the power of family history, stories, myths, legends, and metaphors to help make learning relevant for students. Throughout human history, stories have been fundamental to understanding and valuing the people and lessons of the past. Encourage learners to use their own words with regard to new learning. You might also tie in local or national celebrations. Encourage students to share their own experience. Set up pair shares, small-group discussions, and team projects. Use free association to help learners explore the personal relevance of subjects. You might ask questions such as these: "Have you ever had this happen? If so, how did it feel?" "Could you compare and contrast this to an experience you've had in your own life?"

Emotions

Intense emotions trigger the release of the neurotransmitters adrenaline, norepinephrine, and vasopressin. These chemicals act as signals to the brain, saying, "This is important—remember this." There's little doubt about it: emotions and meaning are linked. You may ask, "Which comes first, the emotion or the meaning?" This is a bit like the proverbial chicken-and-egg question. The systems are so interconnected that chemicals of emotion are released virtually simultaneously with cognition.

Research has uncovered critical links between emotions and the cognitive patterning needed for learning. The "flavor" or "color" of our experiences is likely to make us want either more of it (it was pleasurable) or less of it (it was boring or painful). Further, positive emotions allow the brain to make better perceptual maps, meaning that when we are feeling positive, we are better able to sort out our experiences and recall with more clarity. In fact, Pert (1997) refers to the brain as a little box packed full of emotions.

> The old model of learning separated mind, body, and emotions. We now know differently. Emotions are a critical part of a learner's ability to think rationally and experience meaning.

For the moment, let's say that a learner arrives at school distraught over a dispute at home. He is irritable and inattentive and learns very little. He thinks of class as a waste of time and does not want to be told what to do. Contrast this with a very different experience: A learner has just had a recent success or a positive relationship encounter. The day is rosy, the birds are singing, and she's happy. As a result, she learns better and has positive memories of the class. Here are some specific strategies you can use to reinforce the positive and manage the negative:

What This Means to You

Provide learners with positive and emotionally safe ways to express their emotions—negative or positive—such as the following:

- a mind-calming visualization or relaxation exercise
- physical activity—a walk, a cross crawl, stretching, or games
- dialogue time with partners or a small group, or sharing time
- internal reflection—journal writing, self-assessment, and goal setting
- metaphorical rituals like a "dumping box" near the door so that learners can throw away bad feelings or memories
- role-plays, theater, drama, mime, and simulations
- music—playing instruments, singing, chanting, cheering, and shouting
- debating a controversial issue, playing tug-of-war, or staging an improvisation
- movement—dance, games, exercises, stretching, and play
- excursions, guest speakers, trips, and novel or challenging activities

In a classroom, emotional states are an important condition around which educators must orchestrate learning. Students may be bored with the lesson, afraid of an upcoming test, or despondent about a drive-by shooting. They may be hyperenergized by an upcoming sports competition, an emotional crisis, or a looming deadline. Instead of trying to eliminate learners' emotions by ignoring them (which doesn't work), it makes more sense for us to integrate them into the curriculum. When we ignore the emotional components of any subject we teach, we deprive students of meaningfulness. Emotions drive attention, meaning, and memory. To take advantage of this principle, acknowledge emotions in the learning process.

 **What This Means to You**

Add higher stakes through goal setting or by conducting public performances to evoke emotional investment. Create immersion environments where your entire classroom reflects the subject at hand (e.g., decorate it as a particular city, landmark, or foreign country). Involve the students in the design. Perhaps it's a rain forest, an airplane, a business, or a particular period of time. Encourage students to share their inner worlds with each other. Have them discuss their goals, thoughts, and ideals. Develop greater peer collaboration. Assign cooperative projects. Use partners, long-standing teams, or temporary groups that are activated with specialized activities. Encourage the use of more relationship-driven learning by facilitating apprenticeships with experts. Multiage classrooms, big-brother programs, and community-active adults are perfect examples of support systems that engage deep meaning for learners. Do fewer but more complex projects, especially lengthy multilevel projects with sufficient time and resources provided. For example, students in a science class might plan a five-year trip to Mars. Such a project would involve skills in math, science, problem solving, research, economics, and social studies.

Context

Perception is the act of the brain constructing a map. This process involves brain structures that are responsible for categorization, discrimination, and regrouping. The brain's way of understanding is more through pattern discrimination than through singular facts or lists. The initial stages of processing are largely parallel rather than serial, and they feature analysis results from matching patterns rather than detecting features. We identify an object, for example, by gathering information—often in less than a second—on size, color, shape, surface texture, weight, smell, and movement. The assumption is that a subject can be fragmented into little bits, and when presented with the bits, students will be quite able to assemble the parts and emerge with the whole—even though they've never been provided with an inkling of the whole.

The cortex is both a pattern maker and a pattern detector. The ability to make meaningful sense out of countless bits of data is critical to understanding and motivation. Since the brain's craving for meaning is automatic, patterning occurs all the time. Each pattern that is discovered can then be added to the learner's perceptual maps, relieving the brain of confusion, anxiety, or stress. The brain then "maximizes" again and is ready for more challenge.

The process of creating a pattern or a perceptual map utilizes both the conscious and the nonconscious brain. Every pattern that the brain is able to create can be relegated from the conscious to the nonconscious. From a survival point of view, it is critical to create patterns as quickly as possible.

Also involved in pattern identification are neurons. They don't contain information; they simply translate, conduct, and connect to others that resonate with their own frequency. All cells simultaneously send and receive information. New information, which has no established pattern or frequency, must find uncommitted fields that resonate. Mapping can help trigger these fields. Fields can shift, rearrange, and form new fields (neural mapping). In fact, the more fields tapped, the greater your depth of meaning, feedback, and understanding.

But in this process of establishing a neural, then mental map, the brain is less able to generate other parallel maps because it is thematically distracted. It forms quick hierarchies to extract or create patterns. To the brain, there is a certain survival risk and a vulnerability while a pattern is being created, but the payoff is big. The patterns give context to information that would otherwise be dismissed as meaningless. This desire to form some kind of meaningful pattern out of learning seems innate. Children create games that organize behaviors, and they arrange objects into patterns rather than leave them random. Adults organize dishes, cars, tools, sewing articles, businesses, file cabinets, and book chapters. Researchers believe this patterning may begin on a micro level.

Other areas of neurobiology suggest that pattern making may be innate. In a classic experiment, infants were shown a series of drawings. Each illustration had exactly the same elements as a human face. But only one had them in a coherent shape and form. The others had the eyes, nose, hair, and mouth scrambled. To determine the interest and value to an infant, careful recordings were made of which figures were preferred by gaze time. Infants preferred the pattern of a human face when they were only a few days old. Infants as young as 10 months or less are drawn to, and can recognize, patterns more quickly than nonpatterns. Infants show puzzled looks when presented with scattered, unpatterned material. All of this suggests that we are hardwired to pay attention to certain patterns.

In tests of visual perception, researchers have shown that we are naturals not only at learning pattern discrimination but also at applying it to other models. It's the making of familiar connections (relevance) and the locating of conforming neural networks (pattern making), in fact, that is critical to the formation of meaning. How important is the process of pattern making to the brain? Using the pattern-detecting and pattern-making areas of the brain is critical to proper development. According to Healy (2004), "children who don't learn to search for meaning are often good 'technicians' in the first and second grade because they can deal with isolated data, but when the demands for comprehension increase, they 'hit the wall.' They simply can't assemble it and make sense out of it. Those who can are often thought of as more intelligent" (p. 50).

Exposing learners to interdisciplinary and cross-disciplinary models also exposes them to more patterns, which in turn translates to more relevance, context, and connections. It's the ability to see ideas in relation to others, as well as how individual facts become meaningful in a larger field of information, that is important. How does economics relate to geography? Mathematics to art and music? Ecology to politics?

What This Means to You

Context can be either explicit or implicit. Implicit learning forms a powerful pattern called a *mental model*. Teachers who reveal their own mental models and elicit student models may be surprised at the value. When you open your own windows of the mind, you make the implicit explicit. Ask students how they know what they know through the use of *how* questions: How does democracy work? How does the weather change? How does the body digest food? How do you go about solving problems? These will draw out the patterns of thinking that can expose the boundaries, limitations, and genius in your students.

Pattern detection has been taught exquisitely well by countless teachers. One in particular is former Soviet Union high school teacher Victor Shatalov. The math and science achievement scores of his students ranked among the highest in the world. His success was attributed to the high standards for success he maintained and his "nobody will fail" attitude. He made a practice of describing the mental model he used as he incorporated such techniques as color-coded graphic organizers, frequent shifts from global to detail learning, and active interaction with materials. He emphasized relevance, context, and common patterns. The following teaching strategies can be used to help learners develop good pattern-detection skills:

What This Means to You

- Ask students questions that force them to consider a larger context. For example, "Are high school shootings random, or are they part of a larger pattern?"
- Point out patterns in nature. For example, "Can you see all the leaf shapes in the trees?"
- Introduce the skill of grouping objects, ideas, names, facts, and other key pieces of information.
- Simply read to students; then guide them in establishing some basic patterns depicted in the reading. These might be cycles of cause and effect, problems and resolutions, or intense drama and downtime.
- Ask questions that compare and contrast things in the natural environment.
- Give children the opportunity to play cards, build with blocks, and solve puzzles.
- Incorporate stitchery or sewing with patterns. Sort items related to sewing, building, or other hobbies.
- Assign class projects that require pattern conceptualization (e.g., a classroom library or book-loan system, a school store, a yearbook, a newspaper).

- Pay attention to patterns. Discuss the patterns exhibited by wildlife (e.g., bird calls, migration patterns).
- At the start of each new topic, provide global visual overviews (e.g., overheads, videos, posters).
- Incorporate motor skills. Walk learners through a process that ensures new learning corresponds to a physical place, location, or movement.
- Pre-expose learners with oral previews, applicable games in texts or handouts, metaphorical descriptions, and posted mind maps of the topic.
- Encourage learners to evaluate the pros and cons of a topic, discuss its relevance, and demonstrate their conceptual patterning with models, plays, and projects.

Role-Plays and Games Enhance Meaning

Making learning physical is old hat to most primary school teachers. And the idea of taking academic learning and embedding it within creative expression or entertainment is also centuries old. But does the method of recontextualizing the learning really work? Does brain-based learning research support this type of learning? Yes, it does. This learning allows the brain to make complex perceptual maps, and it has a high likelihood of engaging emotions. Being physical is much more naturally engaging, motivating, and likely to extend learning. When the focus is on performing, rather than learning, stress can be reduced, while creativity increases. Since knowledge is state dependent, what is learned during a role-play may be accessible during that same situation later on. This is the basic premise of self-defense courses that rely on model muggers and other simulation training, such as that used with pilots.

Most important, in these simulation contexts learning becomes more meaningful and enjoyable. More choice and creativity are exercised, and there is minimal negative evaluative pressure. It is easier to push through negative inner thoughts when everyone is caught up in the excitement of producing, planning, researching, and marketing a grand performance. When the stakes are higher, learning may take on more relevance. Reaching multiple goals (e.g., social, artistic, emotional, academic) is easier when the learners' hearts and minds are engaged. The student actors will learn in spite of themselves—by virtue of memorizing lines and creating scenes, if nothing else.

What This Means to You

Students learn much more than they can consciously know when they work together to put on a school play. Many teachers and professors think that active, physical-response learning and role-plays are, well, elementary. Brain research says otherwise. Activate the brain through presentations, skits, mock debates, *Jeopardy* shows, and humorous treatments of commercials, songs, and so on. Include creative and/or entertaining activities as a regular part of the learning process.

Framing Enhances Meaning

Framing is the spin that we, as well as others, put on something to enhance, alter, or diminish meaning. For example, nearly every single political event from Washington gets a spin or a frame put on it so that one political party looks better or worse, depending on motives.

All of us are gifted; the context provides the evidence. You may have many very smart learners, but in the absence of favorable circumstances, their intelligence goes unnoticed. There are many ways to elicit learners' talents by utilizing multiple status roles. Change the learners' status through the use of teams, alter egos, peer tutoring, study buddies, multiage projects, and multigrade projects. In addition, involvement in the community or with other classes provides more opportunity for real-life involvement, novelty, surprise, and meaningfulness.

What This Means to You

Meaning is constructed. Use framing in the classroom to alter the meaning of any activity. Encourage the use of integrated learning. Tap into learners' prior knowledge. Operate from the perspective that learners have to learn how to create meaning for themselves in what they learn. The conditions for meaning making can be encouraged and orchestrated, but it is the learners who must construct the meaning. The genius of this process is that when the teacher gets out of the way of the learners, the learners can create, from scratch, real meaning in the learning.

The brain is designed to seek meaning. Until we provide learners with the resources (time, context, other learners, materials, opportunities) to discover meaning in what we ask them to learn, we will continue to produce robots and underachievers. Correspondingly, until we provide more meaningful forms of assessment, educators will have little incentive to pursue teaching for deep meaning. Students will simply skim a few facts off the top, pass the test, and call it an education. If this constitutes an education, then we're in trouble. Fortunately, however, some educators manage to provide a meaningful curriculum in spite of the continued thrust toward standardized testing and standards-based outcomes.

Part 5

Brain-Compatible Classrooms

20 Enriching the Brain

Typically we think of intelligence as a combination of both environment and genetics. Genetics means "you are mostly what your parents gave you" and "things won't get much better—at least not in the brains department." In fact, for most of scientific history, the prevailing paradigm was that humans have a brain of fixed capacity. We fill our brains with experiences and memories, people thought. Of course, this brain grows some in size after birth—but it was believed that it reached adult size by 10 years old. This traditional wisdom told us that intelligence was a fixed number (IQ), and it stayed that way. This idea of an immutable brain was adopted by many early educators who, once some learners were identified as slow and some as gifted, kept these learners sequestered with peers, as if each had a communicable disease. We now have special ed, regular ed, and gifted ed almost as if we were sorting laundry or nuts, bolts, and washers. The prevailing view—still found in many schools today—is that students will continue to be the way they are right now. This belief is so widespread that it's the dominant model for most public and private schooling.

The "fixed brain" theory is not just dead wrong, but—embarrassingly—it may be doing a great deal of harm. The human brain is so malleable that it can be fixed at artificially low levels by getting a constant diet of a below-average status quo. Millions of students young and old begin to believe that their intellectual destiny is stuck at entry-level testing scores. As a result, millions live far below their biological potential. Here's an exciting thought: Enrichment is the whole purpose of schooling. There is no other reason to send a kid to school unless we are enriching the mind, body, soul, and brain. This chapter is about how to fulfill that potential. Enrichment is an exciting concept, and it can apply to everyone.

GROWING A "BETTER" BRAIN

Can we grow a better brain? The answer seemed to be "no." Many consider Canadian psychologist Donald Hebb to be the original trailblazer in the world of changing brains. Sitting at home and watching as his pets roamed the house, he got an idea. Why not test which was better for an animal—free roving or cage raised? It didn't take long for him to test his hypothesis. Naturally, the free-roving rats did better on maze running. Hebb realized that the brain changes as a result of the environment. His 1949 book, *The Organization of Behavior*, remains a classic to this day.

In 1964, biopsychologist Mark Rosenzweig, of the University of California at Berkeley, led a research team that revealed that rats in an enriched environment indeed grow better brains than those in an impoverished environment (Bennett, Diamond, Krech, & Rosenzweig, 1964; Rosenzweig, Love, & Bennett, 1968). The evidence that an enriched environment could enhance brain development was supported further in groundbreaking research by University of California, Berkeley, pioneer Marian Diamond (see Diamond & Hopson, 1998) and, separately, by University of Illinois researcher William Greenough (Greenough & Anderson, 1991). Based on these pioneering studies and many subsequent to them, we now know that the human brain actually maintains an amazing plasticity throughout life. We can literally grow new neural connections with stimulation, even as we age. This means that nearly any learner can increase his or her intelligence, without limits, using the proper enrichment.

Initial studies with rats were eventually extended to human subjects. The animal studies suggested that, when exposed to an enriched environment, the number of connections in the brain increased by 25 percent. Diamond (see Diamond & Hopson, 1998) found that increasingly enriched environments led to larger and heavier brains, which meant that the nerve cells were better able to communicate with each other. She also saw that larger nerve cells resulted in more support cells and increases in the dimensions of the synapses between cells.

Eventually, we learned that in addition to increased dendritic branching, synaptic plasticity was evident in enriched environments. We now know how the brain modifies itself structurally and that it is dependent on the type and amount of usage. Synaptic growth varies depending on the complexity and type of activity we regularly engage in. For example, when we engage in novel motor learning, new synapses are generated in our cerebellar cortex. And when we engage in repeated motor learning (or exercise), our brains develop greater density of blood vessels in the molecular layer.

An area of the midbrain, the superior colliculus, which is involved in attentional processing, has been shown to grow 5 to 6 percent more in an enriched environment. Using functional magnetic resonance imaging (fMRI) technology, researchers at the University of Pennsylvania discovered that the human brain has areas that are stimulated only by letters, not words or symbols (Ackerman, Wildgruber, Daum, & Grodd, 1998). This suggests that new experiences (e.g., reading) can get wired into the malleable brain. In other words, as we vary the type of environment, the brain varies the way it develops.

The brain changes itself in several ways. First, intrinsic forces, otherwise known as *genetics* or *prewiring*, create a template for processes that drive change in the brain. Second, *experience expectant* processes create massive overproduction of synapses prior to (not after) demand; this occurs when (1) the learning is commonly needed by all members of that species, (2) certain events will reliably occur, and (3) the timing is relatively critical. And third, the brain responds to *experience dependent* processes triggered by environmental stimuli.

A Biological Look at Enrichment

When scientists extended enrichment studies to human subjects, they found definite correlations with the animal studies. University of California, Los Angeles, neuroscientist Robert Jacobs and colleagues found in autopsy studies that graduate students had 40 percent more neural connections than high school dropouts did (Jacobs, Schall, & Scheibel, 1993). The graduate students, who were presumably involved in challenging mental activities, also exhibited 25 percent more overall brain growth than the control group. Yet education alone was not the only differential; the learning experiences needed to be frequent and challenging for the effect to occur. Graduate students who coasted through school exhibited fewer connections than those who challenged themselves daily.

The research by Jacobs and colleagues (1993) on cortical dendrite systems in 20 neurologically normal right-handed humans (half male and half female) evaluated the following variables:

- total dendritic length
- mean dendritic length
- dendritic segment count
- proximal versus ontogenetically later-developing distal branching

These variables are known to relate to the complexity of the brain, the ability to solve problems, and overall intelligence. Jacobs and colleagues investigated several independent variables, as well: gender, hemisphere, and education. The results of their research revealed the following:

Gender: Females had greater dendritic values and variability than males.

Hemisphere: The left hemisphere had greater overall dendritic measurements than the right, but the results were not consistent with each individual.

Education: Level of education had a consistent and substantial effect on dendritic branching; the higher the level, the greater the measurements.

Can enrichment actually make you smarter? The answer to this question is still unclear. But Calvin and Ojemann (1994) say that cortical-area growth does have something to do with being "smart," even though the internal efficiency of our wiring and connections is more significant. A student's early sensory deprivation can play a role as well: as a result of negative experiences, the brain sheds the wrong synapses and ends up malfunctioning (Fuchs, Montemayor, & Greenough, 1990). Retaining excess synapses can be harmful, as in the case of Fragile X mental retardation.

Summary of Enrichment Findings

Enhanced environmental stimulation can affect the brain in many ways. Studies have described at least six fundamentally different effects:

- **metabolism:** chemical allostasis and blood-flow changes (changes in the metabolism and chemical baselines of key brain chemicals)
- **physiological effects:** enhanced anatomical structures (neurons and other cell structures may be larger)
- **mapping:** increased connectivity—new circuitry (far more branching from one neuron to another)
- **responsiveness and learning efficiency:** electrophysiological changes (cells may be much more efficient and have greater plasticity, meaning that one can learn faster)
- **increased neurogenesis and growth factors:** increased production of new brain cells, supporting better learning and memory
- **recovery from tissue, drug abuse, and system damage:** greater capacity to heal when damaged

In working with children, Craig Ramey (1992), at the University of Alabama, found that he could increase intelligence with mental stimulation. His intervention program studied children of low-IQ parents. Divided into two groups (one control group), the children who were exposed to the enriched environment scored significantly higher (20 points) on posttreatment IQ tests. And the results lasted: when the children were retested after 10 years, the effects of early intervention had endured. This provides quite an endorsement for challenging learning environments.

Human Neurogenesis Is Possible

Early studies demonstrated that enrichment of the brain leads to greater spine growth on the dendrites (connection points for cell-to-cell interaction), heavier cell bodies, longer dendrites, and more glial (support) cell growth. As early as 1965, Altman and Das claimed that the mammalian brain can not only grow better dendrites but also grow new cells (*neurogenesis*). The scientific establishment, however, was not ready for this radical claim. The mainstream thinking was that, yes, the human brain can be enriched, but growing new cells was impossible.

Then in 1997, a research effort led by scientists at San Diego's Salk Institute of Neuroscience discovered that neurogenesis is, in fact, a reality in rat brains (at least in the hippocampus; O'Leary, 1997; Van Pragg, Kempermann, & Gage, 1999). A year later, the study was extended to humans, and the findings were reconfirmed (Eriksson et al., 1998). The human brain also has the capability of growing new neurons!

Even though we inevitably lose brain cells each day, new ones can be germinated in a fertile environment. The impact of this finding on the general public has yet to be fully realized, but the scientific community is buoyed by the medical potential of these recent findings. Injuries once viewed as permanent may soon be repairable with accelerated cell-growth prompting. A cure for the dreaded Alzheimer's disease may soon exist. Although we are still a long way from the reality of these prospects, scientists are hopeful.

The Keys to Enrichment

In examining the many enrichment studies that have been conducted over the past few decades, the following common factors have emerged:

Novel Learning

First, to get the enrichment effect, the stimulus must be new. An old stimulus just won't do; it must be novel. Second, the stimulus must be challenging. Routine efforts do little for the brain's growth. Third, the stimulus must be coherent and meaningful. Random input will not enrich the brain. Fourth, the learning has to take place over time. How much time depends on the extent of the neural changes, but the only changes that happen instantly are stimulus-response learning. And finally, there must be a way for the brain to learn from the challenging, novel stimuli; the brain needs feedback. For example, if you're learning to walk a tightrope and you make a mistake, you fall: that's feedback. If you press a lever, you get food or you don't: that's feedback. The more consistent, specific, timely, and learner controlled the feedback is, the better. There you have it! In a nutshell, the critical ingredients for enriching the brain are novelty, challenge, coherence, time, and feedback (see Figure 20.1).

What This Means to You

Create a more multisensory environment. Add posters, aromas, music, and relevant activities. Increase social interaction and group work. Move to novel locations frequently (e.g., take fieldtrips, go outdoors, exchange rooms with another teacher for the day). On a daily basis, modify the environment in some minor way (e.g., seating, displays, bulletin boards). Encourage students to explore new ideas and express themselves creatively. Provide quality, not just quantity, time. Teach and practice critical skills such as logic, categorizing, counting, labeling, language, cause and effect, debate, and critical thinking. Provide positive feedback, and celebrate accomplishments with fun celebrations. Use words from several languages in a variety of contexts. Reduce all forms of severe negative experience, punishment, or disapproval. And most of all, offer students choices so that their learning is meaningful.

Diamond and colleagues have researched a number of enrichment effects, including a thicker cortex (Diamond, Krech, & Rosenzweig, 1964) and increases in the size of neurons (Diamond, Lindner, & Raymond, 1967). In addition, researchers have found increased dendritic length (Green, Greenough, & Schlumph, 1983) and more complex (higher-order) branching on the dendrites

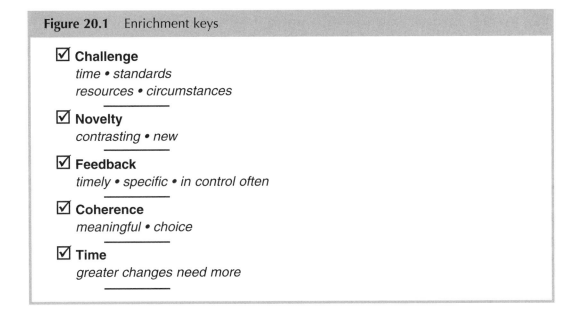

Figure 20.1 Enrichment keys

☑ **Challenge**
time • standards
resources • circumstances

☑ **Novelty**
contrasting • new

☑ **Feedback**
timely • specific • in control often

☑ **Coherence**
meaningful • choice

☑ **Time**
greater changes need more

(Juraska, Fitch, Henderson, & Rivers, 1985), better enabling them to make more future connections (Volkmar & Greenough, 1972). It sounds as if all of these changes would add mass to the brain, and they do: brain weight increases with enrichment (Altman, Wallace, Anderson, & Das, 1968; Bennett, Rosenzweig, & Diamond, 1969).

Arnold Scheibel, director of the Brain Research Institute at the University of California, Los Angeles, has said that unfamiliar activities are the brain's best friend. The fact that the brain is so stimulated by novelty may be a survival response: anything new may be threatening to the status quo and, thus, represents a potential danger. Once we have grown accustomed to an environment or situation, however, it becomes routine, and the reticular formation in our brain begins to operate at a lower level. Once a new or novel stimulus is reintroduced, the reticular formation gets alerted once again, and the brain is stimulated to grow.

The work of Greenough and colleagues (1992) and Black (1989) confirm that for the enrichment effect to occur, the challenges presented must engender learning, as opposed to being mere activity or exercise. When Black isolated other factors, such as aging and stress, from complex environments, he affirmed that it was the learning, not simply the motor activity, that caused optimal brain growth. This tells us that *how* you enrich an environment is critical.

The enrichment effect does not necessarily take months or years to show up. Significant structural modifications in the dendritic fields of cortical neurons have been reported after just four days. Greenough and Anderson (1991) suggest that brain enrichment happens in stages—from surface level to depth growth. They draw four important conclusions:

1. Rats in enriched environments grow heavier brains with more dendritic connections that communicate better. They also exhibit increased synapses, greater thickness in sensory areas, increased enzymes, and more glial cells (which assist in growth and signal transmission).

2. Enriched environments need to be varied and changed often (every 2 to 4 weeks) to maintain the positive differences in rat intelligence. In studies, this meant frequently introducing other rats, more toys, and additional challenges; this holds true for humans as well.

3. Rats of any age can experience increased intelligence if they are provided challenging and frequent new learning experiences.

4. The real world—outside the cages (even the enriched ones)—provides one of the best environments for brain growth.

Schools today are developing greater interest in creating the right kind of enriched environments for students. One of the most convincing arguments comes from the former director of the National Institute of Mental Health, Frederick Goodwin. He says you can't make a 70-IQ person into a 120-IQ person, "but you can change their IQ in different ways, perhaps as much as 20 points up or down, based on their environment" (quoted in Gordon, 1999, p. 298).

Have you ever noticed how much more passion and motivation learners exhibit when they are talking about real-world experiences versus book learning? Real-life learning provides a valuable springboard for delving deeper into the meaning or analysis of things. Some learning opportunities that inspire this type of reflection include field trips, travel or study abroad, library study, the home environment, the park, on-the-job training, a convention, a rally, a special meeting, or vacation—anything rich and varied that naturally occurs in life.

Feedback Spurs Learning

While enriched environments (both mental and physical) are important, research by noted brain expert Santiago Ramon y Cajal (1988) emphasizes that the brain needs feedback from its own activities for optimal learning.

Feedback is critical, but it does not necessarily have to be teacher generated. One of the best ways to encourage self-feedback and boost thinking is to have learners reflect and record audio of their own perceptions. This examination into one's own thinking, sensing, and organizing process provides a powerful vehicle for the brain's development as a problem solver and as a thinker.

> The best feedback is immediate, positive, and dramatic.

A teacher's greatest feedback resource may be other learners. And yet, many learning environments are not organized to take advantage of this asset. Group work and teams are ideal for learning, especially when they are multiage and multistatus groupings. Group work can help learners feel valued and cared for, in which case their brains release the neurotransmitters of pleasure: endorphins and dopamine. This helps them enjoy their work more. Groups also provide a superb vehicle for social and academic reinforcement. When students talk to each other, they get direct feedback on their ideas as well as their behaviors.

The most effective feedback is specific and immediate. Video games and computers both meet this requirement, as does peer editing of a student's story. Also, interaction among learners and with outside sources can provide valuable feedback. A great deal of feedback is obtained nonverbally; facial expressions and body language tell us a lot about our performance on a nonconscious, if not conscious, level. Building a classroom model, playing a learning game, creating a class video, and planning a community project are all activities that provide indirect feedback from the interaction process.

Ideally, feedback involves some learner choice. That is, it can be generated and modified at will. If it's not relevant or if it cannot be immediately applied, however, performance won't be altered. Recall a college class in which your only feedback may have come from a midterm or final exam. That's an example of poor, other-controlled feedback. Fortunately, immediate and self-generated feedback can be achieved in many simple ways. For example, have learners review their own work against performance criteria, provide self-assessment guidelines, post grading criteria, have students review their personal goals, and use computer learning programs if appropriate.

To summarize what we've learned about enrichment, consider the following:

- Learners do best when they are presented with novel stimulation—something out of the ordinary.
- Beware of learner overload. Don't provide too much new material at a time. A presentation of 30 to 90 minutes with intense (preferably nonstop) sensory stimulation is good, followed by a rest period.
- Provide proper downtime after new learning. Repeat new learning 24 to 48 hours after the initial encounter, then daily, and then every other day.
- Interacting with peers, teachers, or other adults regarding the subject matter allows learners to create a conceptual framework for the learning and gather critical feedback.
- Consistent feedback helps learners improve the quality of their understanding and observe their own progress.
- When learners are provided with a roadmap or framework for the new learning—an overall picture of where they are and where they are going— understanding is enhanced.

Activating More of the Brain

Intelligence is largely the ability to bring together random bits of information to inform thinking, problem solving, and analysis. The brain relies on a multitude of circuits to do this effectively. These connections are called *phase relationships* because they tie together simultaneous stimuli. When learners are provided with more consistent feedback and better-quality feedback, they are better able to tie pieces of the learning puzzle together and integrate the information into higher-quality relationships and patterns.

Many of the great thinkers in history (e.g., Leonardo da Vinci) kept elaborate journals of their work. Perhaps these recordings represent a sort of self-feedback mechanism. As a child, you had plenty of environmental stimulation, but you also got all-important feedback. When you first learned to ride a bike, you experienced immediate and conclusive feedback: you either stayed up or fell down. Imagine trying to learn to ride a bike without knowing how you were doing until a month later. You would go nuts! We may be accidentally retarding thinking, intelligence, and brain growth, and ultimately creating slow learners, through lack of feedback and the wide lag time or feedback loop we have built into the typical learning environment.

If after reading this chapter, you want to start increasing the enrichment opportunities in your teaching/learning environment, begin first by simply increasing the frequency and quality of learner feedback. With this intervention alone, you will notice immediate improvement in learners' motivation and achievement.

What Have We Learned?

The results of over 40 years of enrichment studies have suggested that no single experimental variable can account for all of the effects of an enriching environment. Because of the wide variance of models used to study enrichment, both the variables and the effects create a complex puzzle. There is also no standard protocol for all enhanced, complex environmental studies, and while mammals have been used extensively, no one at this time can safely extrapolate all studies to all species. The results are far from final, and more studies always need to be done. Having said that, we can reliably draw some conclusions about the key factors. The single strongest thing to keep in mind is contrast. The greater the contrast from the prevailing or preexisting environment, the greater the benefit. Now, contrast of what to what?

These factors have been shown to create the "delivery" of the contrasting effects:

- **Physical versus sedentary activity**
  the ideal is voluntary, gross-motor-muscle effort
- **Novel, challenging learning versus doing what is already known**
  the ideal is learning tasks that are meaningful to the subject
- **Coherent complexity versus boredom or chaos**
  the ideal is busy, but not overwhelming
- **Managed stress levels versus distress or threat**
  the ideal is low to moderate stress, a healthy concern
- **Good nutrition versus a bland, fatty, or low-nutrient diet**
  the ideal is a balanced, low-fat, high-nutrient diet
- **Sufficient time versus minutes, hours, or days**
  the ideal is weeks, months, or years for the conditions to become lasting
- **Social or community support versus being alone**
  the ideal is having positive status in a safe, affiliated social group

---

Notice what's not on the list. Specific experimenter actions and things—lectures, posters, mobiles, pets, music—have no guaranteed benefit. Each of those might contribute in some way, but no enrichment studies conducted thus far can prove that any specific element helps make for an enriched environment.

How Much Enrichment?

Enrichment is all about contrast. If a student is in an impoverished environment at home for eight hours a day, then gets one hour of enhancement at school, that one hour constitutes only a tiny fragment of the total. That one hour is unlikely to produce substantial long-term benefits, though it's certainly better than nothing—and adding more hours can produce more striking benefits relatively easily. If, in contrast, a student's prevailing environment is already fairly enriched, even five hours a day of positive school enhancement will have to be very targeted to skills and knowledge that the student does not already have to be of value.

How do average students use their 24 hours a day of allotment? Let's use the following as just an average:

- sleep time = 7 hours (varies from 6 to 9 depending on the child)
- daily routines of eating, dressing, grooming, home chores = 3 hours (varies from 2 to 4 hours depending on age, interests, and gender)
- commuting to and from school, doing homework, and relaxing = 3–6 hours (varies from 2 to 4 hours depending on age, interests, and gender)
- school time = 6 hours (varies from 5 to 7 hours depending on grade level or extracurricular activities).

Out of the 6 hours, at least an hour is spent (over an entire year, as an average) on classroom routines, transit time, or testing. This leaves the potential for school enrichment at just 5 hours per day. Remember, this also has to include any time for part-time jobs, video games, studying, or hanging out with friends. This means school time (5 good hours) and "off time" (5 good hours) are both about the same. That's approximately 10 hours a day that are up for grabs for many students. To maximize the enrichment response, you'd want as many of those 10 hours per day to be enriching.

Possibly the entire intake process for so-called enrichment programs may need to be reexamined. They should include a detailed student and parent lifestyle profile. As an example, students who come from homes with just a magazine or a book for reading material and a stay-at-home diet of constant TV are clearly not getting enriched. There are huge opportunities for their brains to become enriched if schools do a strong inventory of students' skills, aptitudes, and interests.

Many of the parents who take their children on airplane trips and to concerts, museums, and fairs, and engage in rich dialogue are most likely doing many positive things for their children, and it's just as important that the schools conduct the previously mentioned inventory. These students may need programs that target lateral enrichment (learning a wider range of skills, developing emotional intelligence). Or they may need more vertical enrichment (the opportunity to dig deeply into individual subjects or skill areas via project learning). If students get into special education programs via testing, the same can be done for the rest of the students.

Changing the Brain—On Purpose!

The enrichment response indicates two primary benefits that may interest educators. The first involves learning and memory; the second involves repair and renewal in cases of brain injury, impairment, and disorders. The first change suggests that we may be able to affect the cognition of all learners, from the average to the gifted. The second change suggests that we may be able to improve the cognition of those with impaired learning, the disadvantaged, or those with brain damage. But there is another option for changing the brain, and parents, educators, and trainers should know how the brain changes in order to better implement their change policies.

The enrichment response is the result of a positive, contrasting environment. But what if you can't change the subject's whole environment? What if you can change only a few localized variables? If the rest of the environment stays the same but the subject is getting a specific skill that's new to the brain, the brain is still likely to change—it's just a different type of change. The ability to change the brain on purpose (i.e., with the cooperation of the subject) can happen because of *neuroplasticity*: the capacity that allows for region-specific changes. It's what occurs when the impact is narrow, such as that of playing the piano over time or being exposed to a localized head trauma. Neuroplasticity is a significant quality that allows for a change in the structure, topology, mapping, or function of the brain—but it can be a negative force, too. People who are consistently violent could literally train and design their brains for more violence. Unfortunately, the evidence suggests that the general capacity for neuroplasticity diminishes a bit with increasing age; fortunately, though, it remains present throughout life.

Enriching the Environment

When a sufficient number of positive factors are brought to bear, it is not unreasonable to speak of enriching the brain. Generally, with environmental enrichment, the changes are less specific to a spot in the brain (though the differences can certainly be located and quantified) and are more of a global experience. In a profound way, environmental enrichment is different from all other forms of experience. It has a far more global and quite widespread effect across the brain that can be summed up as follows:

> Enrichment is a biological response to a positive, contrasting environment in which measurable, global, and synergistic changes occur.

The term *enrichment classes* is commonly used, and people speak of *enriching experiences*. Such phrases tend to involve social, political, and educational definitions that may differ from the biological one I tend to use. But you cannot know if something is an enriching experience before the event itself. Enrichment comes about only as a result of a contrast; without a contrast from the prevailing environment, no enrichment can take place. Make your classroom and your school as big a contrast as you can from the students' daily experience. That's what will maximize brain development.

21

Curriculum in a Brain-Compatible Classroom

Low or No Threat
Prep for Final Performance
High Engagement
Positive Emotional Engagement
Learner Choice
Moderate to High Challenge
Strong Peer Support
Mastery Goals
Sufficient Nonlearning Time
Balancing Novelty and Predictability
Safe for Taking Risks
Moderate Stress
Alternating Low to High Energy
Multimodal Input
Frequent Feedback
Celebrate the Learning

Environment With the Brain in Mind

Strategies for Achieving a Brain-Based Environment
Acknowledgment of Value
Everyone Feels Cared For
Freedom of Expression
Encourage Affiliation
Accountability
Hope of Success
Orchestrated Common Experiences
Physically Safe Environment
Trust of Others
Consistency of Structure

What should be in a school's curriculum? First, we could say that any curriculum should be developmentally appropriate. Most schools are pretty good at seeing to this, although currently reading accountability is being pushed too early in many districts. While some kids are ready to read at age 4 or 5, there are just as many who are ready at 6, 7, or even 8 years old, making for an enormous number of newly diagnosed students with "reading disabilities" who simply need more time. In some cases, there are legitimate disabilities, so it's a tough call.

The second issue is relevancy. Different ages change the relevancy of what our brains want to learn. For example, kids who are 5–12 years old have no interest in credit cards, IRS tax forms, or face-lifts. Their brains are interested in learning new skills, making friends, developing motor skills, and building language skills. At the ages of 12–16, our brains are interested in peer approval, autonomy, mating, career education, and risk taking. At ages 16–25, our brains are most interested in problem solving, mating, prediction, and risk analysis.

You may also ask, "Where is the role of standards in the curriculum?" That's a completely legitimate and practical question. The answer is that it's an economic, ethical, and policy issue. It's not brain compatible to try to match up with the standards. One has to make the best compromises one can. A *brain-compatible approach* means that the curriculum, planning of content, classroom environment, and assessment should all have the brain in mind (see Figure 21.1). The first three items are discussed in this chapter; assessment with the brain in mind follows this chapter.

As an administrator, teacher, or trainer, however, you can experience some immediate success by integrating the practical and simple brain-based strategies presented in this book. A little success encourages more success. So just jump on the bike and start pedaling. Before you know it, you'll be riding like an expert without ever looking back. Remember, too, that no class is 100 percent brain based or 100 percent brain antagonistic. We are all "in process"—moving toward ever greater insights and better implementation.

Many different planning approaches have been suggested to teachers over the years as the "right" way to teach, but the difference between those and planning

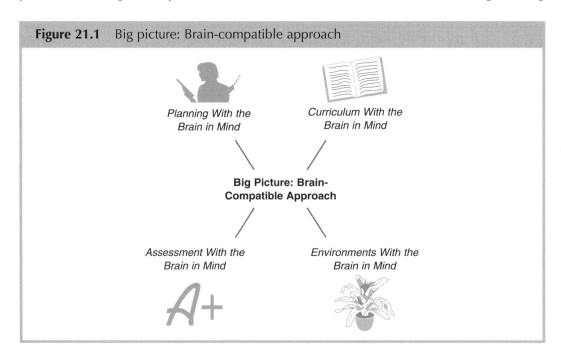

Figure 21.1 Big picture: Brain-compatible approach

Planning With the Brain in Mind

Curriculum With the Brain in Mind

Big Picture: Brain-Compatible Approach

Assessment With the Brain in Mind

Environments With the Brain in Mind

with the brain in mind is the underlying assumption involved. Whereas traditional lesson planning is based on "Plan what there is to teach, then teach it," the brain-based practitioner asks, "What is there to learn, and how can it best be learned?"

CURRICULUM WITH THE BRAIN IN MIND

Many ideas have been established thus far about the function, needs, priorities, and purpose of the brain, but how do we make the leap from brain-based teaching strategies to brain-based content? This chapter explores how what you teach is relevant to how the brain learns best.

No doubt many of the things you already do are good for the brain. And this is no coincidence. Remember, the brain's primary mission is to ensure our survival. Therefore, it is very good at seeking pleasure (e.g., food, social bonding, mating), avoiding pain (e.g., physical harm, embarrassment, negative judgments), and seeking novelty (e.g., finding interesting diversions). These natural tendencies provide the basis for a brain-based curriculum. Our job is to maintain a focus that is meaningful and relevant to the brain.

Brain-Compatible Curriculum

Given what we know about the brain—and its quest for curiosity, affiliation, challenge, and creature comforts—the curriculum elements in Figure 21.2 make a great deal of sense and embody the principles explored throughout this book.

Social Fluency

As human beings, we rely on and learn from each other. In fact, our very survival depends on our relationships with others. Therefore, ensuring that every learner develops the requisite set of social skills to interact productively in the

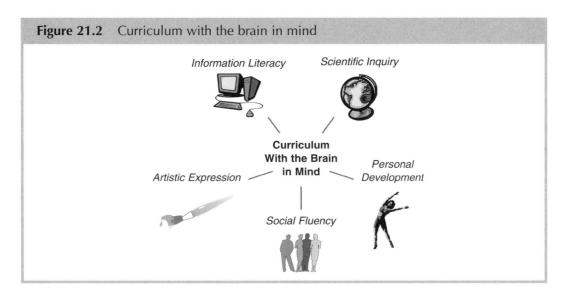

Figure 21.2 Curriculum with the brain in mind

Information Literacy

Scientific Inquiry

Curriculum With the Brain in Mind

Artistic Expression

Personal Development

Social Fluency

world is essential. Humans cannot grow up isolated and expect to succeed in society: The very word *society* implies a complex web of social interactions and rules that provide the basis for a community. What could be more important in the big picture than learning how to get along with others? This aspect of the curriculum ought to include the following subject areas:

Emotional Intelligence

  Identifying and labeling feelings
  Reading others' moods and feelings
  Managing your own moods and feelings
  Controlling impulses, delaying gratification
  Expressing feelings appropriately and productively
  Feeling compassion and empathy for others

Appreciating Diversity

  Accepting the differences of culture, race, religion, ethnicity, and lifestyle
  Exploring the injustice of intolerance
  Acknowledging types of differences
  Understanding the politics of differences and diversity

Language Skills

  Learning how to use the native language accurately and artfully
  Being able to express oneself in a complex social world
  Learning a nonnative language, developing awareness of other languages

Workplace Literacy

  The importance of livelihood
  Careers and jobs
  Bosses, colleagues, and subordinates; the workplace hierarchy
  Getting along in the work setting, problem solving, and conflict resolution

Religious/Spiritual Identities

  The role of religion and/or spirituality
  Similarities and differences among religions
  Religious freedom versus persecution

Appropriate Family Behaviors

  The purpose of family (as a unit of safety)
  Differences in family structures (biological, adoptive, divorced, and nontraditional)
  Functional versus dysfunctional
  A child's rights
  Effecting change in the family unit

Teamwork/Cooperation

    The importance of teamwork
    Group roles
    Competition versus cooperation, the need for both

Conflict Resolution

    The nature of conflict
    Approaches to resolving conflict
    Frames of reference
    Democracy/political action
    The history/role of government
    Types of government
    Approaches to impacting change in a democracy
    Voting

Personal Development

In Maslow's (1943) hierarchy of needs, self-actualization (or the ability to achieve one's goals) lies at the peak of the pyramid, and survival needs (food and shelter) are at the base of the pyramid. Developing the personal power or skills to maximize one's potential is a critical goal in a society that

> These skills ought to be addressed both explicitly and implicitly in an age-appropriate manner and purposefully integrated across the curriculum.

values innovation and achievement. In the past, an emphasis on personal-development skills was reserved for the elite, whose birthright ensured that their basic needs were met. Today, teaching the skills for personal success across the economic divide promises improved access and opportunity for all, regardless of social class. This aspect of the curriculum ought to address the following areas:

Stress Management

    The role of exercise, relaxation, imagery, sleep, and lifestyle choices

Physical Fitness

    Healthy body, healthy mind
    Kinds of fitness: stretching, strength training, aerobics
    Sports and activities
    Body image

Metacognition and Reflection

    Developing self-reflection skills and insight
    Positive inner dialogue
    Learning from mistakes

Recognizing strengths and weaknesses
Analytical skills (e.g., compare and contrast, pros and cons)

Sense of Meaning and Purpose

Self-acceptance, self-esteem, and self-confidence
Loves, passions, and hobbies
Goals and goal setting

Nutrition/Health/Eating Habits

The role of water, hydration awareness
The value of vitamins, minerals, and a good diet
The dangers of additives, growth hormones, herbicides, pesticides, excess fats,
sugars, carbohydrates, dieting, and drugs
Feeding your brain and body

Goal Setting and Achievement

Setting measurable goals and objectives
Decision making and follow through
Vigilance and persistence

Learning-to-Learn Skills

Memory strategies
Note-taking strategies
Study skills, test-preparation skills
Utilizing resources, incorporating feedback, and learning time management

Personal/Ethical Responsibility

What are ethics?
What is integrity?
Agreements, contracts, and dilemmas
Consequences, cause and effect, and risk analysis
Problem solving and whistle-blowing

Artistic Expression

All human beings have a basic need to express their thoughts and feelings,
and many people subsist on the fruits of their artistic/expressive talents (e.g.,
graphic artists, painters, sculptors, writers, architects, jewelers, product/fashion
designers, interior decorators, musicians, performers, actors, conductors, florists).
At the very least, learners need to be exposed to the various means of artistic
expression and, ideally, provided with formal instruction in some of them. This
aspect of the curriculum ought to include the following media:

Music

The history and role of music in society
Types of music

Active versus passive engagement
The parts of music
Singing, reading music, and choral arrangements
Types of instruments
Playing an instrument
Famous musicians

Writing/Storytelling

The role of writing in history
Journal reflection
Poetry
Fiction, nonfiction, and the different genres
Scriptwriting, songwriting, and speechwriting
Famous writers and poets

Dance

Forms of dance
Choreography
The integration of mind, body, and emotions
Famous dancers

Sculpture

Types of media
Role in history
Building, shaping, arranging, and model making
Famous sculptors

Theater

History of the theater
Types of plays and roles
Organizing a production
Famous playwrights, stage performers, and directors

Sports, Hobbies, and Crafts

Quality of life
The role of recreation
Types of activities and inherent risks
The role of physical challenge
Mastery as a means of expression
Hand–eye coordination, motor skills, and balance

Design

Types of designers
The role of aesthetics

The elements of design, form versus function
Computer-aided design, technological factors
Famous designers

Imaging

Types of images (e.g., painting, drawing, montage, photography, graphics)
The role of imagination
Famous artists

Information Literacy

Humans rely on accurate, accessible, and comprehensive information to survive. From newspapers, magazines, meeting minutes, and annual reports to radio, telephone, television, and computer communications, our lives revolve around giving and getting information. How do we access information? How do we process and manage it? This aspect of the curriculum ought to address the following skill areas:

Reading and Writing

The foundations of a modern education
The role of literature
Rules of grammar, syntax, and style
Types of communication
Writing formats
Steps in the writing process
Vocabulary and spelling
Following a set of directions

Hunting and Gathering Skills

Research methods
Priority and analysis skills
Internet search skills

Cognitive Manipulation

Extracting, analyzing, critiquing, sorting, grouping, generalizing, evaluating, synthesizing, presenting, and orchestrating information
Famous inventors, philosophers, thinkers, and strategists

Speaking/Presentation Skills

Reasoning, arguing, debating, persuading, marketing, and sharing information
Famous presenters, teachers, motivational speakers, and politicians

Digital/Technology Skills

Computer skills
Printing, reproduction, and transmission
The impact of innovation, rapid rate of change

Scientific Inquiry

The ability to rationalize and think makes humans unique in the animal kingdom. Asking questions, analyzing situations, conducting experiments, strategizing solutions, formulating plans of action, and interpreting results are basic steps in the scientific process. Whether it's figuring out how to fix a broken water faucet or planning a career, we all need to be good thinkers. The best thinkers understand the natural world and the elements, formulas, rules, and factors that influence it. This aspect of the curriculum ought to address the following areas:

Environmental Studies

Protecting our natural resources
The ecosystem (here and abroad)
Evaluating, problem solving, and political action
Responsible industry, responsible consumerism

Future/Global Studies

Global change, conflict, and relationships
Potential scenarios, problems, and solutions
Planning for the future, the costs of progress
The impact of new scientific discoveries
Astronomy, our solar system, and outer space

Physics/Biology/Chemistry

The nature of reality
The underpinnings of the universe
The elements of science
Famous scientists

Mathematics

Numbers as a universal language
Types of mathematics
A vehicle for problem solving
Business and practical math applications
Rules and formulas
Famous mathematicians

Suggestions for Grades K Through 5

- reduced computer use to a minimum (too early, too much opportunity cost)
- increased language exposure (a great time for learning a second language!)
- mandatory music and arts training (three times a week, 50–60 minutes per session to build strong neural networks for later math and science skills)
- mandatory physical education (30+ minutes per day)
- emphasis on emotional intelligence skills (begin it early, and keep it going)
- increased health education (nutrition, drug/substance awareness, antiviolence training)
- emphasis on learning-to-learn skills, how to utilize information resources versus traditional content and rote memorization

---

Suggestions for Grades 6 Through 12+

- strong emphasis on learning-to-learn skills and lifelong learning
- emphasis on social skills, cooperative learning, teamwork, and interpersonal relations
- exposure to computers; multiple functions and research potential
- deep exploration of a few subjects, rather than surveying a great number
- emphasis on life skills (e.g., financial planning, bookkeeping, career planning, mental health, physical health, recreation, conflict resolution, interpersonal relationships, decision making)
- reduced emphasis on rote learning, semantic learning, and superfluous content

---

 **What This Means to You**

While it's true that teachers aren't at liberty to teach only what they want to teach, it's also true that we have an ethical, moral, and professional responsibility to ensure that every student receives the benefit of our life experience and professional judgment about what learners need to know in order to flourish in the twenty-first century. We are important in the process; if we weren't, we could just teach via television—a proposition that would surely be brain antagonistic. As conductors of the orchestra, we must be fully present and accountable for our learners' performance. Be prepared to meet some resistance as you introduce your modifications to the curriculum. Part of being a brain-based practitioner is acting as an advocate for change. As with anything that requires people to reexamine themselves, pushing for a more brain-friendly curriculum will cause some people to get defensive, territorial, and even aggressive. As you would tell your students: do the best you can, and that is progress enough. Before you know it, you'll be the expert everyone wants to emulate.

PLANNING WITH THE BRAIN IN MIND

What at first may be perceived as a backwards approach to planning is really not. Brain-based learning starts with the learner, not the content. The lesson is based on creating optimal conditions for natural learning. Contrary to traditional belief, we rarely learn in a sequential format (e.g., introduce Unit A, learn it, test students on it, then go to Unit B). We learn best by immersion, by jumping into the fray and then thinking our way out of it. In brain-based learning, we get our feet wet in Unit K, then find solutions in Units A, D, and G. This is real life. Rather than proceeding in a straight line, we move ahead, back, and around like a spiral. That is the brain's natural tendency. This is not to say that planning or structure is not necessary. In fact, planning is more important today than ever because there is more to learn. Rather, the issue is reprioritizing our values as we learn to plan in a way that is natural to the brain.

Immersion-Style, Multipath Learning

The brain simultaneously operates on many levels of consciousness, processing all at once a world of colors, movements, emotions, shapes, smells, sounds, tastes, feelings, and more. It is so efficient at processing information that nothing else in the world comes close to matching human learning potential. Knowing this, you may perhaps find it easier to conceive how this amazing multiprocessor that is the human brain is undernourished, if not starved, in the typical classroom. Many educators unknowingly inhibit the brain's learning ability by teaching in an ultralinear, structured, and predictable fashion.

Even though it seems that we think sequentially—one thought after another—this illusion is far from the reality of the brain's true operating system. Biologically, physically, intellectually, and emotionally, we are doing many things at once. In fact, the brain can't do less than multiprocess. It is constantly registering perceptions (over 36,000 visual cues per hour), monitoring our vital signs (e.g., heart, hormone levels, breathing, digestion), and updating our reality (matching new learning with representations from the past). In addition, the brain is attaching emotions to each event and thought, forming patterns of meaning to construct the larger picture and inferring conclusions about the information acquired.

Many educators have applied the left- and right-brain learning model in their classrooms to help them understand their students' individual learning styles. As long as we keep in mind that this division is not cut and dry, it

> Lockstep, assembly-line learning violates a critical finding about the human brain: each brain is not only unique, it is expanding at its own pace.

can help us plan more inclusive and global lesson plans. In short, we are using both sides of the brain most of the time. In fact, it's impossible to shut them off. Even when we come up with the appropriate answer to a question, the brain continues to process alternative responses and explanations nonconsciously. It literally practices thinking while we aren't even aware of it! So much of the brain's work occurs outside our conscious awareness.

Some scientists say that there is very little learning that the brain does best in an orderly, sequential fashion. The brain uses parallel-processing methods in rapid, serial, visual presentation tasks (Dosher, Han, & Lu, 2004). What this means for learning is that we understand complex topics better when we experience them with rich sensory input, as opposed to merely reading or hearing about them. For example, consider how you learned about the city you live in. Did you learn about it from a guidebook? Or did you learn about it from walking its streets, visiting its attractions, tasting its foods, experiencing its traditions, and interacting with its people?

As children we learned about our neighborhoods from scattered, random input that was messy at times and left room for exploration and manipulation. In fact, most of what we learned as children was imprinted in our memory in this chaotic sort of way. We certainly didn't get lessons from a how-to book on crawling or talking—acts that require complex sequences of precise movements. We figured it out by trial and error. The brain is concerned primarily with survival, not formal instruction. In other words, the brain will concentrate on instruction only if it is perceived as meaningful and only if the brain's primary survival needs have been satisfied. For many students, traditional teaching approaches ignore their individual life circumstances and, therefore, the needs of their brains.

It's easy to formulate a hypothesis about why over 30 percent of the African Americans and nearly 50 percent of Hispanics fail to graduate from high school. To get answers, we could look to the 81,000 students from Indiana University's High School Survey of Student Engagement (HSSSE). The survey was administered in 110 high schools, ranging in size from 37 students to nearly 4,000, across 26 states. It shows that two out of three students are bored in class every day, while 17 percent say they are bored in every class. Yet when kids are in classes that they feel are relevant to either college or a job, attendance and engagement go up. It's not rocket science; simple understanding of our brain says that relevant course work will trump boring course work any day.

The old way of teaching was to take a subject like math, science, or history and divide it into smaller chunks called units, then subdivide the units into weekly and daily lesson plans, and then present microchunks of the whole in a linear fashion. It sounds logical, but it isn't the way our brains learn best.

Imagine yourself as a three- or four-year-old child and you've just received your first bicycle for your birthday. You're excited and want nothing more than to jump on it and go! But wait . . . you can't. Your parents have decided that you should learn to ride your bicycle in the "proper" way first. Replicating the traditional approach used in schools, they insist on teaching you how to ride your bike with the following progression:

Unit A: Safety

Personal safety
Hand signals
Wearing a helmet
Defensive attitude
Neighborhood safety
Possible hazards
Crosswalks
Laws, customs, and rules

Unit B: Bicycle Logistics

History of the bicycle
Types of bikes
Product specifications
Parts of the bike
Tire repair
Costs

Unit C: The Skills of Riding

Proper mount and dismount
Proper use of training wheels
Body positioning
Advanced riding skills

Unit D: Everyday Use

Bicycle storage
Permission
Maintenance

Naturally, before your parents have even completed Unit A, you've lost interest and gone on to do something else. The brain is far more capable than we usually give it credit for. Your natural urge to jump on the bike and try to ride it is really more compatible with the brain. You've already watched others learn to ride, so you ask a few questions, garner support, and get on. Low and behold, after a few falls and fumbles, you learn to ride your bike quite easily.

If you think about it, the way a child generally learns to ride a bike is how you learned some of the most complex things in your life—your native language, for example. Did you study the rules of grammar before you began speaking? Did you take classes in speaking? Were you tested on it? Of course not. Although you received plenty of informal feedback, you weren't taught your native language. Rather, you picked it up.

> The brain learns best in real-life, immersion-style, multipath learning. Fragmented, piecemeal teaching can forever kill the joy and love of learning.

Is it possible that our brain can pick up other subjects as well? Is it possible to learn science, history, accounting, geography, math, life skills, literature, and the arts by default? Of course it is! This, in fact, is how our brains are designed to learn—multipath, in and out of order, on many levels, from a variety of feedback sources, and in various contexts. We learn best with complex learning: moving from chaos to clarity, following our natural passions and interests, exploring issues, focusing on key points, and with a trial-and-error approach. As teachers, we need to plan learning with this in mind. Within the structure of your curriculum, provide flexibility.

> Complex learning is a process that better reflects the way the human brain is naturally designed to learn.

The underlying premise is that our world is an integrated whole and that one of the greatest gifts we can offer our students is a bridge from classroom education to the real world. A brain-based approach to planning urges you to follow the threads woven through the fabric of your students' world. Use textbooks only as supplemental materials. In this fast-moving information age, students need to learn how to rely on multiple sources of information. Include magazines, computers, videos, television, journals, and field trips in your lesson planning.

Brain-Based Planning Strategies

Brain-based lesson planning does not follow a template—mainly because the basic premise of brain-based learning is that every brain is unique, so a one-size-fits-all approach does not work. Learning different things requires different approaches for different people, depending on variables such as prior learning, experience, preferred modalities, and the type of skill being taught. Thus, a toolbox rather than a template is the basis for brain-based lesson planning.

There is a wide range of tools that help encourage the brain to absorb, process, and store experiences and information meaningfully. The following general strategies reflect a brain-based approach to lesson planning. They are followed by a more detailed sequence of guidelines that reflect the seven stages of learning.

 **What This Means to You**

- Pre-expose learners to new material in advance. The more background they have, the greater number of connections they'll make.
- Discover your students' background in the subject, and customize your planning to their experience level and preferred learning style.
- Create a supportive, challenging, complex, no-threat classroom environment in which questions and exploration are encouraged.
- Ensure that your materials and presentation strategies are age appropriate.
- Acquisition happens both formally and informally; provide learning experiences that reflect real life.
- Always plan for elaboration. Presenting is not learning; students must process the learning before they own it.
- Help learners encode learning in their memory with appropriate use of downtime, emotions, real-life associations, and mnemonic techniques.
- Functional integration happens only over time and with repeated reviews.

The Seven Stages of Brain-Based Planning

The following strategies are organized in a sequence that makes sense to the brain. The list is by no means exhaustive: you'll be able to add many more to it based on the demographics of your particular learners. After you've prepared your lesson plans, use the outline as a checklist to ensure that you've planned activities that satisfy the goals of each learning stage:

Stage 1: Pre-exposure. This stage provides the brain with an overview of the new learning before really digging in. Pre-exposure helps the brain develop better conceptual maps.

- Post an overview of the new topic on the bulletin board. Mind maps work great for this.
- Teach learning-to-learn skills and memory strategies.
- Encourage good brain nutrition, including drinking plenty of water.
- Model and practice coping, self-esteem, and life skills.
- Create a strong immersion learning environment. Make it interesting!
- Consider time-of-day brain cycles and rhythms when planning morning and afternoon activities.
- Discover students' interests and background; start where they are in their knowledge base, not where you think they are.
- Have learners set their own goals, and discuss class goals for each unit.
- Post many colorful peripherals, including positive affirmations.
- Plan brain "wake-ups" (e.g., cross-laterals, relax-stretching) every hour.
- Plan activities during which students can move around and choose from a menu of offerings.
- State strong positive expectations, and allow learners to voice theirs, too.
- Build strong positive rapport with learners.
- Read your students' learning states, and make any adjustments as you proceed through the lessons.

Stage 2: Preparation. This is the stage at which you create curiosity or excitement. It's similar to the "anticipatory set" but goes further in preparing the learner.

- Create a "you are there" experience; give learners a real-world grounding.
- Provide the context for learning the topic (can be a repeat of the overview; the classic "big picture").
- Elicit from learners what possible value and relevance the topic has to them personally. They must feel connected to the learning before they'll internalize it. Encourage them to express how they feel it is or is not relevant. The brain learns particularly well from concrete experiences first.
- Provide something real, physical, or concrete. Conduct an experiment, go on a field trip, or invite a guest speaker who is professionally involved with the topic.

- Create complex interdisciplinary tie-ins to the session.
- Provide a "hook," a surprise, or a bit of novelty to engage learners' emotions.

Stage 3: Initiation and Acquisition. This stage provides the immersion. Flood with content! Instead of the singular, lockstep, sequential, one-bite-at-a-time presentation, provide an initial virtual overload of ideas, details, complexity, and meanings. Allow learners to feel temporarily overwhelmed. This will be followed by anticipation, curiosity, and a determination to discover meaning for oneself. Over time, it all gets sorted out brilliantly by the learners. If that sounds like the real world of learning, outside the classroom, you're right: it is.

- Provide concrete learning experiences (e.g., case study, experiment, field trip, interview, hands-on learning).
- Provide activities that employ a majority (if not all) of the multiple intelligences.
- Offer a group or team project that encompasses building, finding, exploring, or designing.
- Attend the theater, put on a skit, produce a commercial, or create a class/school newspaper.
- Provide enough choice that learners have the opportunity to explore the subject using their preferred learning modality: visual, auditory, kinesthetic, and so on.
- A well-designed computer program can be helpful at this stage.

Stage 4: Elaboration. This is the processing stage; it requires genuine thinking on the part of the learners. This is the time to make intellectual sense of the learning.

- Provide an open-ended debriefing of the previous activity.
- Tie things together so that learning across disciplines occurs (e.g., read a science fiction story about outer space while studying the solar system, discuss how literature relates to science).
- Have learners design an evaluation procedure or rubric for their own learning (e.g., write test questions, facilitate peer reviews, design mind maps).
- Have learners explore the topic online or at the library.
- Watch a video, view slides, or see a theatrical production on the topic.
- Stimulate small-group discussions, and have groups report back to the entire class.
- Create individual and/or group mind maps reflecting the new material.
- Hold a school forum, debate, essay contest, or panel discussion.
- Hold a question-and-answer period.
- Have students do the teaching (e.g., in small groups, as class presenters, in pairs).

Stage 5: Incubation and Memory Encoding. This stage emphasizes the importance of downtime and review time. The brain learns most effectively over time, not all at once.

- Provide time for unguided reflection—downtime.
- Have learners keep a journal of their learning.
- Have learners take a walk in pairs to discuss the topic.
- Provide stretching and relaxation exercises.
- Provide a music-listening area.
- Ask learners to discuss new learning with their family and friends.

Stage 6: Verification and Confidence Check. This stage is not just for the benefit of the teacher; learners need to confirm their learning for themselves as well. Learning is best remembered when students possess a model or a metaphor regarding the new concepts or materials.

- Have learners present their learning to others.
- Ask students to interview and evaluate each other.
- Encourage students to write about what they've learned (e.g., journal, essay, news article, report).
- Have students demonstrate learning with a project (e.g., working model, mind map, video, newsletter).
- Let students present a role-play, a skit, or a theatrical performance.
- Quiz students (verbally and/or in writing).

Stage 7: Celebration and Integration. At this point, it is critical to engage emotions. Make it fun, light, and joyful. This stage instills the all-important love of learning. Never miss it!

- Have a class toast (with juice).
- Provide sharing time (e.g., peer sharing, demonstration, acknowledgments).
- Play music, hang streamers, and blow horns.
- Invite another class, parents, the principal, or community guests in to view projects.
- Facilitate a class-designed and -produced celebration party.
- Incorporate the new learning in future lessons. Never introduce something and then drop it. If it's not important enough to refer to in the future, don't waste time on it to begin with.

 **What This Means to You**

As we plan learning with the brain in mind, is critical to ask a different set of questions. Rather than ask "What should I teach?" ask "How will students best learn?" As you plan the learning, keep the focus on the basic principles that support the brain's natural learning tendencies. Follow through from pre-exposure to celebration, making sure that none of the stages in between are skipped. Learning happens over time. Create a complex, integrated, interdisciplinary curriculum that provides for plenty of learner choice. Provide structure, but in an environment that respects each learner's unique nature, needs, and experiences.

Integrating Brain-Based Learning in the Classroom

A good way to work with these guidelines is to write each concept on an index card and then list some of the specific, practical strategies you can do to make it happen. Consider introducing one new concept a week; then be rigorous in your implementation. Remember, you'll still be integrating the concepts from the previous weeks, too; but after a while, your new approach will be automatic.

Pre-Exposure and Priming

Make sure that learners are pre-exposed to the content and context of the new topic at least one week in advance of starting it. This helps establish some background and relevance in the subject and expedites future learning. Post a summary or mind map of the proceeding unit on the bulletin board a couple weeks prior to starting it. Instead of calling students' attention to it, let them notice and ask you about it.

Sufficient Time for Learning

Time is an essential ingredient and is always a factor in the learning equation. The urge to cover more and more content often results in incomplete learning. Provide sufficient time for learning to begin with. Make sure you plan time for review and reflection as well. These are requirements for authentic learning.

Low or No Threat

Interact daily with each learner. Provide frequent, nonjudgmental feedback. Be sure to activate prior learning so that learners draw connections between new subjects and past learning. Manage states without making threats; redirect learners as the need arises. Remember, it's not what you teach, but how they best learn. Keep the focus on learning.

Prep for Final Performance

If you expect learners to take a test to demonstrate their learning, it is your responsibility to prepare them for success on it. We are doing a disservice to learners if they are set up to fail. Every time a student fails or experiences a poor performance, we are reinforcing that self-image. Ensure that learners rehearse for their final performance and that their preparation includes a stress condition similar to that which they'll likely experience at test time. Do not give pop (or surprise) quizzes. Rather, provide ungraded pretests so that learners can discover their strengths and weaknesses before their test scores are final.

High Engagement

Make this statement your mantra: "Involve, don't tell." Get students on the bicycle rather than telling them how to ride it. The bulk of your lesson planning activities ought to engage learners physically and socially so that they are continually interacting and taking action.

Positive Emotional Engagement

Teach learners to manage their own learning states. How students feel is critical to the decision to learn, the quality of learning, and the ability to recall the learning. Reduce negative states by changing activities frequently, providing choice, attending to physical needs (e.g., moving, stretching, providing drinking water, downtime), and keeping the stakes and challenge level high. Be supportive, and provide frequent opportunities for feedback.

Learner Choice

There is a fine line between too little and too much choice, and the balance is related to various factors such as trust, rapport, and past experiences. When you provide a brain-friendly learning environment, learners feel empowered. When they feel empowered, it isn't necessary for them to have a choice in everything because they will trust that you have their best interest at heart. The key element here is perception: if learners perceive that they have power in the relationship, they will demand less of it. We all need to feel that we have some control over our destiny, whether we're 5 or 50 years old.

Moderate to High Challenge

Create enough challenge that what you are asking students to do is worth doing. Any activity can be made more challenging by adjusting any of the following factors: (1) time (increase or decrease the amount of time you give for an activity), (2) standards (raise or lower the final product standards), (3) resources (increase or decrease the availability of resources for doing the task), and (4) circumstances (learners have to do the task silently, or by themselves, or in the dark, or with three partners, or for public performance).

Strong Peer Support

Students will be willing to take on more challenge if they know they can count on peer support. Encouraging positive peer affiliation is an ongoing process that is supported by frequent group assignments and team efforts. Use formal and informal groupings, use frequent pairs activities, encourage socializing at appropriate times, and emphasize cooperative learning. Assist learners in setting up outside study groups and/or paired homework assignments. The old model of learners competing against each other for the best grades ought to be replaced with learners helping each other achieve the best learning results for the greatest number of people.

Mastery Goals

Students, for the most part, do what is expected of them. Set high standards, provide benchmarks, and acknowledge learners for reaching them. Share and post your goals for the class as well as learner goals.

Sufficient Nonlearning Time

The brain is not good at nonstop learning. In fact, not learning is necessary for the brain to process and transfer learning from short- to long-term memory. So make sure your students have sufficient reflection time. Downtime can take the form of journal time, recess, break time, listening to music, lunchtime, or activities such as a walk with a partner.

Balancing Novelty and Predictability

The optimal learning environment provides a balance of novelty/surprise and predictability/ritual. Constant novelty is too stressful for students, while constant predictability is too boring. Too much of one or the other usually results in behavior problems. The best balance is high amounts of both novelty and predictability.

Safe for Taking Risks

Ensure that the culture in your classroom is one that supports emotional safety. Adopt a zero-tolerance policy for teasing, humiliation, put-downs, or name calling. Get learner buy-in by discussing the need for a safe learning environment. Ask learners how it feels to be humiliated or laughed at. Conduct role-plays emphasizing appropriate responses when someone puts another person down. And ask the class to determine what the consequences ought to be for breaking a ground rule. Post a sign to remind learners of their agreements. Always model appropriate responses for such things as incorrect answers: "Good try, Michael; you're using your brain. Do you want to give it another shot? Would someone else like to give it a shot?"

Moderate Stress

A little stress is good; too much is bad. Again, it is the balance that is important here. Stress levels influence learner states. Monitor the tension in your class, and manage it accordingly. If it's too high, it's time for humor, movement, games, or quiet time; if it's too low, it's time to raise the stakes or challenge level.

Alternating Low to High Energy

As mentioned earlier in this book, circadian rhythms are a biological mechanism that moves our energy from low to high and back again along a regular timeline. This roller coaster of energy levels is easier to deal with when you recognize it as a natural aspect of our lives. We are influenced by hourly, daily, weekly, monthly, and seasonal cycles. Acknowledge the influence that these cycles have on learners, and work to accommodate their natural ups and downs. This is another reason that providing choice is so important.

Multimodal Input

Engage as many modalities as possible by providing learners with options and choices. Ensure that learning activities offer auditory, visual, and kinesthetic components. Provide visual aids, guest speakers, partner learning, cross-age tutoring, independent time, computer assistance, audiobooks, and field trips. Remember the importance of the three Vs and the three Cs: variety, variety, variety, and choice, choice, choice!

Frequent Feedback

All of the previous goals are supported by frequent feedback. Ensure that every student gets some kind of feedback every 30 minutes or so each school day. This does not mean you personally have to provide that feedback. Rather, set up mechanisms whereby learners receive feedback from their peers, teaching assistants, and self-reviews, as well as feedback based on grades and your own verbal feedback.

Celebrate the Learning

It's easy after all these demands on your time to forget to celebrate the learning, but this is a critical step for optimal learning. Like the athletic team that celebrates its hard work after each win, learners need to feel acknowledged for their efforts. Celebration also adds an element of fun to the process and engages learners' emotions. From something as casual as a simple high-five to a more elaborate student-planned party, be sure to close each learning session with some kind of a celebration or acknowledgment.

ENVIRONMENT WITH THE BRAIN IN MIND

Strategies for Achieving a Brain-Based Environment

None of us work in a vacuum, and the more we address the whole, the more easily the parts will fall into place. Once you've created a brain-based environment, it's time to seek support from the larger community: the school. A classroom that is the only learning oasis on campus will soon find that it is in jeopardy of being sabotaged. Support on the macro level forms the foundation for long-term success on the micro level, so seek assistance from the larger learning community in achieving the following goals.

Acknowledgment of Value

Ensure that everyone feels a sense of communal contribution. This allows everyone to feel adequate and fulfilled. Daily affirmations, notes of appreciation, and occasional celebrations go a long way toward acknowledging the efforts of everyone in the learning community.

Everyone Feels Cared For

Make sure that no one falls through the cracks. Everyone should be in a peer group, on a committee, or involved in some way with a supportive crew.

Freedom of Expression

Make sure that everyone has a creative voice in the community. It may be volunteering for a local nonprofit, impacting change as a community activist, playing in the marching band, or being on the chess team. For some, it's simply being able to raise their hand in class, get called on, and share their feelings without the fear of humiliation.

Encourage Affiliation

Encourage healthy levels of affiliation among students, parents, teachers, and committee members. Provide many group learning experiences, team efforts, and a variety of bonding activities.

Accountability

We feel accountable when the rules, policies, and norms of the groups at large are consistently enforced by common regulation. As soon as this consistency is broken, we feel we can act with impunity and the system begins to break down.

Hope of Success

Everyone absolutely must feel as if there is hope in his or her efforts. Hope is defined differently by each of us, but the bottom line is that hope is about bettering the situation. Hope may come in the form of potential scholarships, an opportunity to make up a test due to illness, or progress toward higher test scores. Hope is best achieved by progression toward a goal.

Orchestrated Common Experiences

Look for ways to develop common ground on a schoolwide and community-wide basis. Some ideas include assemblies, sporting events, and celebrations.

Physically Safe Environment

Make physical safety a top priority. Do not tolerate bullying, threats, or fighting. Encourage learners to "use their words" and communicate verbally rather than physically. Also eliminate social and emotional distress by making it a safe environment in which learners can make mistakes without embarrassment.

Trust of Others

Trust comes from both the frequency of contact and the predictability of another's behavior. We all want to know that we are safe to express ourselves and that we will be treated fairly and with respect. Practice providing this in all relationships, with students, parents, other teachers, administrators, and the larger world.

Consistency of Structure

A community has to have more than a set of rules, guidelines, and values; it must also have predictable rituals and traditions in which everyone participates. For example, birthdays, holidays, openings, closings, and open houses are all opportunities to strengthen community support.

22

Assessment With the Brain in Mind

Even though the dictionary definition of *learning* is quite simple—to gain knowledge, understanding, or skill by study or experience—when we attempt to measure learning, the complexity of the definition emerges. Even neuroscientists have a tough time agreeing on what constitutes learning. For example, Sally may provide the correct answer to a mathematics equation, but does she understand the underlying rules and formulas, does she recognize the broader context and meaning of the problem, and does she have the ability to apply what she's learned to real-life problem solving? The traditional evaluation of a student's learning disregards these questions altogether. It merely asks, "Did the student get the right answer?"

Why is learning difficult to measure? There are many reasons. First, learning is contextual. We often learn and recall differently or better in one environment than another. Second, learning is temporal. There's a time lag to some learning, and other learning shows up instantly. Third, learning is embedded in diverse and multiple pathways. Some is associative, some is location based, and some is emotional. We can learn symbolically, through our hands or bodies, and we can learn by generalizing. In short, only a small percentage of what we learn is the typical overt text lesson in class. Even a first-year teacher will tell you (rightfully so) that most of what kids learn is not in the lesson plan. Knowing this, what can we do? This chapter highlights some of the brain-based pathways to better assessments.

ASSESSMENT STYLES NOT WORKING

Just because Sammy doesn't demonstrate good reading skills in class doesn't necessarily mean he's a poor reader. When we delve deeper into his learning process, we may discover that in spite of his weak public performance, he reads faster and with better retention than 90 percent of his peers. There could be a number of explanations for this. For example, it is quite possible that Sammy's verbal skills are just on the slower end of the normal development continuum; boys generally develop their verbal skills later than girls. Or Sammy may be underchallenged. Or perhaps the material he's been given lacks meaning for him. Or maybe he's afraid of being ridiculed, judged harshly, or punished for making a mistake. Has anyone bothered to make these determinations?

Unfortunately, we misdiagnose learners often. That's why Sammy is now grouped with the "slower" readers. It won't be long before he perceives himself as a poor reader and associates reading with negative emotions. The worst thing is that the consequences of the superficial assessment are likely long term, if not permanent—all because we missed what was really going on in Sammy's normal development. *Normal development* is a key concept here because most teachers accept the artificial standards erroneously identified as appropriate for each grade level, when, in fact, normal development in children fluctuates by three years. This means that as second graders, Sally may be three years ahead of Sammy in verbal proficiency, and this is perfectly normal.

Mistakes in the Evaluation Process

We have some challenges to overcome in the evaluation process. Formal assessment often ignores the following key brain principles regarding learning and memory:

- Learning takes many forms that are not usually assessed (e.g., spatial, temporal, episodic, procedural).
- Memory is highly state and context dependent. The location of a test may not be where it was learned or where the student will need to know the learning.
- Much of our explicit semantic learning requires tremendous repetition and meaning making to embed for long term retention. On top of that, most explicit learning is at risk for becoming outdated.
- Nutrition and stress make scoring highly variable.
- The brain learns by making mistakes, not memorizing right answers.

On the final point, we could say that neural networks are developed through trial and error: the more experimentation and feedback, the better the quality of the neural networks. Smarter humans don't always get the answers first, and they don't always get them right. But they do eliminate wrong answers better than their peers. And this ability to avoid "bad" choices is developed through trial and error. It isn't developed by someone else telling us the right answer and then having us repeat it back to them. This type of rote learning may produce high scores on a standardized test, but it does not produce high-level thinking. Following are some of the most common mistakes we make in the evaluation process:

Mistake #1: Pushing for Higher Standards Without the Necessary Resources

The new trend toward setting school standards higher is a misguided ploy that will backfire at the expense of children's lives. Because when you raise the bar and tighten the consequences without providing the resources to accomplish the task, we all fail. The more we experience failure, the more vicious the cycle becomes. The result may be short-term improvements in test scores, but what suffer are authentic learning and assessment. Everyone rebels against high-stakes pressure that smacks of control. It's like saying to teachers, "You'll teach them or else. . . ." while saying to learners, "You'll learn or else. . . ." This is the opposite of a threat-free, brain-based learning environment.

There's no doubt that accountability is important, and there are ways to achieve greater accountability without employing draconian measures that reduce teachers to technicians. Already more than half of all new teachers leave the profession within seven years of entering it. Everyone who goes into teaching knows it's not a high-paying job, so the money isn't the issue. The issue is the frustration involved and the lack of rewards and support. When any of us are pressured to perform, we experience stress; the greater the stress, the more learning suffers.

Rather than holding the front lines more responsible for fighting the escalating battle, the "generals" need to take more responsibility and use more strategic means for winning the war. This means investing for the long term rather than gambling with students' (and teachers') lives and self-esteem for short-term results.

With more and more inclusion classes, teachers are seeing greater numbers of kids with special needs, and most teachers lack the training to deal with them. For starters, consider how many of the common problems in the following list you have been trained to identify and act on. Do you know the symptoms of these conditions? Do you know what to do once you identify a potential problem? Do you know which cases should be referred out? Don't feel bad if the answer is no. The fact is, most teachers don't; yet between 25 and 40 percent of all students today face challenges related to one or more of these special needs:

- abuse and/or neglect (e.g., physical/sexual/emotional, sleep deprivation, learned helplessness, fear, high stress)
- mental disorders (e.g., antisocial disorder, anxiety disorder, attachment disorder, depression, posttraumatic stress disorder, obsessive compulsive disorder, bipolar, borderline personality disorder, eating disorders, schizophrenia, oppositional defiant disorder)
- learning disorders (e.g., attention deficit hyperactivity disorder, auditory processing deficits, reading deficits, dyslexia)
- physical disabilities (e.g., mild autism, brain injury, epilepsy, diabetes, fetal alcohol syndrome, motor skill deficits, seizures, Tourette's syndrome)
- substance dependency (e.g., drugs and/or alcohol, food, cigarettes, caffeine)
- cultural issues (e.g., refugee status, language deficits, values differences, high stress)
- poverty issues (e.g., nutritional deficits, learned helplessness, high stress, peer/social ridicule)

Teachers are expected to ensure that all learners meet the new standards, but where are the increased training programs to support their efforts? Ideally, districts should provide more comprehensive inservice programs to help meet the increased demand on teachers, but even this will not provide an overnight solution. The overall impact of raising standards without increasing the stability of the infrastructure is higher stress, lower morale, and greater teacher turnover. Is this what our teachers, kids, and schools need?

Mistake #2: Lockstep Testing Ignores Brain Development

Cognitive psychologists have established a pretty good idea of how and when the brain develops in childhood, but the fact is that determining what is critical for children to learn at each grade level is not a precise science. Although certain learning tasks (e.g., reading in first grade) make good general sense, it is quite another thing to mandate that all first graders exhibit a particular reading level or face remedial measures. This pressure-cooker formula reflects the outdated demand model of learning. It implies that if your learners don't demonstrate the prescribed benchmarks by the assigned time, you are not doing your job right. However, it fails to acknowledge that brains develop differently and some are not ready for reading in first grade.

What one student is doing academically does not necessarily relate to another student. Their backgrounds may be a world apart. The bell curve may have served learners at one time, but in the diverse culture we live in today, the bell curve does not reflect reality. The only thing that really matters is how students are doing compared to their previous performance. When we recognize the wide variation in human development, we begin to see how the faulty assumptions of the old assessment model hinder learning.

> Comparing one student to another is one of the most irrelevant and damaging assessment strategies ever devised.

Mistake #3: Short-Term Testing Ignores How the Brain Learns

The first problem related to this mistake is that authentic learning takes time. Research has clearly demonstrated that giving a test only once per year is a poor way to assess student functioning. Salthouse (2007) administered 16 common cognitive and neuropsychological tests and found that the variation between someone's scores on the same test given three times over two weeks was as big as the variation between the scores of people in different age groups. It's as if, on the same test, someone acted like a 20-year-old on a Monday, a 45-year-old the following Friday, and a 32-year-old the following Wednesday. This major inconsistency raises questions about the worth of single, one-time test scores and suggests that repeating the tests within a month gives a more accurate range of scores. The likelihood is that no administrators would allow for that kind of change in testing since many complain that testing already takes up too much time.

The second problem is that most of what's important is not being measured. We've all witnessed students who vehemently resist new ideas or face learning challenges, only to see them emerge years later more well rounded and successful in life than the straight-A students. And we've all witnessed the straight-A students—those who met grade expectations, filled in all the boxes correctly, and got good marks—not succeed in the real world. To use a metaphor, consider this: if you keep pulling up your newly planted fruit tree to see how it is doing, you will damage its root system, and you won't learn anything about its long-term health. Testing students before they are ready creates frustration, disillusionment, and a distrust of the system. Learning takes time to germinate; provide fertilizer and water, tend to the earth around it, but keep in mind that rushing its maturity won't make it grow any faster.

> Biologically, the best, most valuable, and deepest learning does not produce any tangible results for a considerable time.

Mistake #4: Most Testing Ignores Building-Block Learning

Some subjects prepare learners for later learning. These so-called prep subjects may be important, but they are difficult to measure. For example, research has suggested that early music exposure helps learners develop subsequent math and science skills. Does this mean that we should grade learners on their mastery of a musical instrument? Or does it mean that we ought to expose learners to classical music? How should we assess the learning of music, or should we?

When we compare music with physical education, we see a similar dilemma. How should we grade learners who may not exhibit great athletic prowess but who run around and participate as best they can? Are these students not building spatial, counting, and problem-solving skills; strengthening their cardiovascular systems; lowering their stress levels; building social skills; receiving settling benefits; and experiencing a low-threat learning environment for trial-and-error learning in spite of their lack of athletic talent? Music and physical education are two examples of curriculum activities that are important to subsequent learning yet problematic to assess.

Mistake #5: Most Testing Ignores Real-World Applications

Certainly it is possible to measure whether students have memorized something or are able to summarize a topic, but does this reflect what we want to teach? In a competitive global society, will learners be best served by such ability? Or will there be a greater advantage in having high-level thinking and conceptual-analysis skills; knowing how to work in a team environment; being highly motivated to achieve; and/or being able to solve problems through model building, research, systems analysis, and good communication skills?

We waste huge amounts of student and teacher time by filling up brains with trivia that will not be remembered one year later. National and state assessment designers were sold a bill of goods; they bought into the "cultural literacy" ideology that insists a graduate should have memorized a heap of facts. But content-based knowledge is always accessible to anyone who has a computer, a television, a phone, a fax machine, or even a library card. Asking learners to memorize an increasingly larger body of facts to be replayed at test time is ludicrous, irrelevant, and ultimately a poor use of valuable class time.

We need to do fewer things, but do them better. We ought to focus on developing positive learners who exhibit critical thinking ability, basic skills proficiency, a love of learning, and the capability to work with others in a cooperative manner. To achieve these goals, we need to reduce (not increase) the content we test on and update our evaluation criteria. Even with today's so called high standards, many high school graduates still can't name the past five presidents, what countries make up NATO, who authored the Declaration of Independence, or who was in the War of 1812. Why do we continue to waste valuable school time teaching things learners have already demonstrated they don't learn?

OVERVIEW OF BRAIN-BASED ASSESSMENT

Most of the time when we think we are assessing learning, we are merely getting feedback on how well a student plays the game of school. Perhaps more disturbing is the fact that what we normally assess is superficial and irrelevant to the brain. Not only do we need to reevaluate our fundamental premises about assessment, we need to broaden our evaluation techniques so that learners receive the benefit of a fair and authentic assessment process.

Authentic Assessment

Authentic assessment reflects a commitment of moving beyond quantity of learning to quality of learning; that is, asking the tougher questions and broadening our definition of *learning*. Accurately assessing learners is part science, part art. Most teacher-education programs fall short in this department. We are taught that the way to evaluate learning is to test students with quantifiable instruments that can be scored and defended expediently. Authentic assessment requires more than this from the teacher, and it rejects the notion that quality of learning can be accurately assessed simply by observation and testing means. Authentic assessment asks *why* when a learner performs short of our expectations.

Now that we've reviewed what's wrong with the traditional assessment approach, let's explore what's right. The following five areas provide a basis for authentic assessment (see also Figure 22.1):

1. Content (what learners know)

2. Emotions (how learners feel about it)

3. Context (how learners relate it to the world)

4. Processing (how learners manipulate data)

5. Embodiment (how deep the learning goes; how learners apply it)

Let's make what's important more measurable, rather than making what's measurable more important.

These areas are inclusive of mind, body, and heart, as well as past, present, and future. Learners may express what they know using multiple media such as drawings, charts, lists, dialogues, actions, demonstrations, debates, or maps.

Content

The prevailing wisdom is that the old-style true/false and/or multiple-choice/matching tests are out of step with authentic assessment. And this is true to a certain extent; however, there is still a place for traditional testing, so long as its limitations are recognized. For example, learners who have not mastered the language (perhaps they are nonnative speakers, have a learning disability, or are disabled) may or may not (depending on the individual circumstance) be better assessed by answering questions in a traditional test format. And traditional testing can help us assess all learners to some degree, albeit narrowly.

The critical question, though, is this: How much weight should old-style content tests be assigned in the overall assessment package? I'll give you a direct

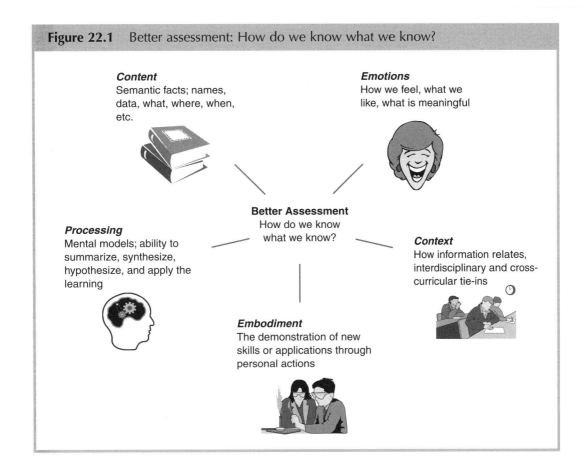

Figure 22.1   Better assessment: How do we know what we know?

Content
Semantic facts; names, data, what, where, when, etc.

Emotions
How we feel, what we like, what is meaningful

Better Assessment
How do we know what we know?

Processing
Mental models; ability to summarize, synthesize, hypothesize, and apply the learning

Context
How information relates, interdisciplinary and cross-curricular tie-ins

Embodiment
The demonstration of new skills or applications through personal actions

answer: less than half. Much of our knowledge is demonstrated only with prompting; that is, our memory is triggered by cues. This is why answering essay questions is usually more difficult than answering a multiple-choice question. So multiple-choice and true/false questions aren't necessarily bad; it's just that we shouldn't rely on them as much as we traditionally have for assessing learners.

What This Means to You

Don't throw out the true/false, matching, or multiple-choice tests completely; just don't make them the mainstay of your assessment program. In addition to tests or quizzes, give learners an opportunity to demonstrate their knowledge in their preferred learning modality. See that you assess more than content knowledge. Evaluate learners' progress over time. And make sure that they are well aware of the various ways they can demonstrate learning. Ask yourself the tough questions when students don't seem to be working up to their potential. Try to get a picture of their unique experience. Show an interest in their feelings. What might be interfering with their concentration? If your district is enforcing standards-based outcomes and you don't feel supported, do what you would expect your own learners to do: ask for help, and be specific about what you need.

Emotions

We remember events that tap into our emotions. Likewise, we will remember learning that taps into our emotions. How students feel about a topic or subject is critical. Either they like it or they don't; if they don't, they won't likely want to explore the subject again. When we tap into learners' positive emotions, the learning becomes more meaningful.

As we increase students' awareness about the different types of learning and how we learn (metacognition), we help them understand why some subjects are easier for them than others. Draw a distinction for them between knowledge (usually surface knowledge) and meaning (something that clarifies what's happening in our world or extends our existing natural knowledge). Surface knowledge will be forgotten shortly after a test is given, while what's intrinsically meaningful to the individual learner will be lasting. This is why comparing students to one another is erroneous. The faulty premise that students should all be learning the same thing at the same time is based on a model that disregards the importance of personal relevance and normal differences in the developmental process.

Give learners the opportunity to discuss what is personally meaningful to them and how the subjects they're studying connect to their own lives. If we want to evaluate authentic learning, we need to start here. Rather than "testing" students, why not interview them? Let's acknowledge the importance of emotions in the educational setting by addressing rather than ignoring them. This, consequently, is the learning that makes education rewarding, rich, and timeless. It's also the kind of learning that spurs intrinsic motivation, while superficial knowledge requires constant external reinforcement and ultimatums. As we focus on authentic learning and engaging emotions, classroom management flows more effortlessly and naturally.

Context

In assessing students more accurately, we definitely need to consider their ability to generalize or contextualize what they've learned. In other words, we need to ask, "Now that you have learned ABC, how does this apply to DEF?" Many believe that applying knowledge is strongly related to real-life, survival skills, and what could be more important than this? Intelligence is closely related to the ability to generalize learning from one platform to another, which requires planning, metacognition, and both inductive and deductive reasoning skills. While teaching students about thinking and learning, we are also providing them with the framework to be productive and to succeed in the world.

It's important for learners to be able to ask questions and formulate thinking in a safe environment where exploration of concepts, feelings, and emotions is encouraged. Ask learners how they know something and where it fits into their life. Demonstrate how learning can be deep, shallow, impertinent, or profound. Asking more or fewer questions is irrelevant; it's the quality of the question that counts. Keep in mind that the answer to one well-formed open-ended question can provide a more authentic and comprehensive basis for assessment of learners than how they did on a 20-question surface-level test.

Expect learners to demonstrate the depth and quality of their learning with mind maps, cross-subject debates, integrated subject demonstrations, and panel discussions. These projects provide a strong basis for assessing learners' ability to generalize their learning.

Processing

Some areas of processing are easier to assess than others. For example, it's pretty easy to determine whether students can summarize and draw conclusions. But what about the more important and complex processing skills? How do you measure learners' ability to hypothesize, form mental models and comparisons, sort and manipulate data, present and defend their position, and ultimately apply the principles? Although these are tough criteria to measure, they are strong indicators of the depth of learning. In the big-picture analysis, it is the cognitive skills—not the content—that will be the primary measure of a student's long-term success in today's world.

Embodiment

When learners *embody* learning, they have incorporated it into their life in a meaningful way. Student who take the initiative to solve a problem or influence others with their knowledge are demonstrating that they have internalized the learning and are able to act on it in a real-life context. Schools that encourage this depth of learning are on the cutting edge. Examples of projects that encourage this level of integration are yearbooks, school papers, school stores, internships and work-study, travel-abroad programs, theater productions, competitive athletics, and other extracurricular activities. It is very difficult to measure a learner's degree of embodiment on a multiple-choice, true/false, or matching test. Even an essay test does not really demonstrate how well a learner has embodied the learning; rather it suggests how well a learner can talk (or more specifically, write) about the learning. This does not necessarily reflect actions or integration of the learning.

Ideas for Assessing Authentic Learning

Outlined below are some ideas for evaluating a student's content understanding in ways that reinforce their learning without inducing the anxiety state usually associated with testing. These strategies also give emotions a seat at the assessment table. Remember (and remind students) that much of the value in the assignments is in the emotional responses they elicit, and in the planning and production processes. The finished product is important, but focusing on issues such as problem solving, interpersonal relations, conflict resolution, accountability, group dynamics, follow-through, and self-assessment throughout the life of the project are also critical learning functions.

1. **Internet newspaper.** Have students create an online school newspaper that covers relevant learning topics. Emphasize multiple points of view,

personal experiences, and the process necessary for creating an accurate finished product (i.e., writing drafts, checking facts, dividing responsibilities, editing, proofreading, presenting).

2. **Class yearbook.** Create a class yearbook, and start by brainstorming. What should be included? What events of the year will go down in history? What music was popular? What was learned? Include students' artwork, poems, photographs, and other contributions.

3. **Wall-sized mural.** Have the class choose a theme related to what you're learning. Then map out an image depicting the subject matter on a large piece of butcher paper. Once the sketch is completed, everyone can participate in the painting of it. When it's done, hang it in a conspicuous location for all to enjoy. If the mural is really good, you might want to see if there's interest from the community in having the mural painted in a public area. Civic projects are great for meaning making and building relevance.

4. **Storyboards.** Disney cartoonists pioneered the concept of storyboarding. Start with a sequence of roughly drawn pictures that capture the action or key events of a story or topic. Put them up on a wall as a timeline illustration or a visual history of the subject.

5. **Student-generated tests or quizzes.** Establish some basic criteria, and then have students decide what's important to be tested on and what's not. Have them write the questions.

6. **Multimedia creation.** Have students make a video, a PowerPoint presentation, or a CD that will help others learn the subject they are studying. Insist on good quality, and ensure that learners have access to the necessary resources and equipment.

7. **Pre/posttest comparisons.** Design pre- and postsurveys that examine learners' feelings about a subject. Not all of the questions have to deal overtly with the subject of emotions. You might ask on a science survey, for example: Do you watch the Discovery Channel on TV or read science magazines and books? Have you ever done a science experiment? If so, how did you feel about it? On a scale of 1 to 10 (with 1 being low and 10 being high), what's the likelihood that when you grow up your career will involve an aspect of science? You get the point. What you're trying to do is get a reading on learners' emotional reactions to the subject. At the end of the term or unit, have students complete the same survey again, and compare the differences between the two surveys.

8. **Storytelling.** Have students write or tell a story about the subject. This gives them an opportunity to relate feelings and emotions through the eyes and voice of a fictional character. This strategy also reinforces personal meaning.

9. **Learning logs.** Have students keep a freeform or structured journal about their learning. Journal writing is a strong and reflective medium for expressing emotions. Encourage learners to relate subject matter to their own lives while describing real-life applications for the content.

10. **Demonstrations/student teachers.** Have learners demonstrate an application for the learning or facilitate a group experience. Teach them how to act as peer or student teachers. As you know, teaching others is a great way to reinforce your own learning. It is also a nonthreatening way to evaluate depth of learning and applications to real-life situations.

11. **Community projects.** Students can actively demonstrate their learning with community projects, such as volunteering for a special event or becoming an activist for an important cause. It may be a social, ecological, or business concern. One high school junior in Portland, Oregon, frustrated by her school's closure of the arts and music program, began a letter-writing campaign that eventually resulted (through her persistence) in a benefit performance by singer/songwriter Jackson Browne. The concert raised enough money to save the arts and music program, and the student definitely got a real-life boost in her self-confidence and social skills.

12. **Theatrical performance.** Produce a play or a skit that relates to the current unit of study. Give students the opportunity to plan the process, the content, and the final production. Keep the emphasis on having fun, while also reinforcing learning.

13. **Model making.** This is a particularly good way to measure learners' depth of understanding with regard to physical laws and scientific principles, while keeping the focus on experimentation and exploration. Again, the emphasis ought to be on the process as well as the final product.

14. **Artwork/drawing.** Not only is art a good medium for exploring emotions, it is a safe way for students to express themselves. It is also a great way to channel concentration and energy and to manage states. When approached as a downtime activity, it can also help learners subconsciously process content and integrate learning.

15. **Sculpture.** Many students optimally demonstrate their learning (and learn best) with hands-on activities that allow them to manipulate concepts and physical objects. Creativity and risk taking are also encouraged as learners design works of art that draw out their emotions and challenge them.

16. **Music.** Have learners use music to represent and extend their learning. They can set key words and concepts to music and then perform it, or they can come up with their own idea.

17. **Commercials/short films.** Give learners the opportunity to translate their learning into a short film or a commercial. Emphasize the process more

than the final product. Assist them at each stage, from brainstorming the topics as a group, writing the script, and auditioning for the key roles to rehearsing, filming, and editing. This project requires a vast array of skills that will be invaluable in the students' future work and personal lives.

18. **Case study problem.** Give students an opportunity to design, build, and demonstrate their learning with a physical representation of the topic or unit. Observe what parts of the task they like and excel at and what parts are problematic for them. To get the process started, you might want to suggest a problem related to the content they're learning—preferably one that can be solved in a variety of ways.

19. **Group discussions.** Give groups of learners a task or problem and some ground rules. Then observe how individuals participate in the process. After they solve the problem, provide some discussion and reflection questions that help them focus on the process they used. Have a spokesperson for each group report on the group's process to the rest of the class.

20. **Informal interviews.** Much can be assessed about students' learning simply by talking to them in a casual, relaxed manner. Informally interview students, and have them interview each other. The ability to formulate questions, extrapolate answers, and synthesize the information in writing will be extremely valuable to students' future learning and work life.

21. **Game design.** Have students incorporate current learning into a game, such as Simon Says, Monopoly, Jeopardy, Wheel of Fortune, Concentration, card games, or a ball toss.

22. **Personal goals.** Have students create a set of personal learning goals. Teach them how to make the goals measurable. Emphasize the importance of short- and long-term objectives. Teach them how to integrate their goals into their own ongoing self-assessment program. Encourage them to reevaluate their goals on a regular basis and to track their progress.

23. **Mind mapping.** As a group or alone (or both), have students create a mind map of their current learning. A mind map is a webbed, thematic graphic organizer that illustrates information and connections between topics with colorful doodles and lines connecting topics. These open-ended depictions of students' thinking processes can provide an excellent vehicle for evaluating learning. The process also reinforces learners' understanding of relationships, themes, and associations between ideas.

24. **Debates.** Debates provide a forum for learners to defend their learning and verbalize their knowledge. Half of the value is in preparing for the debates. Expect an array of emotions to surface as learners struggle with presenting a point of view that may not necessarily reflect their own. Be very specific about your criteria for assessment so that learners understand they are not being graded on what they say but how they say it and how well prepared they are.

25. **Miniconference.** Have students plan (and carry out, if you're really brave) a miniconference on a topic related to the current unit of study. This is an opportunity for students to gather information from the community at large, invite speakers, organize logistics, and pull off a special event with higher-than-usual stakes involved.

26. **Time lines.** Have learners create a chronological graphic time line that reflects the historical development of the topic they're studying. This project can help you evaluate research skills as well as learners' integration of the subject with related learning.

27. **Montage/collage.** Using any combination of media, have students create an original work of art that reflects their learning. Emphasize freedom of expression and originality. There is no right or wrong way to approach the task. One popular technique is to cut out and arrange print images that resonate with the learners and draw connections between concepts. Looking through magazines for photographs is also a great way to get students sparked for goal setting. Have them make a collage that incorporates their short- and long-term goals.

All of these evaluation strategies respect differences in developmental stages and reflect the type of learning that is difficult to measure in the short run. Rather than presenting learners with a barrage of standardized tests (or pulling up the fruit tree to see if it's growing properly), we water, fertilize, and appreciate the organism, knowing fully that by nurturing it, growth happens.

FOCUSING ON FEEDBACK

Grades are too often relied on as the primary means of student feedback. This strategy reflects a "too little, too late, too general" approach that is doomed to fail. By contrast, when we concentrate on ensuring learner feedback from multiple sources (including self-assessment) every 30 minutes, learners begin to view feedback as healthy guidance rather than critical judgment.

Not only is feedback important to the brain, it is important to all stakeholders in the education system: parents, teachers, administrators, and the community at large.

> The brain hunts for feedback to ensure its survival, growth, and progress.

Tips for Improving Feedback

- more often, and immediately after a mistake
- more task oriented, not person oriented
- the greater the specificity, the better
- the more emotionally weighted, the better (within reason)

What This Means to You

To optimize learning, make it a rule that learners get feedback every 30 minutes. This does not mean you personally have to talk to each student every half hour. Although this would be ideal, it is highly unlikely that you would realistically be able to keep this up over the long haul. Rather, incorporate various forms of feedback that don't all rely on you. Teach learners how to assess themselves: provide self-quiz materials, rubrics, and guided reflection activities. Also use group and partner assessment techniques, such as holding discussions in which learners get ideas validated or reshaped; setting up peer teaching opportunities, debates, partner mind-mapping activities, group observation/feedback exercises, team discussions; or simply asking for a show of hands in response to reflection questions. The most effective feedback is nonjudgmental: it simply takes note, observes, and gently guides learners toward the agreed-upon goal.

We know that reporting is essential, yet many teachers agree that grading students in the traditional manner has strong disadvantages. What are the alternatives in a brain-based school? It is fully possible to approach grading in a more holistic manner; that is, by utilizing the following strategies to guide learners on a daily basis and eventually report their progress for the term.

Brain-Friendly Assessment in a Nutshell

- Increase feedback from yourself and other sources (including other students).
- Encourage group work; include discussion groups, long-term team projects, theatrical productions, brainstorming, debates, and games.
- Encourage learners to use self-assessment techniques; introduce rubrics, study groups, and self quizzes.
- Replace external rewards of any kind with acknowledgment of the intrinsic rewards of success.
- Focus on substantial long-term group assignments that impact the larger community as well as the learners.
- Keep all student work in a portfolio file, and refer to their progress often.
- Compare learners only to themselves, not other learners.
- Emphasize mastery rather than a bell-shaped (or any-shaped) curve.
- Discuss your assessment philosophy and approach with all stakeholders (how and why it works as well as your expectations).
- Post your grading policy/approach in a highly visible location in the room; make it colorful and attractive so that students won't perceive it as a threat but rather as a friendly reminder.

Many schools are currently moving toward this model. They are doubling and tripling the quantity of feedback students get. And they are getting learners involved in setting criteria for assessment. Even many major universities are recognizing the weaknesses of traditional standardized achievement tests and rigid once-a-term testing. They are also beginning to emphasize consistent feedback and a more holistic approach to grading.

Outcome-based learning, in which students have little say in the process, is outdated and obsolete but we still see a reliance on this demand model at the highest levels of education. We can do all the insisting we want, but students (and teachers) don't perform better with more stress and threat. Punishing with disapproval when demands aren't met is not a long-term solution. A long-term solution recognizes the importance of happier, threat-free students and teachers who feel supported by a compassionate, caring, and fair system that recognizes everyone's natural desire to succeed in life.

> Multiple-choice, true/false, and fill-in-the-blank tests are not brain antagonistic; they're simply part of the overall assessment process. Each can help reveal some of what students know, but alone they present an incomplete picture of authentic learning.

Improving Test Scores

While the thrust of this chapter was to explore more authentic ways to assess learners, keep in mind that testing is still a reality in our school systems and will likely be for a long time. Therefore, we need to prepare learners for this aspect of education. There are very few "points of power" when it comes to improving test scores; however, the following tips can positively impact student performance and test-taking skills.

Tips for Boosting Test Scores

- Improve the original learning. Use the strategies in this book to see that students integrate the learning in meaningful ways.
- Teach study skills and memory-enhancing techniques, such as mnemonics.
- Review learning at frequent intervals: after one day, one week, and one month.
- Rehearse the test. The questions don't have to be exactly alike; there is value in the process itself. Try to duplicate the stressful conditions, however, and recognize that the more similar the practice session is to the final session, the more helpful it will be.
- Teach students how to approach the various types of tests and test questions. For example, discuss time restraints, quick scanning techniques, prioritizing, self-imposed time limits, test-taking objectives, types of questions, and educated guessing.
- Prepare learners to manage their own states. We can all get discouraged or frustrated, but these states can be devastating during a test. Teach students how to do deep breathing for relaxation; emphasize the value of positive self-talk; discuss issues of posture, hydration, lighting, and resting the eyes; and address the impact of high-energy foods eaten prior to testing.
- Make students aware of what they can and can't do during testing. Can they stand, walk around, or take a stretch break? Will they have access to

water, or can they bring their own? Can they suck on hard candies or chew gum as a stress reducer? Can they use any learning aids?

- After the test, provide a debriefing session during which students can discuss their experiences and feel supported. Testing is a stress-inducing experience and one that should not be left unaddressed. Lead learners in a discussion about how they might better prepare for the next test if they feel they did poorly, or about what study techniques they want to repeat for the next test if they feel they did well.

23 Brain-Based Reform

This chapter invites you to ask questions about the process of school change. Taking a brain-based perspective, the questions are a bit unusual. First, from the point of view of the brain, how does change happen? Second, what kinds of change make sense? Third, where, when, and who should be making the changes? And finally, how do we ensure that the changes are systemic and not trivial?

As a generalization, the human brain prefers stability (keeps stress down) with some novelty (adds excitement). Most of us find that too much change is stressful and too little novelty is boring. This preference is what maintains many large organizations (e.g., schools, businesses), and as a rule, it maintains the same structure and processes. Any school change can invoke stress in the staff because stress results from a perceived loss of control. That's why many say, "I don't mind change; I just don't like being changed." Consequently, the more that staff are involved, and the more in control they feel, the less stressful the process becomes. Keep this in mind as you prepare your school for change.

HALLMARKS OF BRAIN-BASED REFORM

I have never advocated developing a school based 100 percent on brain research, and I never will. That just doesn't make sense. The reality is that other factors deserve attention, too. We must consider the interests of parents, districts, school boards, staff, students, and states. We must also consider safety, weather, and local culture. One way to think about how schools influence the brain (aside from the obvious answer: giving an education), is to address these five issues:

- curriculum (what we teach)
- instruction (how we teach it)
- environment (where we teach it)
- assessment (how we measure what we teach)
- staff development (the change process)

Based on everything you now know about the brain and learning, what do you think are the hallmarks of brain-based reform? Do you think the traditional restructuring approach, such as enforcing outcomes-based standards, will result in the kind of change that our schools desperately need? If not, why? Do you think there's a way to reform the reforms so that they are student centered and teacher supported? Asking ourselves questions such as these will help us embody the learning we've done so far.

Ways of Improving Student Achievement

The key issues that need to be addressed, if we hope to improve student achievement across the board (and which are often neglected), include the following:

- Most school staff (including teachers, assistants, and administrators) are overwhelmed by the enormous responsibility they have to turn out learners who test well. The more we emphasize outcomes-based standards based on grade level, the more distress and feelings of resignation teachers experience. Positive change is unlikely to happen in this physiological and emotional state.
- Many educational systems are increasing the accountability load on teachers without enhancing their training, resources, and support. Most communities are unwilling to fund the requisite staff-development time necessary to make

substantial changes. This is partly a problem of ignorance and partly a problem of trading in long-term reform for short-term results that provide immediate gratification for special-interest entities, such as politicians.

- Classrooms today are dramatically less homogenous than they were just a couple of decades ago. Teachers are expected to prepare for the next grade learners who don't speak (never mind understand) the language. Along with language barriers, learners from a multitude of cultural, ethnic, and religious backgrounds pose issues related to norms and values. Some students have never been in one classroom for a complete year; others have known only violence; some are undernourished; others have been taught that the way to survive is to dominate others. In addition, students with special needs are being mainstreamed into classes of 30 students and one teacher. Their special needs can range from physical to emotional or mental. What teacher wouldn't be overly challenged in such an environment?

- All of the prior concerns are exacerbated when teachers have only a few weeks or years of classroom teaching experience. This is like throwing a rookie lion trainer into a pit of lions and saying, "We're leaving now, but we expect you to train these dangerous animals to perform the following stunts. Unfortunately, we can't provide you with much assistance, but we'll be sure to return at the end of the term to determine if you were capable of meeting our expectations."

- Most of the restructuring changes are token substitutes for real reform. Substantial change requires a long-term commitment that addresses mental models, paradigm shifts, present weaknesses, training shortcomings, and infrastructure decisions that support real learning. Most administrators are in denial about how significant the changes must be and how challenging it really is to affect change on this level.

Environmental Control for Learner Achievement

To achieve better results in learner achievement, we need to focus on the factors we have the most control over: environment, environment, environment! When a more responsive environment supports students, their behaviors change quickly. In spite of all the educational reforms that are in the works, there is a critical element that will do more to motivate learners than any other:

Make schools more like real life. Integrate the curriculum, incorporate real problems, organize simulation activities, supply plenty of novelty and feedback, and seek student cooperation by earning their interest and respect.

Schools, businesses, and organizations of all kinds can implement top-down restructuring measures all they want, but until they make the true distinction between what motivates learners in real life and what is going on in their respective environments, the result will always be the same: naturally good, curious, and motivated individuals will become demotivated, unempowered, and branded "lazy." Rather than expending more energy on judging learners, we need to spend more time determining how we can best serve and nurture them.

Authentic school reform must be committed to long-term, personal, systemic, and organizational change—anything less is doomed to fail.

Educational leaders who are committed to true and substantial reform will learn from past mistakes. We've gone down these fatal paths before. It's time to try something new based on what we now know about the biology of learning.

Fatal Paths to Avoid

- conducting only high-stakes testing (creates teaching to the test and causes student's brains to "minimize"); instead, create more frequent assessment, use multiple assessment strategies, and provide a rich and constant stream of feedback to learners in both the long and short term
- increasing staff pressure to achieve outcomes-based standards (more stress without support disempowers teachers and learners alike)
- using assessment practices that focus only on immediate and/or easily measured results (many aspects of authentic learning cannot be measured); instead, focus on both the most useful data and the joy of learning
- expecting teachers to increase student achievement results without providing the additional training and support necessary to meet the needs of diverse student populations (inclusion will backfire unless teachers are intensively trained to deal with physical, mental, and emotional disorders, as well as cultural differences and non-English-speaking learners)
- incorporating testing standards that don't account for the one- to three-year range of cognitive and developmental differences that are perfectly normal in children and teens
- reinforcing high teacher control of kids in classrooms (creates resentment and learner apathy)
- encouraging "stand and deliver" teaching practices that rely on lecture, lecture, and more lecture
- encouraging punitive discipline measures, rewards, bribery, and control tactics; school is not prison, so make learning fun, treat students with respect and dignity, and expect them to want to learn for the sake of learning

Include the Brain in the Reform

The issues of stress and control are key to understanding the process of reform. Generally, the more out of control we are, the greater the stress we experience. If your only goals are to achieve the standards, you'll miss out on the bigger goal: to enrich every student's brain and develop a better person. Many schools find that when curriculum and assessment standards are combined with the goal of providing a brain-based education, a better process and result emerges. The following instructional approaches work because they fit with the brain research on learning:

1. Provide variety of instruction. Uniqueness is the rule, not the exception, when it comes to brains. There is a wide variety of genetic and environmental variables that influence the brain every day. These variables change the filtering, processing, and output of the brain.

2. Use error correction daily. The brain rarely gets explicit learning right the first time. It often sacrifices accuracy for simply "getting it done." Effectiveness is usually more important than accuracy.

3. Use short instructional segments. We have attentional and input limitations. It's tough to maintain focus for extended periods of time. Too much input overloads our cognitive and emotional systems. Most input is implicit.

4. Enrich the environment every chance you can. Environment affects the brain. Social, physical, academic, and cultural environments have the capacity to change the brain. The longer a brain is in any environment, the more committed the nervous system becomes to that environment.

5. Keep adjusting what you do. We have highly adaptive brains. They are constantly changing; it's all a matter of degree. Both structures and systems are malleable through learning, nutrition, and stress. Enrichment is an example of environmental effects on the brain, as is skill building (neuroplasticity is engaged).

6. Manage the emotional states. We have integrated mind/body/emotional states. These signatures, of both chemical and neural assemblies (such as stress), influence our attention, memory, learning, meaning, and behavior.

7. Manage the positives, and limit the intense negatives. We often develop a dependency on rewards of some kind. We crave positives and strive to avoid negatives. The brain often becomes addicted to predictable rewards (e.g., TV, gambling, drugs, adrenaline). Big positives and lots of small course-correction negatives are good for the brain.

8. Shape and influence meaning proactively. The brain seeks and creates meaning. The more important it is, the greater the attention we should pay to influencing the shaping of it.

9. Influence perception more than reality. Perception, not reality, becomes our experience. Prior knowledge changes how the brain organizes new learning. Change the way you perceive the world, and you change your experience. Remember, experience drives change in the brain.

10. Manage students' memories because memories are malleable. Memory is the result of learning and the basis for prediction. But some memories are encoded poorly, changed, not encoded, or not retrieved. In addition, memories are never fixed; they can be changed by accident or on purpose. Engage multiple learning and memory systems. We learn and store our learning at least a dozen different ways.

11. Use novel repetition. We need reinforcement, but our brains also seek novelty. Use repetition three to four times in the first hour, but only after error correction. The students need to do the repetition, not the teacher.

12. Teach estimation and prediction skills daily. Prediction is our strongest survival skill, yet schools rarely focus on strengthening it.

13. Ask for student input; then incorporate it. In study after study, students ask for more engaging curriculum, less boring instruction, more frequent assessment, and stronger teacher-student relationships. These match up well with what drives motivation and achievement in schools.

14. Social structures. The brain is highly influenced by social conditions. Make strong, prosocial contact a priority. Implement the use of peer counselors, mentoring programs, clubs, homeroom sharing groups, and other positive contact programs.

15. Arts and physical education. Make both of these a mainstay of your school, and ensure that all kids get 30 minutes a day of each of these by qualified staff.

16. Collaboration. Create teacher-to-teacher support networks that encourage sharing, rapport, and problem solving.

Schools that incorporate the brain-based learning methods outlined in this book are consistently more successful than those that don't. But then how do we define success? Quite simply, systematic success means fewer dropouts; deeper authentic learning; and increased enjoyment, critical thinking, risk taking, and creativity. Success is teaching learners about learning—how to do it and the intrinsic benefits derived from it. But this requires more than just applying a few brain-based techniques. A brain-based school must concentrate on becoming a learning organization. Pulling from *Ten Steps to a Learning Organization* (Kline & Saunders, 1997) and *The Fifth Discipline Fieldbook* (Senge, Kleiner, Roberts, Ross, & Smith, 1994), the following sequence of steps is recommended for transforming a school into a learning organization.

Seven Steps to Transforming Your School Into a Learning Organization

1. Assess the Existing Culture. This requires observation over time and a safe environment in which people can tell the truth about their perceptions regarding the organization. Use both formal and informal means to determine what works and what doesn't. What is the predominant thinking? What overt and covert

assumptions are influencing the environment? How are decisions made and supported (or not supported)? The findings (if they're honest) may result in some despair, but only after the truth is acknowledged can the real work begin. Does the staff understand the basic brain-based principles? How strong is the implementation of those principles?

2. Build a Collective Vision. This involves identifying a mutually agreed-upon mission statement and collective vision. Based on discussions, reflections, and consensus, map out the steps in a visually stimulating manner. Avoid identifying specific strategies at this time. Post the mission map or vision statement in a highly visible location. Having said this, nothing is more important than getting the staff invested in the process. All the team building in the world does little good if staff members dislike the process or disagree with the goals.

3. Establish a Learning Climate. Identify and promote positive teaching practices that will aid the organization in reaching its vision. Share what's working on a consistent basis. Reward appropriate risk-taking behaviors with acknowledgments and celebrations. Allow for mistakes, celebrate lessons learned, and supply lots of feedback; this goes for both students and teachers. Remember, your aim is to produce good learners, not robots.

4. Encourage Personal Mastery. Support each member of the learning team in creating a personal vision, a guiding life statement, and both long- and short-term personal goals. Unless each member of an organization is making progress and feeling empowered, an uncomfortable dissonance is created. Keep a staff library shelf in the lounge from which inspirational books and videos can be borrowed. Offer "Learning to Learn" workshops or "Learning for Life" seminars for staff and faculty, and include personality profiles and learning modalities/styles assessments. Become a great learner. As you model lifelong learning, others will be more likely to follow. If you believe it, live it.

5. Promote Team Learning. Make a commitment to staff collaboration with group and partner learning. Set up your planning meetings with this in mind. Through discussion, reflection, and team activities, staff and faculty will provide each other with valuable feedback while processing and sharing their knowledge. Encourage team members to view each other as valuable resources. When we restructure our learning organizations into sideways, rather than vertical, power structures, we increase participation and accountability at all levels by default. Foster cooperation and teamwork.

6. Systems Thinking Is Everyone's Business. Seek to understand the key relationships that influence your organization. This is partly a matter of trial and error and partly a matter of asking the right questions frequently enough. It may feel like you're only slowly chipping away at a granite boulder, but creating systematic change takes time. Discover what key statistical indicators your school uses to assess quality of learning. Focus on individual policy changes, one at a time, until eventually critical mass is reached and the organization's investments become aligned with brain-based practice. Keep the focus on how one person's actions can influence the whole.

7. Nourish the Dream

All the seed planting in the world will produce nothing unless you nourish the dream. *Kaizen* is a Japanese word that means never-ending improvement. Make this your school's 10-year theme. Be satisfied with incremental improvements. Create a scorecard for the organization so that team members can chart overall progress. Encourage team members to also create scorecards that reflect their own personal progress. Get people together often to reflect on mutual needs and concerns, share successes, and celebrate milestones. Great schools take nothing for granted, and their staff members have an attitude that "we can always get better." The best staff are willing to take risks to get better, even if they are already good. One has to be willing to risk being good in order to be great.

> The number-one thing that successful learning organizations do well is support people in embracing change.

To assess how brain-friendly your learning organization is, answer the following questions:

How Brain-Friendly Is Your School?

- Do team members act differently around management?
- Do team members act differently around certain staff?
- Are people afraid to speak their mind to others or to management?
- Do staff and faculty feel free to try out new ideas without fear of reprisal?
- Is the overall feeling of the learning community one of satisfaction or frustration?
- Do teachers think of themselves as learning catalysts, rather than instructors?
- Are there frequent discussions about educational practices and policies, or is the culture steeped in gossip and pot stirring?

Your answers to these questions will shed light on the kind of learning climate that exists in your organization. In general, you'll know that your school is a learning organization when the following things are happening:

- The school's prevailing vision often emerges in discussions and policy revisions.
- Team members feel their work is meaningful and makes a difference.
- Team members work together frequently and well; they don't drag each other down or make unilateral decisions without regard for the rest of the group.
- Team members feel free to share their successes, concerns, and setbacks with others in a regularly scheduled support meeting.

- Team members are encouraged to inquire further when they feel that an action is unjust or out of line with the organization's vision. There are very few (if any) "sacred cows" (topics off limits for discussion).
- There's a great respect for differences. Personal experiences, diverse opinions, and individuality are valued rather than squelched or feared.
- The focus is on continued growth and desired change. The majority of school members are committed to improving themselves and the organizational climate. The emphasis is on becoming the best learning organization possible.
- As you walk around campus, students appear to be enjoying themselves.
- Learners regularly do extra work on their own, and they meet in groups outside class.
- Students bring things from home to share at school, even when it's not assigned.
- Tardies and absences are minimal.
- Teachers are highly regarded and spoken well of by students in private.

Learning organizations will succeed well into the twenty-first century, not because they are better at predicting what change will be necessary but because they are better at changing when necessary. Even if we could predict the future, we would still not always agree on how to interpret it, react to it, or prepare for it. Any learning organization worth its salt will be made up of individuals with varying value systems, and conflict among these is natural. But a learning organization that is experienced in working with diverse opinions and value judgments will be more efficient at coming to consensus. The infrastructure will be in place and the team members well versed in the process. The learning organization has established a culture of learning its way into the future.

ASSESSING THE LEARNING COMMUNITY

Is it really possible to measure the degree to which a school is brain based? The answer is both yes and no. Like an automotive engine, a school can have many things wrong with it and still work, just as it can have many things right about it and still not work. Brain-based learning communities are not perfect; rather we ought to view ourselves on a continuum with "brain-based practices always implemented" on one side and "brain-based practices never implemented" on the other. The reality is that most of us will fall somewhere in between. The deep-seated problems that educational systems are facing won't simply fall away once we've declared ourselves to be brain-based schools. It is an ongoing process. If a school declares that it has reached brain-based perfection, it is likely off base. The model itself is one of continuous improvement and recognition of the need for constant vigilance. Much of the true quality of a brain-based learning organization is in the process itself. To sum up, brain-based schools maintain brain-friendly practices most of the time.

If you don't live it, you don't believe it.

What This Means to You

To discover the interest level among others at your school, start a conversation about brain-based learning during lunch or prep times. Keep a list of good suggestions that come to you. Even if only a few others show interest at first, organize a regular time for information sharing. Support from others will grow exponentially as awareness increases. Meanwhile, implement positive changes in your own classroom, and watch for progress. You have little to lose and much to gain. Schools around the world are incorporating the strategies outlined in this book. If you can't find support for your efforts immediately inside your organization, you can find it outside.

Becoming a Local Expert

Learn as much about the subject as you can; try out some applications; integrate what works and throw out what doesn't work. Before you know it, you'll be teaching others. Expand your contacts and associations. Relate your learning beyond yourself and your students to the larger community. Making connections on a larger scale is often referred to as *natural knowledge*. Form support groups, hold meetings, sponsor activities, write newsletters, and participate in a brain-based training network.

Speak on the topic at your school, in your district, and in the community. Make sure you role model the principles you're advocating. You would be surprised how many people lecture on brain-based learning for a lengthy period of time, never realizing that they are doing exactly what they are saying doesn't work. Create materials you can share with others. Include your name, phone number, e-mail address, and references so that interested individuals can follow up and learn more.

It's not easy, but it's simple. Take the first step and start walking. Get support, and turn your good ideas into a movement. Learning can work for everyone. And it can begin with you. Take action right now. You're in good company.

References

Ackerman, H., Wildgruber, D., Daum, I., & Grodd, W. (1998). Does the cerebellum contribute to cognitive aspects of speech production? A functional magnetic resonance imaging study in humans. *Neuroscience Letters, 247*(2), 187.

Allen, L. S., & Gorski, R. A. (1991). Sexual dimorphism of the anterior commissure and massa inter media of the human brain. *Journal of Comparative Neurology, 312,* 97–104.

Altman, J., & Das, G. D. (1965). Autoradiographic and histological evidence of postnatal hippocampal neurogenesis in rats. *Journal of Comparative Neurology, 124,* 319–335.

Altman, J., Wallace, R. B., Anderson, W. J., & Das, G. D. (1968). Behaviorally induced changes in length of cerebrum in rats. *Developmental Psychobiology, 1,* 112–117.

Amabile, T. (1989). *Growing up creative.* New York: Crown.

Ankey, C. D. (1992). Sex differences in relative brain size: The mismeasure of woman, too? *Intelligence, 16,* 329–336.

Arenson, K. (1998, January 15). Test gap between sexes narrows. *Toronto Globe and Mail,* p. A15.

Asbjornsen, A., Hugdahl, K., & Hynd, G. W. (1990). The effects of head and eye turns on the right ear advantage in dichotic listening. *Brain and Language, 39,* 447–458.

Asher, J. (1966). The learning strategy of the total physical response: A review. *Modern Language Journal, 50,* 79–84.

Bandler, R. (1988). *Learning strategies: Acquisition and conviction.* [Videotape]. Boulder, CO: NLP Comprehensive.

Bangert, M., & Altenmüller, E. O., (2003). Mapping perception to action in piano practice: A longitudinal DC-EEG study. *BMC Neuroscience, 4,* 26.

Bennett, E. L., Diamond, M. C., Krech, D., & Rosenzweig, M. (1964). Chemical and anatomical plasticity of the brain. *Science, 146,* 610–619.

Bennet, E. L., Rosenzweig, M. R., & Diamond, M. C. (1969). Rat brain: Effects of environmental enrichment on wet and dry weights. *Science, 164,* 825–826.

Benton, D. (2001). The impact of the supply of glucose to the brain on mood and memory. *Nutrition Reviews, 59*(1), S20–S21.

Benton, D., & Roberts, G. (1988). Effect of vitamin and mineral supplementation on intelligence of a sample of schoolchildren. *Lancet, 1*(8578), 140–143.

Black, J. E. (1989). Effects of complex experience on somatic growth and organ development in rats. *Developmental Psychobiology, 22,* 727–752.

Bliss, T. V. P., & Lomo, T. (1973). Long-lasting potentiation of synaptic transmission in the dentate area of the anaesthetized rabbit following stimulation of the perforant path. *Journal of Physiology, 232,* 331–356.

Brener, N. D., Billy, J. O. G., & Grady, W. R. (2003). Assessment of factors affecting the validity of self-reported health-risk behavior among adolescents: Evidence from the scientific literature. *Journal of Adolescent Health, 33,* 436–457.

Brophy, J. (1983). Research on the self-fulfilling prophecy and teacher expectations. *Journal of Educational Psychology, 75,* 631–661.

Brown, S., Martinez, M. J., & Parsons, L. M. (2006). Music and language side by side in the brain: A PET study of the generation of melodies and sentences. *European Journal of Neuroscience, 23,* 2791–2803.

Buzan, T. (1974). *Use both sides of your brain.* New York: E. P. Dutton.

Caine, G., & Caine, R. (1991). *Making connections: Teaching and the human brain.* Alexandria, VA: Association for Supervision and Curriculum Development.

Calvin, W., & Ojemann, G. (1994). *Conversations with Neil's brain.* Reading, MA: Addison-Wesley.

Campbell, D. (1983). *Introduction to the musical brain.* St. Louis, MO: Magnamusic.

Casolini, P., Kabbaj, M., Leprat, F., Piazza, P. V., Rouge-Pont, F., Angelucci, L., et al. (1993). Basal and stress-induced corticosterone secretion is decreased by lesion of mesencephalic dopaminergic neurons. *Brain Research, 622,* 311–314.

Chang, E. C. (2001). *Optimism and pessimism: Implications for theory, research and practice.* Washington, DC: American Psychological Association.

Conn, R. (2003). Drinking water can help your diet. Retrieved January 16, 2008, from www.eurekalert.org/pub_releases/2003-02/wfub-dwc020303.php

Csikszentmihalyi, M. (1990). *Flow: The psychology of optimal experience.* New York: Harper & Row.

Damasio, A. (1994). *Descartes' error: Emotion, reason, and the human brain.* New York: Putnam and Sons.

Davis, P. (1999). *Aromatherapy: An A–Z* (rev. ed.). Essex, England: C. W. Daniel.

DeBono, E. (1970). *Lateral thinking.* New York: Harper & Row.

Deci, E. L., & Ryan, R. M. (1987). The support of autonomy and the control of behavior. *Journal of Personality and Social Psychology, 53,* 1024–1037.

Dember, W., & Parasuraman, R. (1993, February). Remarks before the Annual Meeting of the American Association for the Advancement of Science, Boston.

Dhong, H. J., Chung, S. K., & Doty, R. L. (1999). Estrogen protects against 3-methylindole-induced olfactory loss. *Brain Research, 824,* 312–315.

Diamond, M., & Hopson, J. (1998). *Magic trees of the mind: How to nurture your child's intelligence, creativity, and healthy emotions from birth through adolescence.* New York: Dutton.

Diamond, M. C., Krech, D., & Rosenzweig, M. R. (1964). The effects of an enriched environment on the histology of the rat cerebral cortex. *Journal of Comparative Neurology, 123,* 111–120.

Diamond, M. C., Lindner, B., & Raymond, A. (1967). Extensive cortical depth measurements and neuron size increases in the cortex of environmentally enriched rats. *Journal of Comparative Neurology, 131,* 357–364.

Dishman, R. K., Berthoud, H. R., Booth, F. W., Cotman, C. W., Edgerton, V. R., Fleshner, M. R., et al. (2006). Neurobiology of exercise. *Obesity, 14,* 345–356.

Dosher, B. A., Han, S., & Lu, Z. L. (2004). Parallel processing in visual search asymmetry. *Journal of Experimental Psychology: Human Perception Performance, 30,* 3–27.

Drake, S. (1996). Guided imagery and education: Theory, practice, and experience. *Journal of Mental Imagery, 20,* 1–58.

Drevets, W. C., & Raichle, M. E. (1998). Reciprocal suppression of regional cerebral blood flow during emotional versus higher cognitive processes: Implications for interactions between emotion and cognition. *Cognition & Emotion, 12,* 353–385.

Driesen, N. R., & Raz, N. (1995). The influence of sex, age, and handedness on corpus callosum morphology: A meta-analysis. *Psychobiology, 23,* 240–247.

Dunn, K., & Dunn, R. (1992). *Bringing out the giftedness in your child.* New York: John Wiley & Sons.

Earthman, G. (2002). *School facility conditions and student academic achievement.* Los Angeles: University of California, Los Angeles, Institute for Democracy, Education, and Access. Retrieved January 16, 2008, from http://repositories.cdlib.org/cgi/viewcontent.cgi?article=1011&context=idea

Edwards, B. (1979). *Drawing on the right side of the brain.* Los Angeles: J. P. Tarcher.

Eriksson, P. S., Perfilieva, E., Bjork-Eriksson, T., Alborn, A. M., Nordborg, C., Peterson, D. A., et al. (1998). Neurogenesis in the adult human hippocampus. *Nature Medicine, 4,* 1313–1317.

Fedulov, V., Rex, C. S., Simmons, D. A., Palmer, L., Gall, C. M., & Lynch, G. (2007). Evidence that long-term potentiation occurs within individual hippocampal synapses during learning. *Journal of Neuroscience, 27,* 8031–8039.

Fiske, S. T., & Taylor, S. E. (1984). *Social cognition.* Reading, MA: Addison-Wesley.

Flanagan, J. R., Vetter, P., Johansson, R. S., & Wolpert, D. M. (2003). Prediction preceded control in motor learning. *Current Biology, 13,* 146–150.

Ford, M. (1992). *Motivating humans.* Thousand Oaks, CA: Sage.

Frank, J. D. (1985). Further thoughts on the antidemoralization hypothesis of psychotherapeutic effectiveness. *Integrative Psychiatry, 3,* 17–26.

Fuchs, J. L., Montemayor, M., & Greenough, W. T. (1990). Effect of environmental complexity on size of the superior colliculus. *Behavioral and Neural Biology, 54,* 198–203.

Gardner, H. (1983). *Frames of mind: The theory of multiple intelligences.* New York: Basic Books.

Giancotti, F. G., & Ruoslahti, E. (1999). Integrin signaling. *Science, 285,* 1028–1032.

Gillberg, M., Anderzen, I., Akerstedt, T., & Sigurdson, K. (1986). Urinary catecholamine responses to basic types of physical activity. *European Journal of Applied Physiology, 55,* 575–578.

Glasser, W. (1999). *Choice theory: A new psychology of personal freedom.* New York: HarperCollins.

Goleman, D. (1995). *Emotional intelligence: Why it can matter more than IQ.* New York: Bantam Books.

Gordon, E. (1999). *Skill wars: Winning the battle for productivity and profit.* London: Butterworth-Heinemann.

Gratton, G., Coles, M. G., & Donchin, E. (1992). Optimizing the use of information: Strategic control of activation of responses. *Journal of Experimental Psychology, 121,* 480–506.

Green, E. J., Greenough, W. T., & Schlumph, B. E. (1983). Effects of complex or isolated environments on cortical dendrites of middle-aged rats. *Brain Research, 264,* 233–240.

Greenough, W. T., & Anderson, B. J. (1991). Cerebellar synaptic plasticity: Relation to learning versus neural activity. *Annals of the New York Academy of Science, 627,* 231–247.

Greenough, W. T., Withers, G., & Anderson, B. (1992). Experience-dependent synaptogenesis as a plausible memory mechanism. In I. Gormezano & E. Wasserman (Eds.), *Learning and memory: The behavioral and biological substrates* (pp. 209–229). Hillsdale, NJ: Lawrence Erlbaum.

Griesbach, G. S., Hovda, D. A., Molteni, R., Wu, A., & Gomez-Pinilla, F. (2004). Voluntary exercise following traumatic brain injury: Brain-derived neurotrophic factor upregulation and recovery of function. *Neuroscience, 125,* 129–139.

Harmon, D. B. (1951). *The coordinated classroom.* Grand Rapids, MI: American Seating Company.

Harper, C. G., & Kril, J. J. (1990). Neuropathology of alcoholism. *Alcohol and Alcoholism, 25,* 207–216.

Healy, J. M. (2004). *Your child's growing mind: Brain development and learning from birth to adolescence.* New York: Broadway.

Hebb, D. O. (1949). *The organization of behavior.* New York: John Wiley & Sons.

Hellige, J. B. (1993). *Hemispheric asymmetry.* Cambridge, MA: Harvard University Press.

Hermann, N. (1996). *The whole brain business book.* New York: McGraw-Hill.

Heschong Mahone Group. (2007). *Daylighting and productivity—CEC PIER.* Retrieved January 13, 2008, from www.h-m-g.com/projects/daylighting/projects-PIER.htm

Hillman, C. H., Motl, R. W., Pontifex, M. B., Posthuma, D., Stubbe, J. H., Boomsma, D. I., et al. (2006). Physical activity and cognitive function in a cross-section of younger and older community-dwelling individuals. *Health Psychology, 25,* 678–687.

Iacoboni, M., & Dapretto, M. (2006). The mirror neuron system and the consequences of its dysfunction. *Nature Reviews Neuroscience, 7,* 942–951.

Iacoboni, M., Molnar-Szakacs, I., Gallese, V., Buccino, G., & Mazziotta, J. C. (2005). Grasping the intentions of others with one's own mirror neuron system. *Public Library of Science Biology, 3*(3), e79.

Ivry, R., & Fiez, J. (2000). Cerebellar contributions to cognition and imagery. In M. Gazzaniga (Ed.), *The new cognitive neurosciences* (pp. 999–1012). Cambridge, MA: MIT Press.

Jacobs, B., Schall, M., & Scheibel, A. B. (1993). A quantitative dendritic analysis of Wernicke's Area in humans: Gender, hemispheric and environmental factors. *Journal of Comparative Neurology, 327,* 83–111.

Johnston-Brooks, C. H., Lewis, M. A., Evans, G., & Whalen, C. K. (1998). Chronic stress and illness in children: The role of allostatic load. *Psychsomatic Medicine, 60,* 597–603.

Juraska, J. M., Fitch, J. M., Henderson, C., & Rivers, N. (1985). Sex differences in the dendritic branching of dentate granule cells following differential experience. *Brain Research, 333,* 73–80.

Jussim, L. J., Madon, S., & Chatman, C. (1994). Teacher expectations and student achievement: Self-fulfilling prophecies, biases, and accuracy. In L. Heath & R. S. Tindale (Eds.), *Applications of heuristics and biases to social issues* (pp. 303–334). New York: Plenum Press.

Kandel, E., & Hawkins, R. (1992, September). The biological basis of learning and individuality. *Scientific American,* 79–86.

Kandel, M., & Kandel, E. (1994, May). Flights of memory. *Discover,* 32–38.

Kazdin, A. (1976). The rich rewards of rewards. *Psychology Today, 10*(6), 98, 101–102, 105, 114.

Kazdin, A. E. (1977). *The token economy: A review and evaluation.* New York: Plenum Press.

Khalsa, D., Ziegler, M., & Kennedy, B. (1986). Body sides switch dominance. *Life Sciences, 38,* 1203–1214.

Kimura, D., & Hampson, E. (1993). Neural and hormonal mechanisms mediating sex differences in cognition. In P. A. Vernon (Ed.), *Biological approaches to the study of human intelligence* (pp. 375–397). Norwood, NJ: Ablex.

Kitabatake, Y., Sailor, K. A., Ming, G. L., & Song, H. (2007). Adult neurogenesis and hippocampal memory function: New cells, more plasticity, new memories? *Neurosurgery Clinics of North America, 18*(1), 105–113.

Klein, R., & Armitage, R. (1979). Brainwave cycle fluctuations. *Science, 204,* 1326–1328.

Kleiner, S. M. (1999). Water: An essential but overlooked nutrient. *Journal of the American Dietetic Association, 99,* 200–206.

Kline, P., & Saunders, B. (1997). *Ten steps to a learning organization* (2nd ed.). Arlington, VA: Great Ocean.

Klutky, N. (1990). Geschlechtsunderschiede in der gedächtnisleistung für gerüche, tonfolgen, und farben [Sex differences in memory performance for odors, sequences, and colors]. *Zeitschrift für Experimentelle und Angewandte Psychologie, 37,* 437–446.

Knecht, S., Breitenstein, C., Bushuven, S., Wailke, S., Kamping, S., Floel, A., et al. (2004). Levodopa: Faster and better word learning in normal humans. *Annals of Neurology, 56*(1), 20–26.

Kohn, A. (1993). *Punished by rewards.* New York: Houghton Mifflin.

Kramer, A. F., Erickson, K. I., & Colcombe, S. J. (2006). Exercise, cognition, and the aging brain. *Journal of Applied Physiology, 101,* 1237–1242.

LaRue, A., Koehler, K. M., Wayne, S. J., & Chiulli, S. J. (1997). Nutritional status and cognitive functioning in a normally aging sample: A 6-year reassessment. *American Journal of Clinical Nutrition, 65,* 20–29.

LeDoux, J. (1996). *The emotional brain.* New York: Simon & Schuster.

Leff, H. L., & Nevin, A. (1994). *Turning learning inside out: A guide for using any subject to enrich life and creativity.* Tucson, AZ: Zephyr Press.

Liberman, J. (1991). *Light: Medicine of the future.* Santa Fe, NM: Bear.

Locke, E. A., & Latham, G. P. (1990). Work motivation and satisfaction: Light at the end of the tunnel. *Psychological Science, 1,* 240–246.

Maslow, A. H. (1943). A theory of human motivation. *Psychological Review, 50,* 370–396.

May, C., Hasher, L., & Stoltzfus, E. (1993). Optimal time of day and the magnitude of age differences in memory. *Psychological Science, 4,* 517–525.

McKinley, M. J., & Johnson, A. K. (2004). The physiological regulation of thirst and fluid intake. *News in Physiological Sciences, 19,* 1–6.

McNay, E. C., McCarty, R. C., & Gold, P. E. (2001). Fluctuations in brain glucose concentration during behavioral testing: Dissociations between brain areas and between brain and blood. *Neurobiology of Learning and Memory, 75,* 325–337.

Meece, J. L., Wigfield, A., & Eccles, J. S. (1990). Predictors of math anxiety and its influence on young adolescents' course enrollment intentions and performance in mathematics. *Journal of Educational Psychology, 82,* 60–70.

Middleton, F., & Strick, P. (1994). Anatomical evidence for cerebellar and basal ganglia involvement in higher cognitive function. *Science, 266,* 458–461.

Moberg, P., Agrin, R., Gur, R., Reuben, C., Turetsky, B., & Doty, R. (1999). Olfactory dysfunction in schizophrenia: A qualitative and quantitative review. *Neuropsychopharmacology, 21,* 325–340.

Molloy, J. T. (1988). *New dress for success.* New York: Warner Books.

Nandam, L. S., Jhaveri, D., & Bartlett, P. (2007). 5-ht₇, neurogenesis and antidepressants: A promising therapeutic axis for treating depression. *Clinical and Experimental Pharmacology and Physiology, 34,* 546–551.

National Association for Music Education. (n.d.). *Scores of students in the arts.* Retrieved January 21, 2008, from www.menc.org/information/advocate/sat.html

O'Leary, D. M. (1997). *The lifespan development of individuals: Behavioral, neurobiological and psychosocial perspectives.* New York: Cambridge University Press.

Orlock, C. (1998). *Know your body clock.* New York: Barnes & Noble.

Ornstein, R. (1991). *The evolution of consciousness: The origins of the way we think.* New York: Simon & Schuster.

Pakenberg, B., & Gundersen, H. J. G. (1997). Neocortical neuron number in humans: Effect of sex and age. *Journal of Comparative Neurology, 384,* 312–320.

Pantev, C., Oostenveld, R., Engelien, A., Ross, B., Roberts, L. E., & Hoke, M. (1998). Increased auditory cortical representation in musicians. *Nature, 392,* 811–814.

Pauli, P., Bourne, L. E., Diekmann, H., & Birbaumer, N. (1999). Cross-modality priming between odors and odor-congruent words. *American Journal of Psychology, 112,* 175–186.

Pellegrini, A. D., & Bohn, C. M. (2005). The role of recess in children's cognitive performance and school adjustment. *Educational Researcher, 34*(1), 13–19.

Pereira, A. C., Huddleston, D. E., Brickman, A. M., Sosunov, A. A., Hen, R., McKhann, G. M., et al. (2007). An in vivo correlate of exercise-induced neurogenesis in the adult dentate gyrus. *Proceedings of the National Academy of Sciences of the United States of America, 104,* 5638–5643.

Peretz, I., & Zatorre, R. J. (2005). Brain organization for music processing. *Annual Review of Psychology, 56,* 89–114.

Pert, C. (1997). *Molecules of emotion.* New York: Scribner.

Posner, M., & Badgaiyan, R. (1997). Time course of cortical activations in implicit and explicit recall. *Journal of Neuroscience, 17,* 4904–4913.

Proverbio, A. M., Brignone, V., Matarazzo, S., Del Zotto, M., & Zani, A. (2006). Gender differences in hemispheric asymmetry for face processing. *BMC Neuroscience, 7*(1), 44. Retrieved January 7, 2008, from www.biomedcentral.com/1471-2202/7/44

Ramachandran, V. S., & Blakeslee, S. (1998). *Phantoms in the brain.* New York: William Morrow.

Ramakrishna, T. (1999). Vitamins and brain development. *Physiological Research, 48,* 175–187.

Ramey, C. (1992). High-risk children and IQ: Altering intergenerational patterns. *Intelligence, 16,* 239.

Ramon y Cajal, S. (1988). *History of neuroscience.* New York: Oxford University Press.

Rauscher, F. H., Shaw, G. L., Levine, L. J., Wright, E. L., Dennis, W. R., & Newcomb, R. L. (1997). Music training causes long-term enhancement of preschool children's spatial–temporal reasoning. *Neurological Research, 19,* 2–8.

Reis, S., & Diaz, E. (1999). Economically disadvantaged urban female students who achieve in schools. *Urban Review, 31,* 31–54.

Restak, R. (1994). *The modular brain.* New York: Scribner.

Rhodes, R. E. (2006). The built-in environment: The role of personality and physical activity. *Exercise and Sport Sciences Reviews, 34,* 83–88.

Riggs, C. (1997). The impact of aerobic dance on the self-concept of female exercisers (Doctoral dissertation, University of Wyoming, 1997). *Dissertation Abstracts International, 57,* 7-A.

Rosenthal, R. (1991). Teacher expectancy effects: A brief update 25 years after the Pygmalion experiment. *Journal of Research in Education, 1*(1), 3–12.

Rosenthal, R., & Jacobsen, L. (1968). *Pygmalion in the classroom: Teacher expectation and pupils' intellectual development.* New York: Rinehart & Winston.

Rosenthal, R., & Jacobson, L. (1996). Teachers' expectancies: Determinants of pupils' IQ gains. *Psychological Reports, 19,* 115–118.

Rosenzweig, M. R., Love, W., & Bennett, E. L. (1968). Effects of a few hours a day of enriched experience on brain chemistry and brain weights. *Physiology & Behavior, 3,* 819–825.

Russell, I. J., Hendricson, W. D., & Herbert, R. J. (1984). Effects of lecture information density on medical student achievement. *Journal of Medical Education, 59,* 881–889.

Salthouse, T. A. (2007). Implications of within-person variability in cognitive and neuropsychological functioning for the interpretation of change. *Neuropsychology, 21,* 401–411.

Sampson, A., Dixit, S., Meyers, A., & Houser, R. (1995). The nutritional impact of breakfast consumption on the diets of inner-city African-American elementary school children. *Journal of the American Medical Association, 87,* 195–202.

Sapolsky, R. (1992). *Stress, the aging brain, and the mechanisms of neuron death.* Cambridge, MA: MIT Press.

Sapolsky, R. (1996). Why stress is bad for your brain. *Science, 273,* 749–750.

Sapolsky, R. (1999, March). Stress and your brain. *Discover,* 116.

Sapolsky, R. M. (2004). Is impaired neurogenesis relevant to the affective symptoms of depression? *Biological Psychiatry, 56,* 137–139.

Schiffer, F., Teicher, M. H., Anderson, C., Tomoda, A., Polcari, A., Navalta, C., et al. (2007). Determination of hemispheric emotional valence in individual subjects: A new approach with research and therapeutic implications. *Behavioral and Brain Functions, 3*(1), 13. Retrieved January 7, 2008, from www.behavioralandbrainfunctions.com/content/3/1/13

Schnaubelt, K. (1995). *Advanced aromatherapy: The science of essential oil therapy.* Rochester, VT: Healing Arts Press.

Schnaubelt, K. (1999). *Medical aromatherapy: Healing with essential oils.* Berkeley, CA: Frog.

Seligman, M. E. P. (1998). *Learned optimism: How to change your mind and your life.* New York: Pocket Books.

Senge, P. M., Kleiner, A., Roberts, C., Ross, R., & Smith, B. (1994). *The fifth discipline fieldbook.* New York: Doubleday.

Shors, T. J., Miesegaes, G., Beylin, A., Zhao, M., Rydel, T., & Gould, E. (2001). Neurogenesis in the adult is involved in the formation of trace memories. *Nature, 410,* 372–376.

Squire, L. R. (1992). Memory and the hippocampus: A synthesis from findings with rats, monkeys, and humans. *Psychological Review, 99,* 195–231.

Stickgold, R., & Walker, M. P. (2007). Sleep-dependent memory consolidation and reconsolidation. *Sleep Medicine, 8,* 331–343.

Sullivan, T. E., Schefft, B. K., Warm, J. S., Dember, W. N., O'Dell, M. W., & Peterson, S. J. (1998). Effects of olfactory stimulation on the vigilance performance of individuals with brain injury. *Journal of Clinical and Experimental Neuropsychology, 20,* 227–236.

Tomporowski, P. D. (2003). Effects of acute bouts of exercise on cognition. *Acta Psychologica, 112,* 297–324.

Tonegawa, S. (1995). Mammalian learning and memory studied by gene targeting. *Annals of the New York Academy of Sciences, 758,* 213–217.

Valle, J. D. (1990). The development of a learning styles program in an affluent, suburban New York elementary school. *Reading & Writing Quarterly, 6,* 315–322.

Valtin, H. (2002). "Drink at least eight glasses of water a day." Really? Is there scientific evidence for "8 x 8"? *American Journal of Physiology, 283,* 993–1004.

Van Praag, H., Christie, B. R., Sejnowski, T. J., & Gage, F. H. (1999). Running enhances neurogenesis, learning, and long-term potentiation in mice. *Proceedings of the National Academy of Sciences of the United States of America, 96,* 13427–13431.

Van Praag, H., Kempermann, G., & Gage, F. H. (1999). Running increases cell proliferation and neurogenesis in the adult mouse dendate gyrus. *Nature Neuroscience, 2,* 266–270.

Vance, D. (1999). Considering olfactory stimulation for adults with age-related dementia. *Perceptual and Motor Skills, 88,* 398–400.

Vaynman, S., & Gomez-Pinilla, F. (2006). Revenge of the "sit": How lifestyle impacts neuronal and cognitive health through molecular systems that interface energy metabolism with neuronal plasticity. *Journal of Neuroscience Research, 84,* 699–715.

Velle, W. (1992). *The nature of the sexes: The sociobiology of sex differences and the "battle of the sexes."* Groningen, Netherlands: Origin Press.

Volkmar, F. R., & Greenough, W. T. (1972). Rearing complexity affects branching of dendrites in the visual cortex of the rat. *Science, 176,* 1445–1447.

Vuontela, V., Rämä, P., Raninen, A., Aronen, H. J., & Carlson, S. (1999). Selective dissociation between memory for location and color. *NeuroReport, 10,* 2235–2240.

Wallin, N. L., Merker, B., & Brown, S. (1999). *The origins of music.* Cambridge: Massachusetts Institute of Technology.

Weinberger, N. M. (2004). Music and the brain. *Scientific American, 291*(5), 88–95.

Williams, J. M., & Anderson, M. B. (1997). Psychosocial influences on central and peripheral vision and reaction time during demanding tasks. *Behavioral Medicine, 22,* 160–167.

Wolverton, B. C. (1997). *How to grow fresh air: 50 houseplants that purify your home or office.* New York: Penguin.

Wurtman, J. (1986). *Managing your mind and mood through food.* New York: Harper & Row.

Yin, J. C., Wallach, J. S., Wilder, E. L., Klingensmith, J., Dang, D., Perrimon, N., et al. (1995). A drosophila CREB/CREM homolog encodes multiple isoforms, including cyclic AMP-dependent protein kinase-responsive transcriptional activator and antagonist. *Molecular and Cellular Biology, 15,* 5123.

Zohar, A., Degani, A., & Vaaknin, E. (2001). Teachers' beliefs about low-achieving students and higher order thinking. *Teaching and Teacher Education, 17,* 469–485.

Index